ANGLOPHONE AFRICAN DETECTIVE FICTION 1940-2020

AFRICAN ARTICULATIONS

ISSN 2054-5673

SERIES EDITORS
Stephanie Newell & Ranka Primorac

EDITORIAL ADVISORY BOARD
Akin Adesokan (Indiana University)
Jane Bryce (University of the West Indies)
James Ferguson (Stanford University)
Simon Gikandi (Princeton University)
Stefan Helgesson (Stockholm University)
Isabel Hofmeyr (University of the Witwatersrand)
Madhu Krishnan (University of Bristol)
Lydie Moudileno (University of Southern California)
Grace A. Musila (University of the Witwatersrand)
Caroline Rooney (University of Kent)
Meg Samuelson (University of Adelaide)
Jennifer Wenzel (Columbia University)

The series is open to submissions from the disciplines related to literature, cultural history, cultural studies, music and the arts.

African Articulations showcases cutting-edge research into Africa's cultural texts and practices, broadly understood to include written and oral literatures, visual arts, music, and public discourse and media of all kinds. Building on the idea of 'articulation' as a series of cultural connections, as a clearly voiced argument and as a dynamic social encounter, the series features monographs that open up innovative perspectives on the richness of African locations and networks. Refusing to concentrate solely on the internationally visible above the supposedly ephemeral local cultural spaces and networks, African Articulations provides indispensable resources for students and teachers of contemporary culture.

Please contact the series editors with an outline, or download the proposal form www.jamescurrey.com. Only send a full manuscript if requested to do so.

Stephanie Newell, Professor of English, Yale University stephanie.newell@yale.edu
Ranka Primorac, Assistant Professor in English, University of Southampton r.primorac@soton.ac.uk

Previously published volumes are listed at the back of this book

ANGLOPHONE AFRICAN DETECTIVE FICTION 1940–2020

The State, the Citizen, and the Sovereign Ideal

Matthew J. Christensen

JC JAMES CURREY

© Matthew J. Christensen 2024

All Rights Reserved. Except as permitted under current legislation
no part of this work may be photocopied, stored in a retrieval system,
published, performed in public, adapted, broadcast,
transmitted, recorded or reproduced in any form or by any means,
without the prior permission of the copyright owner

The right of Matthew J. Christensen to be identified as
the author of this work has been asserted in accordance with
sections 77 and 78 of the Copyright, Designs and Patents Act 1988

First published 2024
James Currey
Paperback edition 2026

ISBN 978-1-84701-387-3 (hardback)
ISBN 978-1-84701-395-8 (paperback)

James Currey is an imprint of Boydell & Brewer Ltd
www.jamescurrey.com
and of Boydell & Brewer Inc.
www.boydellandbrewer.com

Our Authorised Representative for product safety in the EU is Easy Access System
Europe - Mustamäe tee 50, 10621 Tallinn, Estonia,
gpsr.requests@easproject.com

A catalogue record for this book is available
from the British Library

The publisher has no responsibility for the continued existence or accuracy of URLs for
external or third-party internet websites referred to in this book, and does not guarantee
that any content on such websites is, or will remain, accurate or appropriate

In memory of my grandparents,
who shared with me the love of reading and puzzle-solving

Contents

List of Illustrations	viii
Acknowledgements	ix
Introduction	1

Part 1: Africanizing Detective Fiction's Un/Sovereign Subjects

1	Dispossession, Rescue, and the Sovereign Self in the Colonial-Era Detective Story	29
2	Sovereign States: Police Investigators, Secret Agents, and Sleuthing Citizens after Independence	59
3	Decolonization Arrested	93

Part 2: Neoliberal Noir

4	Neoliberal Noir	115
5	Seriality, Stasis, and the Neoliberal State	143
6	Managed Risk and the Deadly Allure of Transparency	169
	Conclusion: The Future Imperfect	185
	An Anglophone African Detective Fiction Bibliography, 1940–2023	193
	Bibliography	201
	Index	219

Illustrations

1	Cyprian Ekwensi, *Yaba Round-about Murder* (1962, Tortoise Books)	69
2	David G. Maillu, *Benni Kamba 009 in the Equatorial Assignment* (1980, Macmillan Pacesetters)	73
3	Valentine Alily, *Mark of the Cobra* (1980, Macmillan Pacesetters)	78
4	Wahome Mutahi and Wahome Karengo, *The Miracle Merchant* (2003, Phoenix Publishers)	125
5	Rosina Umelo, *Finger of Suspicion* (1984, Macmillan Pacesetters)	171

Full credit details are provided in the captions to the images in the text. The author and publisher are grateful to all the institutions and individuals for permission to reproduce the materials in which they hold copyright. Every effort has been made to trace the copyright holders; apologies are offered for any omission, and the publisher will be pleased to add any necessary acknowledgement in subsequent editions.

Acknowledgements

Writing this book has been a work of detection as much as it has felt at many times like a criminal heist. Uncovering and piecing together the history of Anglophone African detective fiction has involved no small effort of ferreting clues, identifying suspects and witnesses, weighing evidence and motivation, and fitting together the pieces of a puzzle for which there was no clear picture to aim. But like a complex heist, producing this book has relied upon a network of accomplices, plausible alibis, specialized tools and resources, and the occasional bad influence. Moreover, in the continual pleasure the writing has given me, I have never felt anything less than that I was getting away with something.

Encouraging me in this particular heist were Anja Oed, who, along with Christine Matzke, invited me to give a paper at the 8th Jahnheinz Jahn Symposium, on African crime fiction, and Simon Gikandi, whom I deeply appreciate for not taking no for an answer to his request that I write an essay on the history of Anglophone African mysteries, detective stories, and thrillers for his volume *The Novel in Africa and the Caribbean*. In writing that essay I came to appreciate the historical depth and extraordinary richness of African detective fiction and the urgency with which its stories need telling. Mine is but one of those stories.

Crucial funding and other forms of institutional support came from the National Endowment for the Humanities Summer Stipend program, the American Council of Learned Societies Faculty Fellowship, the SUNY Stony Brook Humanities Institute, the University of Texas Rio Grande Valley Faculty Development Leave Program, UTRGV Office of Global Engagement, and the financial and administrative support of two college deans, Dahlia Guerra and Walter Diaz, and three department chairs, Pamela Anderson-Mejias, Caroline Miles, and Doug LaPrade. I would be remiss not to mention Liza Porras, Nora Duran, Adelina Sifuentes, Sarah Munoz, Monica Denny, Elena Reyna, and the many other administrators, support staff and work study students laboring behind the scenes to make my life as a faculty member easier.

This book benefitted greatly from the discussion and feedback that comes from collaboration in its different guises. Jane Elliot's and Gillian Harkins' invitation to contribute an essay to a special issue of *Social Text* on 'Genres of Neoliberalism' was both generous and essential for inspiring the critical framework that would come to inform the entire book. Emily Johansen's and Alissa G. Karl's invitation to write a piece for an issue of *Textual Practice* on

'Neoliberalism and the Novel' proved crucial for testing out the implications of certain ideas about genre. Several conferences and panels generated unusually productive discussion and feedback: the Yale University 'Crime and its Fictions in Africa' conference organized by Jacob Dlamini, Jeanne-Marie Jackson, and Nathan Suhr-Sytsma; the University of Wisconsin, Madison symposium 'Forms of Informality' organized by Matthew H. Brown and Victor Goldgel; the 'Things that Repeat' panel at the American Comparative Literature Association conference organized by Eleni Condouriotis and Lauren Goodlad; and the 'Genres of Violence in African Writing' panel that I organized for a Modern Language Association meeting and that Mukoma Wa Ngugi, Stephanie Bosch Santana, and Laura Murphy so kindly joined.

Esther de Bruijn, Marisa Palacios Knox, Shirley Jennifer Lim, and Katherine Sugg took time away from their own writing to read and comment on chapters. My arguments are significantly sharper as a result. Danika Brown, Rebecca Mitchell, Marci McMahon, and Shawn Thomson gave insightful feedback on grant and fellowship applications and the book proposal. Richard Yarborough, Carla Calarge, Robert Affeldt, Ed Cameron, Catie Merla-Watson, and Randall Monty posed helpful questions and pointed me to resources that I might have overlooked.

I thank Pim Higginson and Tsitsi Jaji for early encouragement; Moradewun Adejunmobi, Simon Gikandi, and Jane Elliott for recommendation letters; Steven Nye for the reference to a delightfully obscure Gambian detective novel; and Lloys Frates for proposing the idea of a study of African detective fiction long before I was prepared to take on such a project. I also thank Matthias Krings for so generously sharing his entire digital collection of *African Film* and *Boom* look-reads. I was not able to use much from these photonovels, but I hope to soon. I also need to acknowledge Krings' home institution, the Mainz African Studies Centre at Johannes Gutenberg Universität for securing me office space, administrative support, and library privileges during even the briefest of visits.

A book like this is only as good as the libraries and archives from which it draws. Interlibrary loan offices at the University of Texas, Rio Grande Valley and SUNY Stony Brook never balked at the dozens of requests that at times I put in nearly daily. The New York Public Library's Schomburg branch, the Jahnheinz Jahn Library of African Literature, the University of London's SOAS special collections, and the British Library's Newspaper collection were treasure troves. I might never have written this book had I not come across a Kenyan detective novel sitting atop a box of unprocessed materials at my old friend John Durham's Bolerium Books. Thank you to John and the other antiquarian dealers who had the books I needed, especially during the many months when the Covid-19 pandemic shuttered libraries.

Chapters 4 and 6 include revised material from previous publications. I thank Duke University Press journals for permission to include analysis and arguments from 'African Popular Crime Genres and the Genres of Neoliberalism', *Social Text*, 31(2) (115) (2013), 103–121. I thank Rüdiger Köppe Verlag for permission to repurpose portions of 'Violable States: Postcolonial Sovereignty, Neoliberalism, and Generic Failure in Tony Marinho's Biothriller *The Epidemic*', in A. Oed and C. Matzke (eds), *Life is a Thriller: Investigating African Crime Fiction* (2012), 77–88. I thank Taylor & Francis Journals for permission to include an updated version of 'Managed Risk and the Lure of Transparency in Anglophone African Neoliberal Noir', *Textual Practice*, 29(2) (2015), 315–333.

No work of scholarship is as unassailable as the final explanation of whodunit given by the old-fashioned murder mystery detective. Nor should it aim for that standard. My analytical conceptualization and argument are, however, considerably more defensible for the magnifying glass-level scrutiny to which my external readers subjected this manuscript. It is difficult for me to imagine a more knowledgeable and rigorous pair of evaluators. Any faulty logic, missed evidence, and unclear writing survives despite their best efforts.

Ranka Primorac and Stephanie Newell saw the promise in this project even before I fully understood that there was a project. Jaqueline Mitchell, Megan Milan, Nick Bingham, Christy Beale, the entire team at James Currey/Boydell & Brewer, and copyeditor Nicholas Jewitt, made sure that the resulting book is better and more beautiful than I could have hoped. Three cheers to you all. Appreciation also goes to David Martinez for additional copyediting and for the fine index and to Julienne Alexander/YSSRS Creative for the elegant cover illustration.

My deepest gratitude is always for Shirley Jennifer Lim. Her commitment to illuminating overlooked cultural histories, her passion for the written word, and her boundless faith in me keeps me going every day.

Introduction

Nigerian novelist Kole Omotoso pinpoints the central challenge facing African detective fiction writers, namely 'how to prosecute the people who are powerful enough to totally ignore the process of law. The private dick angle doesn't work; somebody has to do more than this' (1979: 10). The conflict between the classic British whodunit's implicit promise of legal justice and the entrenched fallibilities of Nigeria's judicial system animates Omotoso's claim. For him, the scenarios and resolutions of the typical British mystery cannot credibly accommodate Nigerian realities. To plausibly provide the pleasures of suspense and catharsis, detective stories must reflect the worlds in which their readers live. Omotoso's example of legal accountability for the rich and powerful is less uniquely African than he suggests as other global crime mysteries play on the same dynamic. He also overlooks the elasticity of the 'private dick angle' to account for a wide range of social and judicial scenarios, including the Nigerian situation. Yet Omotoso's question about how African detective fiction writers will represent the law and the courts, notions of criminality and justice, and the relationship between the citizen and state more broadly signals the imperative for African writers to interrogate what kinds of stories their detective fiction should tell and, most significantly, to what ends.

By the early 1940s, African writers had already begun answering Omotoso's question. Rather than replicate British manor-house mysteries with little more than an Africanization of character names, the earliest writers turned the tyrannies of colonial policing and the challenges of achieving equitable justice under colonial judiciaries into rich material for suspenseful and convincing detective stories. Over time, other African writers would do the same with the criminalization of state institutions by self-dealing politicians, the authoritarianism of military rule, and the neoliberal elevation of unbridled self-interest to a public virtue. Ghana's R.E. Obeng was possibly the first to reimagine the detective genre for an African context, in 1942, with his collection of mystery stories featuring the detective Issa Busanga. Nigeria's Cyprian Ekwensi followed Obeng later in the decade with his first two investigation narratives and was joined in the 1950s and '60s by writers from South Africa, Ghana, and Ethiopia. In the years since, African writers have churned out hundreds of detective stories, novellas, and novels in English, French, Portuguese, Arabic, Amharic, Yoruba, Hausa, Swahili, Northern Sotho, Tswana, Zulu, and other African languages and across an ever-expanding array of whodunits, political thrillers, courtroom dramas, journalistic investigations, anti-corruption investigations, truth-commission thrillers, police procedurals, feminist counter-procedurals, and other subgenres of crime and comeuppance, each in their own way domesticating the genre to local social worlds.

The effect of this Africanization of the detective story is only partially ludic. In the act of crafting new types of characters and narrative conflicts to match local social dynamics, Africa's crime mystery writers also harness for local contexts the cultural labor that the detective genre can be made to perform. Over the course of the genre's long global history, that cultural work has taken many forms, ranging from the psychoanalytic to the metaphysical to the political. For African writers, one of the detective genre's most important labors is its capacity for appraising the social and structural conditions that impinge upon a society's ability to secure the rights and protections of its citizens. As a literary genre entwined historically with the consolidation of the modern state and its legal and juridical regimes, the detective story provides its writers with an especially rich narrative framework for probing the limits and possibilities of governance, governmentality, and citizenship. African writers repeatedly mobilize this capacity to assess the conditions and contradictions of the political sovereignty of the state and the personal sovereignty of the citizen, sovereignties that take on heightened significance under the conditions of coloniality and postcoloniality. The fundamental obstacle to achieving the liberty, security, and self-governance envisioned at the time of political independence, the body of fiction suggests, is the state itself. Never sovereign in the ways that modern states are presumed to be, the postcolonial African state is shown repeatedly to be the conduit for continued forms of colonial and neocolonial domination or for the exertion of rule by individuals who have either commandeered the institutions of the state or who have supplanted the bureaucratic state altogether. For its readers, African detective fiction asks a fundamental question about survival: how do individuals and communities manage risk and resources when the presumed conceptual vehicle for securing them is radically unstable? This question prompts a second: despite its instabilities, can the modernist postcolonial nation-state be recuperated to achieve sovereign futures? By re-articulating these questions during each transformation in the historical relationship between the state and citizen, from the late-colonial to the neoliberal eras, African detective fiction continually revisits and re-energizes the founding promises of decolonization.

This book traces the history of these critical articulations through a focused study of Anglophone African detective fiction. Africa's English-language crime mysteries do not necessarily grapple with the problematics of sovereignty in more complex or more revealing ways than other linguistically categorized

African detective fiction traditions.¹ Anglophone detective fiction does, however, stand out for its substantially greater historical depth, geographic breadth, and thematic cohesiveness. Since the 1940s, African writers have published over 200 detective stories in English-language newspapers, magazines, and novels. Distributed widely across Africa's diverse cultural and political geographies, the Anglophone texts share aesthetic characteristics and thematic preoccupations that reflect the transnational networks of production, circulation, and influence in which they have been created and consumed. Taken together, these commonalities and histories distinguish Anglophone African detective fiction from other Europhone and African language crime writing. For these reasons Africa's Anglophone detective fiction offers an especially clear expression of the crime mystery's critical possibilities.

Investigation and Discovery: Defining Terms

This book's focus is on detective fiction, as opposed to the broader category of crime fiction, of which the detective story is a part but also from which it stands apart. Put differently, while most Anglophone African detective stories are crime stories, not all Anglophone African crime stories are detective stories. I emphasize this fact because while Anglophone African detective fiction shares certain thematic and critical preoccupations with crime fiction broadly, it develops these themes and articulates these critiques in generically specific ways. It is this specificity that this book seeks to comprehend. I insist on this specificity with the acute understanding that all genres are inherently amorphous, ever evolving, and blurred at their edges, few more so than the detective story. For reasons to do with detective fiction's efficacy in deconstructing a given social order's organizing assumptions, the genre has, moreover, been borrowed widely and appealed to a heterogeneous array of writers who have improvised freely on its form, language, characters, and other generic attributes. At this point in the detective genre's global history, determining what is or is not a detective story is less a function of absolute norms, of which there are possibly none, than of texts being recognized as such by readers, cultural intermediaries, and institutions.²

What makes a detective story recognizable as a detective story? For the purposes of this book, I highlight three attributes. First, when acts of murder, theft, sabotage, or other criminal activity put plots in motion, the solving of criminal mysteries and/or the containment of villainy take precedence over

---

1 Scholarship on African language detective fiction is sparse. For a sampling see Assefa (1989) on Amharic writing, Chigidi (1997) on Shona writing, Oed (2012) on Yoruba writing, and Khamis (2012) on Kiswahili writing.
2 For a discussion of the role of cultural intermediaries and institutions in the formation of genres, see Adejunmobi (2017).

the villainy itself. Second, in detective stories, narrative codes of investigation and discovery are central. Third, detective stories typically unfold as quests for justice, whether that justice be private or public, legal or moral, or actual or ideal. Even texts missing an obvious detective or that deconstruct the formal structures of the detective genre can be viewed as detective stories if they marshal the reader's generically conditioned expectations for any of these fundamentals. What is important is the 'family resemblance' (Dimock 2006: 86). Regarding nomenclature, I employ the terms 'detective story' and 'crime mystery' interchangeably to avoid repetition and because, while detectives need not necessarily solve criminal mysteries nor do mysteries necessarily require crimes in need of solving, rare is the Anglophone African detective story in which a crime of some sort does not feature prominently.

As a generic family, detective fiction in Africa encompasses a diverse array of variants. Included among these are the aforementioned puzzle-clue mysteries, thrillers, police and courtroom procedurals, journalistic investigations, and espionage adventures, but also medical mysteries, historical mysteries, schoolyard mysteries, falsely-accused-individuals-proving-their-innocence mysteries, and any number of other iterations of the detective story's basic outline. There are discernible and sometimes substantial aesthetic, stylistic, and thematic differences among them. Few readers would confuse a police procedural with a biothriller for instance. Other readers might distinguish as separate genres, with distinct ideological orientations, a mystery from a detective story or a detective story from an espionage thriller. The differences among journalism investigations, police procedurals, spy thrillers, medical mysteries, and their generic kin are not inconsequential, and reading them for their specificities is often essential for understanding the contextually specific uses to which Anglophone African writers have put the detective genre across place and time.

Detective Fiction and the State

The state and the problems of sovereign self-rule preoccupy Anglophone African writers of detective fiction for much the same reason that the state preoccupies a wide spectrum of African expressive artists. As Tejumola Olaniyan explains, the twentieth- and twenty-first-century African state has been incredibly productive in generating literature, music, and other forms of expressive and modernist culture that exists in significant part to proclaim, with no small irony, 'the illegitimacy of the new state and its authority' (2017: 5).[3] Olaniyan enumerates

---

3 A full catalogue of scholarship on popular culture and politics would be impossible. A few standout studies include Tejumola Olaniyan (2004 and 2018), Tsitsi Jaji (2014b), Nanimata Diabate (2020), Matthew H. Brown (2021), Emily Callaci (2017), Carmela Garritano (2013), and Akin Adesokan (2009).

just a few of the many disjunctions between the state and the people that have spawned so much cultural activity:

> the strangeness of [the state's] structure, the systemic ease with which its rules are disregarded with impunity especially by those who rule, its alien and alienating language, its overtly vulgar class character, its enthronement of money as the solvent of all values (in newly and unevenly monetized societies), its imponderable bureaucracy, its radically different codes of access to personal fulfillment and participation in the public realm – not with hard work and integrity but simply money, some smattering of Western education and, later on, possession of weapons and coercion. (5)

At times corrupt, at others violent and coercive, frequently absent, and forever haunted by the authoritarian legacies of colonial governance, the state, Olaniyan argues, has struggled to ensure the rights and protections of citizenship that were promised at the time of independence and that continue to animate so many electoral campaigns. The precise valences of state illegitimacy, as well as crisis and fragility – the specificities of which will be touched on throughout this book – vary from country to country and year to year.

Insofar as 'crime is a critical prism through which a society might come to know itself, might measure itself against its own ideal self-image, might contemplate ways and means of perfecting itself' (Comaroff and Comaroff 2016: 5), African writers have turned repeatedly to crime plots to appraise the problematics of structural inequality, interpersonal insecurity, and the easy seductions of power in the colonial and postcolonial state. These meditations feature just as prominently in the 'serious' novels of Ngũgĩ wa Thiong'o, Wole Soyinka, Chinua Achebe, and Alex La Guma as they do in lurid and oftentimes titillating popular fiction novels such as Nkem Nwankwo's *My Mercedes is Bigger than Yours* (1975), K. Bamfi Adomako's *From Undergraduate to Prostitution* (1988), and Ben R. Mtobwa's *Najisikia Kuua Tena* [*I Feel Like Killing Again*] (1985). Africa's crime fiction cannot be argued to uniformly decry the illegitimacy of the state and its authority, but the crimes it frequently narrates unfold in the spaces produced by the disjunctures that Olaniyan describes. Anglophone Africa's detective fiction concentrates this meditation by focusing not only on criminal activity and motivation but also on the state's capacity to regulate social and economic relations.

In this respect, African writers build on a longer global history of detective fiction. In his provocative transnational genealogy of British, American, and French crime fiction, Andrew Pepper contends that 'the development of crime fiction is bound up with the consolidation of the modern, bureaucratic state; that is to say, with the policing, governmental, and judicial apparatuses set up to enforce the law, and with the new techniques and technologies of governing established to produce a more secure world' (2016: 1). Pepper highlights the 1720s as a key period in the development of modern European and American crime writing, when novelists such as Daniel Defoe, working in the context of the emergence of the modern state system, first treat 'crime and punishment in a self-conscious manner' and begin 'to demonstrate an awareness of the tensions between the right and need to punish, and inadequacies and failures of the bodies charged with this task' (4). The self-conscious narrativization of these tensions gains momentum, Pepper argues, over the following century in the writings of a variety of authors, including, among others, Eugène-François Vidocq, Mary Elizabeth Braddon, and Émile Gaboriau, and witnesses its formalization with the innovation of the detective figure, whose invention is often credited to Edgar Allan Poe but whose presence was already evident in Vidocq's *Memoirs* (1828) and, outside of Pepper's immediate geographical frame, in China going back to the tenth century.[4] A longstanding Anglo-American-centric narrative of the detective story's development marks the 1930s as a pivot point, prior to which Poe, Doyle, Christie, and their counterparts crafted reassuring tales of the benevolent power of the state and after which Dashiell Hammett, Raymond Chandler, and their hard-boiled acolytes laid bare the systemic corruption of modern life under a soulless modern state. But Pepper's transnational reading of crime fiction – though still confined to the narrow France-Britain-America nexus – reveals that from its beginnings, even in Poe and the so-called golden-age British writers, modern 'crime fiction … tends to produce a contradictory account of the state as both necessary for the creation and maintenance of collective life and central to the reproduction of entrenched socio-economic inequalities, to the point that this tension becomes the constitutive and foundational feature of the emerging genre' (2016: 1–2).

Similar contradictions and tensions mark Anglophone African detective fiction's account of the state. The small but growing body of scholarship on the writing has isolated some of its countervailing propensities, identifying on the one hand modes of counter-hegemonic critique and on the other modes of reaffirming existing power relations. Overlooked in all but a few of these studies is what I see as the complex interplay of both critique and affirmation that characterizes so much of the history of Anglophone African detective fiction and that gives the genre so much of its cultural and social nuance. The existing scholarship nevertheless usefully illuminates the basic terms with which Anglophone African detective fiction writers engage the problems of the state and the sovereign ideal. A brief survey of these arguments will, I trust, help clarify my arguments to come.

---

4   On China's detective fiction and non-fiction, see Robert van Gulik (1976) and Louise Nilsson, David Damrosch, and Theo D'Haen (2017).

Julia Augart sums up one strain of thinking on Anglophone African detective fiction when she asserts that Kenya's detective and crime novels regularly take 'a critical stance towards their country, and to the social problems of the postcolonial state' (2018: 82). In this reading, Anglophone African crime mystery writers wield the genre for progressive, if not radical, political ends. In her study of Botswanan writer and High Court judge Unity Dow's novels, Sonja Darlington offers as an example of this politics Dow's mobilization of the criminal investigation plot to develop a feminist critique of 'policemen, cabinet members, lawyers, judges, businessmen and community leaders who use their professional roles in Botswana to obstruct the rights of women and children' (2013: 80). Sabine Binder reads post-transition South African crime mysteries featuring women detectives along parallel lines. In a context where the 'formal equality granted to South African women under the constitution remains incomplete ... especially [for] economically disadvantaged women of colour', Binder argues that many of the country's women-authored 'fictional detectives ... not only operate as agents of the established criminal justice system, but adhere to forms of so-called "restorative justice", which is victim based and relies on remedial measures. By working for more equality and striving to remedy the law's masculine discourse, they are able to find different versions of "truth" and justice' (2021: 134). Anja Oed and Christine Matzke add that '[i]ncreasingly, African crime fiction depicts the intricate connection and pitfalls of globalization, i.e. the way hegemonic global organisations prey on African resources, thus establishing neocolonial structures of exploitation and dependency', adding that frequently 'a particular government or state apparatus is represented as complicit in the misuse of local assets' (2012: 11, 12).

Other critics highlight how African detective novelists activate the genre's implicit promise of truth and certainty and its normative reliance on Enlightenment understandings of reason and rationality to assess persistent postcolonial problematics. Magalí Armillas-Tiseyra offers the clearest expression of this reading in her analysis of Chris Abani's *The Secret History of Las Vegas* (2014). The novel, she argues, 'both invokes and refuses the epistemic certainties typically promised by the detective plot. In place of solving a mystery and depicting a subsequent return to order, the novel proffers a principle of hermeneutic skepticism that is attuned to multiplicity, simultaneity, and discontinuity', ultimately 'turning critical attention to the power dynamics that structure the present' (2022: 49).[5] While the state per

---

5 Festus Kalua reads Unity Dow's *The Screaming of the Innocent* as a similar project 'to debunk essentialist and purist claims about culture, dismantle and destabilize the continuities and constancies of her tradition, and negotiate her identity in the temporal in-between of her past-present in which her culture can be named only in a manner of discursive uncertainty' (Kalua 2009: 50).

se falls outside of Armillas-Tiseyra's focus, her insights about how detective stories can enunciate hermeneutic skepticism and uncertainty highlights the availability of the genre to question the Enlightenment precepts that undergird the sovereign ideals and juridical, developmentalist, and bureaucratic modes of governmentality that shape the modern state globally. In the African postcolony, where the legal apparatus still largely operates on the principles of British (or French or Portuguese) jurisprudence, this critical capability opens the genre to explorations of the enduring 'strangeness' of the state's structure and struggles for legitimacy (Olaniyan 2017: 5).

Along these lines, Leon de Kock proposes that the South African 'crime-detective fiction' produced in the profoundly unstable first two decades of the country's political transition from apartheid tyranny to progressive liberal democracy 'serves as a measure of an unreadable present and an unplottable future, appraised in relation to an eternally unsettled past' (2016: 11). '"Crime" in South African discourse', de Kock explains, 'is a problematic signifier, capturing very incompletely a more generalised scene of social instability' (43). The transition from apartheid rule generated significant social anxiety as the country struggled to achieve the racial redistribution of resources, risk, and policing promised by the new democratic state. Exacerbating anxieties was the simultaneous transfer of sovereign authority away from the state to global corporations and international institutions prompted by a hegemonically ascendant neoliberal capitalism. De Kock and others read the heightened anxiety about crime and lawlessness as symptomatic of a generalized fear about the capacity of the neoliberalized state to manage social and economic relations within and across its borders.[6] De Kock proposes that, as a genre prone to overplotting, the detective story can thus make the 'bewildering, unreadable postapartheid topography' knowable (45). 'The "solving the crime" approach', de Kock adds, 'acts as an analogy for detecting the source of public misgovernance or private malfeasance, or (as often occurs) both' (8). Miriam Pahl (2018) suggests that detective fiction serves a similar function in a variety of other contexts that are not encumbered by the same apartheid history but that are, like South Africa, under comparable neoliberal pressures.

These studies offer an especially clear conceptualization of how the detective story's narration of crime and justice can elicit readerly reflection on law-breaking as a sign of the state's and the citizen's sovereign existence. In doing so they illuminate how the detective story lays bare a catalogue of problems confronting the postcolonial state's exercise of its presumptive authority. The state's excesses, its easy capture by narrow class interests, and its many racial, ethnic, gender, urban/rural, and regional fault lines become at different times

---

6   See also Rita Barnard (2008).

and in different ways visible in narratives about law-breaking and the battle to stop it. So too do the post-Independence African state's limited resources and its compromised authority as a sovereign entity under neocolonial and neoliberal global capitalism. In this narration, the detective story exposes the precarity of daily life for most individuals in the colony and postcolony as well as the states of exception and exclusion in which they can easily find themselves. Put differently, African detective fiction's private eyes, amateur sleuths, journalists, cops, and spies perform what Christine Matzke and Susanne Mühleisen describe as 'social detection' in which investigations serve less to revel in the detective's – and author's – ingenuity than to make visible the social conditions that facilitate violations against persons, property, and society (2006: 8).[7] For Ranka Primorac, this aspect of African detective fiction underscores an inherent future orientation. Insofar as crime mysteries establish justice as the theoretical endpoint of criminal investigation, detective protagonists conjure 'up the possibility of a national counter-world in the making' (2012: 29).

Anglophone African detective fiction's contradictory account of the state becomes readily visible in the countervailing propensity for an apolitical escapism that some critics argue reaffirms existing power relations for its refusal to engage with the problems of the day. This dismissal might be expected given F.R. Leavis's outsized impact on the pedagogical constitution of university English department curricula across Britain's former colonies and the long critical shadow cast by the Frankfurt school critiques of the mass culture industry.[8] But even thinkers situated outside those frameworks question the detective genre's political efficacy. In his haunting 1963 memoir of growing up in South Africa, Bloke Modisane divulges that during the periods when the weight of apartheid oppression became too crushing and his journalism for *Drum* magazine and its sister publications felt insufficient to the task of challenging South Africa's racist political and social order, he would write 'escapist trash, about boxers with domestic problems, respectable pickpockets,

---

7 Scholars of postcolonial, feminist, African American, and other non-culturally dominant detective fictions often highlight the importance of social detection even if they use different terminology. For a few examples not mentioned elsewhere in this introduction, see Yumna Siddiqi (2008), Nels Pearson and Marc Singer (2009), Ed Christian (2001), Patricia Walton and Manina Jones (1999), Stephen Soitos (1996), Paula Woods (1995), and Ralph E. Rodriguez (2005).

8 On the Leavisite university curriculum in former British colonies, see Apollo Amoko (2010: especially pages 5–10). For discussions of the differences between European/American and African material conditions of cultural production and their implications for debates about the mass culture industry, see among others, Stephanie Newell (2002a); Karin Barber (1987), and Pim Higginson (2017). For a discussion of Francophone African detective fiction as a 'popular', as opposed to mass culture literature, see Hervé Tchumkam (2012).

hole-in-the-wall housebreakers, private detectives and other cardboard images' for the 'yellow African magazines' (139). Kenyan writer Hilary Ng'weno explains that he explicitly crafted his detective thriller *The Men from Pretoria* (1975) with this sort of escapism in mind. He imagined his target audience as the 'average young person who has left school and is seeking two or three hours of light entertainment without having to worry too much about the deeper processes of thought. I believe this is the major reading public in East Africa today' (1979: 159). Ng'weno's fellow Kenyan, Henry Chakava, founded Spear Books in 1974 for a similar presumed audience.9 About the detective and romance novels that Spear and other African presses published, Chakava quipped, 'it is better to read local trash than imported trash' (1977: 86–87). Though, on that point, Nigerian playwright and cultural critic Femi Osofisan is less sanguine. Writing in the 1980s about the popularity of Macmillan's and Fontana's African-authored detective fiction and romances, Osofisan despairs: 'because of the massive spread of western culture into the cities all over the globe, our own masses in the third world have come too to be corrupted by these same inferior, mind-drugging means of entertainment' (2008: 314).

Making one of the most vociferous cases for the detective genre's ideological conservatism is Mukoma Wa Ngugi. A literary scholar and author of two detective novels, *Nairobi Heat* (2010) and *Black Star Nairobi* (2013), Mukoma details why he believes that detective fiction as a genre inherently reaffirms existing power relations. First, Mukoma contends that, unlike literary fiction, African detective stories can rarely be read as 'a meditation on the larger issues' because the larger issues merely 'become the backdrop that makes the plot possible' (2018: 159). Second, according to Mukoma, violence in detective fiction is always individual and never the source of revolutionary agency in what he describes as the Fanonian sense. 'In *Things Fall Apart*', he writes, 'individual acts of violence transform the whole society', whereas in Ghanaian detective novelist Kwei Quartey's '*Wife of the Gods*, individual actions transform individual lives' (159). Mukoma claims no more political significance than that for the violence in his own detective novels.10 Mukoma never clarifies how individual acts of violence are not social; violence is after all a fundamentally social act. Regardless of the distinction, Mukoma's third, and perhaps most important contention is that 'even in times of great upheaval the detectives and

9   Chakava explains that Spear, which would go on to publish several crime novels, 'was aimed to attract the low-brow reader's leisure time, as opposed to going to a movie or a football match, watching TV or chatting with a neighbor. The language was controlled and the length was fixed between eighty to ninety-six pages, in the belief that the African reader was young and had a short concentration span' (Chakava 1997: 160).
10 Despite Mukoma's attestation that the big issues are never more than background in his detective novels, Eleni Condouriotis (2017) argues that he continually brings history into and out of the narrative foreground.

criminals are working within society, working within the rules even as they break them' (159). For this reason, he suggests that while political and social conflict are good for putting crime plots in motion, the genre itself perforce reproduces dominant value systems and/or specific governing regimes more commonly than it challenges them.[11]

Implicit in Mukoma's contention is that the detective story offers the opportunity for a reassertion of the forms of authority that legitimate the modern state as the most salutary political formation for maintaining collective life. This line of argumentation has led many scholars of the genre to argue that detective stories inevitably reproduce existing relations of power and domination. Dennis Porter (1981), for instance, advances the case that the detective story should be read as a component of Althusser's ideological state apparatus, insofar as the genre generates consent for the police, military, and other components of the capitalist state's repressive machinery. Such arguments about the relation of the detective story to the state have also prompted more than one writer to contend, as British mystery novelist Dorothy Sayers does in her 1929 essay 'An Omnibus of Crime', that 'the detective-story proper could not [flourish] until public sympathy had veered around to the side of law and order', adding the jingoistic and racist contention that 'even today, the full blossoming of the detective-stories is found among the Anglo-Saxon races ... In the Southern States of Europe the law is less loved and the detective story is less frequent. We may not unreasonably trace a connection here' (1946: 74–75).[12]

As is clear from the accelerating production of detective fiction across the African continent since the 1940s, the detective genre can flourish where the sympathy for institutions of law and order is lacking and where the larger part of the reading public is not merely unsympathetic to the forces of law and order but outright hostile to them. To borrow Sayers's formulation, we may

---

11 On this point, Mpalive-Hangson Msiska's argument that Kenyan detective fiction promotes 'a particular ideal of masculinity as the privileged and dominant mode of African subjectivity' serves as a reminder that a patriarchal discourse continues to haunt Anglophone African detective fiction broadly (Msiska 2009: 136). Similarly, Binder suggests that even texts featuring female detectives put their protagonists in the contradictory position of 'asserting a claim to power and equality *within*' patriarchal institutions thus rendering them 'compromised to varying degrees as agents of' these institutions (Binder 2021: 133).

12 A half century later, the Mexican critic Carlos Monsiváis reiterates Sayers's underlying point, declaring that 'in Mexico there does not exist nor does it appear probable that there will exist a detective novel or literature of conspiracy and espionage' (qtd in Close 2008: 28). This is because, in Mexico, where few people have any confidence in the rule of law, Monsiváis contends, a 'police force unanimously judged corrupt retains no credibility: if this literature were to aspire to realism, the accused would almost never be the real criminal and, unless he were poor, would never receive punishment' (28).

not unreasonably trace a connection here.[13] To wit, Modisane tells us that in hindsight he came to recognize 'the sociological significance of what I was doing, that with a central idea behind them I could use my stories as a reflection or a study of our society' (1963: 139). And, perhaps more tellingly, Mukoma admits that 'as a scholar and reader I have found the divide between the literary and the popular to be a false opposition' (2018: 154). He continues:

> the reality for my generation, which grew up at the height of the neocolonial dictatorships with all its serious punishable ridiculousness (for example, it was illegal to dream and talk about the president's death and you needed a permit to gather more than five people), was that we read the literary alongside the popular – James Hadley Chase, Frederick Forsyth, and Robert Ludlum. But we also devoured popular fiction by African writers like David Maillu, Meja Mwangi, Mwangi Ruheni, and John Kariamiti … They were entertaining to read, but considering the Kenya of the 1980s, where the literary writers like my father, Ngũgĩ wa Thiong'o, were in exile or in detention, it was the popular writers who kept us reading and thinking about neocolonial Kenya. (154)

Even Osofisan eventually attempted a detective novel. He published the result, *Pirates*, under the pen name Okinba Launko with Lagos's Lantern Books in 2009. One might read into the pseudonym a continued disavowal of the genre fiction that Osofisan had found so offensive two and a half decades earlier. But the novel itself, while not especially well executed, attempts to bring to the crime mystery formula some of the same critical engagements with the problems of Nigerian social and political life that make Osofisan's self-consciously serious fiction and drama so important to the African literary canon.

Mukoma's seemingly contradictory messaging highlights the tension in the scholarship surveyed above between a desire for Fanonian political commitment and a lingering fear that African trash fiction is still trash fiction. In other words, Africanist detective fiction scholarship is just as encumbered by the weight of the conservative-ideological binary as is the scholarship on any other national or linguistic crime mystery tradition. Varying degrees of attention, or more frequently inattention, to how so-called conservative and

---

13 Other regions of the Global South have seen a similar growth in detective fiction writing. Among these, Mexico's *neopoliciaco* shares the most in its aesthetics and thematics with African detective fiction. Glenn Close's (2008) insights on the Mexican genre have helped me nuance many of my own. For another excellent analysis of the *neopoliciaco*, see Persephone Braham (2004). Pablo Piccato (2017) has been equally influential for examination of detective fiction in relation to the state.

so-called radical ideological imperatives actually operate has made it difficult to register the multi-layered story that detective Anglophone African fiction has been narrating about the state and sovereign authority since the late-colonial era. I share Pim Higginson's perspective, outlined in his study of Francophone Black Atlantic crime fiction, that to take crime fiction on its own terms requires readers to acknowledge the texts' much more complex relation to 'an ideological enterprise', including the possibility that they reject such a relation altogether (2011: 26). Andrew Pepper stresses that the same is true for the American, British, and French texts in his study. He insists that

> critical approaches that pay too much attention to the genre's capacities for imposing and advocating dominant ideologies or disciplinary norms, or, for that matter, those that overplay its political radicalism or deviancy or indeed its willingness to service politically progressive agendas, cannot do justice to the specificity of the genre's relationship to the justice system. (2016: 2)

Higginson's solution to the constraints of a reductive binary logic is to read crime fiction as a manifestation of what he terms the 'frivolous literary'. He explains that Francophone Black Atlantic authors of crime fiction authorize 'a radically new attitude toward the business of writing itself: 'pleasure ... writing that is, in the eyes of a Western tradition of recuperative instrumentalization of the other's cultural production, frivolous' (2011: 27). By 'recuperative instrumentalization', Higginson has in mind those critics who impute resistance politics onto crime writers who themselves make no explicit claims to or disavow such a politics. Recuperative reading, he suggests, co-opts 'the literary ... in the name of a political project' (16, 19). This co-optation in turn fixes African and other Black Atlantic writers in a narrow space in the 'hierarchical ordering of writerly aesthetics' of representing Black experience ethnographically through testimony and protest fiction (4). By contrast, 'the frivolous literary' draws attention to the act of writing as a source of pleasure and of 'the right not to be engaged' (18), not to mention as a source of individual financial gain. With this focus on entertainment Higginson does not so much dismiss the resistant potential of genre fiction as to relocate it. By emphasizing frivolity in relation to the literary, Higginson redirects the critical eye from questions of ideology to the subversive resistance to Western epistemes that overdetermine the relationship between writing and racial subjectivity. Commercial entertainments written with both the writer's and reader's pleasure in mind assert agency through refusal of these epistemes and through the embrace of joy. This is, Higginson writes, 'a meaningfully defiant gesture – though resolutely not a revolutionary one' (18).

Higginson's notion of the frivolous literary calls to mind Tsitsi Jaji's and Lily Saint's contention that genre's broader critical productivity in African expressive arts is also a function of its potential for resistant playfulness. In what they see as the 'rapturous abundance' of African expressive genres, Jaji and Saint identify a spirited challenge to taxonomy itself. 'In its African incarnations, and in an era of ambivalence', they write, 'genre expresses rebellion, more the artist's tool of insurgency than the critic's cuff of discipline' (2017: 153). The rebellion they see is in part against the hierarchies of aesthetic value, so often determined in the Global North at the cost of African cultural prestige. Jaji and Saint argue that the rebellion of African expressive genres is also mobilized against Aristotelian taxonomies with their pathological obsession with purity, and against the very conception of classification itself, especially insofar as it continues to underwrite colonial and racial domination (154). This 'rapture' is not simply reactionary. African artists often work around genre constraints rather than against them, Jaji and Saint emphasize. Genre consequently becomes a form of play, not for form's sake only, but as a way of elaborating 'postcolonial African experience' (152). Which is to say, 'genre, politics, and play in the postcolony not only coexist but are, in fact, co-constitutive' (152).

Understandings of genre such as those proposed by Higginson and Jaji and Saint offer powerful critical frameworks for reading Anglophone African detective fiction outside of the straitjacket of ideological binaries. Emphasizing the defiance of writerly and readerly pleasure can be especially useful, for example, when making sense of the devious detectives crafted by Black South Africans writing during the escalation of apartheid law-making in the 1950s or the tongue-in-cheek counter-espionage agents brought to life during Nigeria's intermittent military dictatorships in the 1970s.[14] Pleasure in these contexts stands as its own politics. So too does the embrace of storytelling not defined strictly by protest or 'the endless dialectic of tradition and modernity, village and city, orality and writing' (Higginson 2011: 8). Any study of Anglophone African detective fiction must thus attend to the act of writing itself as a site of critical engagement.

However, I am less willing to relinquish the progressive ideological import of Anglophone African detective fiction to the degree that Higginson suggests we do for Francophone crime fiction. This is not to suggest that Higginson lets go of ideological exegesis completely. He does not. It is perhaps a difference between the Francophone canon that he analyzes and the Anglophone one that I read, but, viewed collectively, Anglophone African detective stories and novels rarely let the reader forget the crises, fragilities, or excesses that characterize

---

14 My capitalization of 'Black' here and throughout the book reflects the recent move to capitalize the term by newspapers such as the *New York Times* and style guides such as the *Chicago Manual of Style*. See Coleman (2020).

socio-political life in the African postcolony. Decade after decade, these texts meditate on the state of the state, narrating, to borrow a phrase from Tejumola Olaniyan, 'a biography of the state' (2015). When the state is under scrutiny, questions of ideology are never far removed. Thus, I read Anglophone African detective fiction in terms similar to those Pepper proposes for the French, British, and American texts in his study. Anglophone African detective fiction cannot be reduced to a simple conservative-progressive binary. Nor can it be described at the level of the individual text or in the aggregate as either exclusively affirming or exclusively critiquing excesses of state power. The reality is much more multifaceted. In Anglophone African writing, affirmation and opposition often operate in entangled, mutually constituting ways, giving new inflections to so-called conservative and so-called radical ideological articulations.

A recurrent example of this entanglement is the way that writers activate the genre's potential to make detectives symbolize the Law in ways that call attention to the chasm between the ideal of the Law and its uneven and often oppressive application.[15] With the exception of the protagonists of the police procedural, Africa's fictional detectives generally toil outside the state's institutions of law and order, and sometimes in antagonism with them. However, they almost always endeavor, often in the face of sure failure, to ensure that the rule of law is followed, that victims of crimes receive the recognition they are due under the law, and that the villains get appropriate sanction. From the earliest Anglophone African detective stories written during the years of 'aggressive boot-stamping' colonial police regiments (Ekwensi 1954: 124) through the politics of the belly and criminalization of the state decades of the 1970s and '80s then into the period of widespread neoliberal governance reform when austerity-minded governments further shifted the burdens of risk and security from the state onto individual citizens,[16] African writers have continually reimagined this 'conservative' function to counter-hegemonic ends. Private detectives, investigative journalists, civic-minded citizens, and police constables go about their solving of criminal mysteries whether or not social and political conditions

---

15 Again, not all detective stories, African or otherwise, hinge on law-breaking, nor do all detectives serve the state directly. Poe saw his Dupin mysteries as stories of ratiocination, not as crime mysteries per se. The suspense he envisioned derived from the tension stemming from the challenge of solving a seemingly impossible puzzle under spatial and temporal constraints. Variants of the mystery genre, such as metaphysical detective stories, including those by Jorge Luis Borges or Umberto Eco, remain primarily focused on puzzles of an epistemological nature. For scholarship on metaphysical detective fiction, see Howard Haycraft (1941), Michael Holquist (1971), and Patricia Merivale and Susan Sweeney (1998).

16 The phrase 'politics of the belly' is taken from Jean-Francois Bayart (1993). The phrase 'criminalization of the state' appears in a wide range of publications, but the primary reference here is to Jean-Francois Bayart, Stephen Ellis, and Beatrice Hibou (2009).

permit justice to be served. In this way, they affirm basic moral and legal values much the same way that a character such as Agatha Christie's Hercule Poirot does. But instead of generating consent for anti-democratic social, economic, and political relations that might exist in the postcolony, affirmation more often functions to sustain a vision of an idealized sovereign African state. This sort of idealization does double duty insofar as it measures the distance between existing and expected social orders, thereby providing another framework for critique. Not every Anglophone African crime mystery focalizes the state or the sovereign ideal in this way, but, in my reading, many do.

Another example of where I see entanglement is in the liberal ideologies that periodically surface in Anglophone African detective fiction. Crime mysteries, at least in Britain and the United States, are often read as expressions of liberal values. As one narrative goes, the classic whodunit of Poe, Doyle, and Christie presumes a fundamental liberal social equilibrium that is predicated on rational self-interest, civic solidarity, and individual liberty, which the criminal act disrupts in no small part by transforming everyone into a suspect. The detective restores this equilibrium by identifying and expelling from society a single criminal (or criminal syndicate), thereby reassuring the community of characters within the narrative and the reader alike of the overarching safety and security of the normative liberal social order. From the first publication of Poe's Auguste Dupin stories in the 1840s, the Anglo-American iterations of the genre have elucidated the daily anxieties of private property ownership, the fears of internal and external others, and the desire for the stable, bounded structures of family, town, and nation. The classic Anglo-American whodunit quickly came to be, as Sean McCann puts it so eloquently, 'a paean to those humble bourgeois virtues in the guise of a parable of their disappearance' (2000: 14).

Rarely do Anglophone African detective stories pretend the pre-existence of a liberal social order available for easy restoration. For that matter, the Anglo-American crime mystery tradition has never been so neatly arranged as the narrative suggests. Even for Poe and Doyle, a liberal social equilibrium was always more an ideal than a reality, predicated as it was on the insular homosocial world of the detective and his 'Watson' rather than on the brute inequalities of nineteenth century Paris or London. What does frequently carry over into Anglophone African detective fiction is the expectation of a reassuring but not overbearing hand of a liberal state that guarantees citizens their rights to a Lockean self-possession and that is otherwise organized to let individuals get on with their lives free from impediment. Arthur Maimane's fiercely individualistic and entrepreneurial private detective O. Chester Morena, for example, conducts his criminal investigations as an assertion of sovereign selfhood in resistance to the apartheid South African state's organizing logic of racialized dispossession. Unity Dow's characters similarly demand that Botswanan rule of law be applied equitably so that women enjoy the same legal recognition as rights-bearing citizens that men do. Kwei Quartey's Darko Dawson mysteries offer their protagonist as a model of meritocratic achievement in a Ghanaian society in need of alternatives to old-boy networks and patronage hierarchies. The detectives in many other texts endeavor to ensure institutional and governmental accountability to the citizenry. Not all detective mysteries are so liberal-minded, of course. Rodwell Musekiwa Machingauta's *Detective Ridgemore Riva* (1994) celebrates authoritarianism at its most draconian and Ulysses Chuka Kibuuka's anarchic *For the Fairest* (1991) casts the nation-state of any kind as an irrelevance.[17] And even for those Anglophone African texts that encode liberal values, their liberalism is only partially that of Mill or Burke. In its diverse iterations, Anglophone African detective fiction's liberalism is shot through with a postcolonial recognition of the colonial legacies and neocolonial structural inequalities that compromise any individual state's claim to liberally defined political sovereignty.

In this respect, Anglophone African detective fiction mobilizes, but also significantly expands, hard-boiled noir's frame of reference. McCann (2000) argues that where the most conservative expressions of the classic British whodunit had depicted the nightmarish inversion of the liberal capitalist order only to reaffirm core liberal values, the hard-boiled detective story turned a deeply suspicious and cynical eye on the precepts of liberal society. For Dashiell Hammett, Raymond Chandler, James M. Cain, and the other writers who helped develop the American hard-boiled mode, the institutions of liberal society are seen to be indifferent to the survival of individual citizens, free association 'protects only the right of the strong to exploit the weak', and rational self-interest functions merely as a cover for rapacious greed (McCann 2000: 23, 29). Jennifer Fay and Justus Nieland add that noir, the French term for hard-boiled crime fiction, gave writers and filmmakers new tools for examining 'human agency as increasingly governed by forces beyond reason or rational control, not only within the human (passion, madness, paranoia, trauma, and the like), but beyond and abstracted from human capacity in the very modernity of the modern world' (2009: 8). One aspect of the modern world that came under special scrutiny was the state.

With few exceptions, Anglophone African detective fiction refracts its expectation for liberal governance through noir-tinged narratives. Detectives battle, not always successfully, to secure their client's and, by extension, their community's safety and autonomy in a world defined by some combination of rapacious social relations, institutional corruption, and state tyranny. If American hard-boiled crime fiction illuminates liberalism's crises and contradictions, dismissing the liberal conceits of rational self-interest and

---

17 On Machingauta's authoritarian aesthetics, see Primorac (2005).

benevolent governance as bankrupt and forever overwhelmed by darker human impulses and uncheckable institutional power, Anglophone African noir offers less by way for critiquing liberalism itself than it does for assessing the conditions preventing its realization in postcolonial societies. The legacies of colonial authoritarianism and colonial racism, the winner-take-all logic of global capitalism, and the World Bank's control over governing priorities come under its focus.[18] Moreover, if what noir does is enunciate social anxieties about modernity, Anglophone African noir speaks to the deep anxieties about the state, as both the locus of the modernity of the modern world and as the principal source of material and epistemic insecurity for its citizens.

World Literature as Method

If my reading of liberalism or noir – or any of my periodic declarations about normative features of the detective genre for that matter – appears to overly yoke Anglophone African detective fiction to an Anglo-American canon, it is a consequence of the writers' declared influences. Keen readers and, in many instances avid cinema-goers, African novelists have been deeply familiar with the Anglo-American crime mystery canon. 1930s-era records of the Carnegie Non-European Library Service in South Africa, for instance, reveal that its patrons were enthusiastic readers of mysteries, especially those of Agatha Christie and Arthur Conan Doyle (Sandwith 2018: 25, 31). Sherlock Holmes references abound in novels across regions and decades. Kole Omotoso explains that *Fella's Choice* was his deliberate attempt to write 'an African James Bond' (1979: 10). David G. Maillu's character Benni Kamba 009 is just one of the many additional Bond allusions. *Drum* magazine's writers in the 1950s looked to the hard-boiled detective fictions of Leslie Charteris and Peter Cheyney. Arthur Maimane draws extensively from Hammett and Chandler in his serialized detective stories for the magazine.[19] James Hadley Chase's imprint is large and deep. Ulysses Chuka Kibuuka (2009) cites Chase as an influence on his noir

---

18 An important, though still underrecognized precursor to this aspect of Anglophone African writing can be found in African American novelist John Edward Bruce's fiction. Twenty years prior to the first American hard-boiled stories, Bruce had already employed the crime mystery's conventions in *The Black Sleuth* (1907, 2002) to illuminate the violence inherent in the United States' racialized enforcement of legal protection and sanction, and did so within a trans-Atlantic, anticolonial narrative framework. While it is unlikely that any Anglophone African writer would have had access to *The Black Sleuth*, even after its reprint as a stand-alone novel in 2002, Bruce's mystery anticipates many of the ways that Anglophone African writers will expand noir's critical frame to speak also to the problematics of race, coloniality, and postcoloniality.

19 Colette Guldimann (2019: 270-1) drew my attention to the Hammett and Chandler allusions.

detective writing, as does Helon Habila (2013) in explaining his rationale for establishing Cordite Books, a crime-focused imprint of Nigerian publishing house Parrésia. A character in Sekelani S. Banda's *Dead Ends* recalls a Chase novel read in childhood (Banda 2000: 68), and Rosina Umelo goes so far as to have her protagonist nickname his tenacious lawyer "Hadley Chase" (1985: 109).[20] Meja Mwangi adapted his detective thriller, *The Bushtrackers* (1979), from the script for *Revenge*, the movie African American filmmaker Gordon Parks Jr. was shooting in Kenya when he died. Mukoma Wa Ngugi identifies Walter Mosely's Easy Rawlins novels as an influence on his development as a fiction writer (2018: 154). Less clear are other global transcolonial circuits of influence on Anglophone African writing. But even here, many African writers signal a familiarity, for example, with Asian martial arts films.

As African writers absorbed the detective genre's Anglo-American history and sought to make sense of the genre's possibilities for themselves, they also filtered their ideas through one another. Cyprian Ekwensi published in South Africa's *Drum*; *Drum* was distributed in Nigeria, Ghana, and Kenya; and *African Parade* explicitly copied *Drum*'s aesthetic for Central African Federation readers.[21] Similarly, in the 1970s and '80s, Macmillan's Pacesetters series established a continent-wide audience for its popular fiction titles so that readers and aspiring writers in any given place were as likely to come across detective novels by Nigerians, Zimbabweans, and Kenyans as they were those by their compatriots. The resulting intertextual influences are never anything less than multidirectional. Locally published and distributed novels such as Omotoso's *Fella's Choice* and Hilary Ng'weno's *The Men from Pretoria*, for example, reveal more than a hint of inspiration from Drum Publications' Lance Spearman crime fighting and counter-espionage adventures, which circulated multinationally as photonovel look-reads in the late 1960s, and quite clearly spawn an entire subcategory of Pacesetters novels that followed, beginning in the late 1970s. Anglophone African detective fiction writers continue to debate one another, especially about the political and social tenor of their shared literary endeavor: Kenya's Mukoma, as indicated earlier, calls into question the revolutionary capacity of Ghanaian Kwei Quartey's police procedurals, and Quartey (2021) in turn raises the alarm about Unity Dow's graphic depiction of the evisceration of a prepubescent girl.

Anglophone African writers are far from unique in their engagements with other global texts and writers. Pepper reminds his readers that

---

20 Writing in the 1980s, Cyprian Ekwensi (1986: 105, 107) bemoaned the fact that Nigerian readers were still regularly devouring James Hadley Chase at the expense of African writers, noting further that the country's Kingsway department store chain had recently featured a display of forty-five of Chase's titles and none by Africans.
21 For details about *African Parade*, see Stephanie Bosch Santana (2014).

> Vidocq's *Memoirs* were simultaneously translated into English and circulated in London, influencing writers on both sides of the Channel; Poe read Vidocq, Émile Gaboriau read Poe, and Doyle read Gaboriau; Simenon and Hammett read each other's work and both were championed by André Gide ... [Chester] Himes only wrote his Harlem crime stories once he emigrated to France and only then at the urging of his Parisian editor. (2016: 8)

Further, as Higginson (2011) reveals, Himes was consumed eagerly by subsequent generations of Francophone African crime writers. In their introduction to *Crime Fiction as World Literature*, Louise Nilsson, David Damrosch, and Theo D'Haen point out that 'crime fiction circulates in ways that go quite beyond common understandings of the diffusion of the novel from European centers to non-Western peripheries, as traced by Franco Moretti, or the competition for recognition in Paris or New York emphasized by Pascale Casanova' (2017: 2).[22] One cannot deny the detective genre's linguistic and national traditions, as my use of the term 'Anglo-American detective fiction' and as the various studies of South African crime fiction attest. And there are more than enough Nigerian texts to speak of Nigerian detective fiction. But these lineages are never separable from the transnational circuits and circulations along which detective fiction has long traveled. In its aesthetic developments and polyvalent critical engagements, detective fiction is resolutely global. Anglophone African writers recognize this and, through these circulations and crosscurrents, insert themselves as active agents into the detective genre's global history.

While I insist on African genre fiction's globality, my focus is on what makes Anglophone African detective fiction an *African* articulation, which is to say contextually specific to recognizable African realities but not necessarily radically distinct from its counterparts elsewhere. Thus, I am alert to Wai Chee Dimock's caution that where genres share distinguishable attributes across global zones, as is the case with detective fiction, those similarities should be viewed 'as probabilistic and distributional; it has less to do with common ancestry than with an iterative structure of comparable attributes, issuing from environments roughly similar but widely dispersed. What matters here is not lineage, but a phenomenal field of contextually induced parallels' (2006: 86). I am equally attentive to Stephanie Newell when she asserts that the production of so much of Africa's popular literature '*outside* the genre-determining relationships that characterize Western popular fiction' has freed the continent's creative artists from rigid literary formulas and opened them to 'wider varieties of intertextual currents' (2002a: 4, emphasis original). To Newell's point, Anglophone Africa's

---

22 See also Stewart King (2014).

detective fiction writers freely absorb, discard, combine, and recombine elements of the detective tale's many subgenres, not to mention influences from Asian martial arts, American Blaxploitation films, and even the picaresque to fashion texts that are simultaneously generically recognizable and contextually specific.

Raymond Williams shares Dimock's view that genre 'is neither an ideal type nor a traditional order nor a set of technical rules' (Williams 1977: 185). However, he departs from Dimock's conceptualization of autonomous genre formation when he asserts that genres are nevertheless historically rooted and routed and 'that there are undoubted continuities of literary form through and beyond the societies and periods to which they have such relations. In genre theory, everything depends on the character and process of such continuities' (182–183). On the problem of how to make sense of generic continuities in African contexts, I follow Newell, but only up to a point. Treading a path between Dimock and Williams, Newell argues that any continuities from the metropole to the postcolony are limited to form and aesthetics. About a literary genre's themes and meanings, she contends that: 'When dominant Western genres such as the romance and thriller are put into operation by writers who are situated geographically and economically outside the centres of mass-production, then the ideologies commonly associated with the genres are detached' (2002a: 4). By Newell's reasoning, detective fiction's longstanding reproduction of Western liberal values, its propensity to generate consent for the state's repressive apparatus and for capitalist social relations, its recurrent misogyny, and so forth should disappear from African crime mysteries while new ideologies accrue in their place. While I share this latter position, that genres can take on ideological articulations not apparent in other parts of the world, I would not go so far as to assert that 'the ideologies commonly associated with the genres are detached'. Detached implies a severing, an erasure of residual traces that, in my reading, fails to adequately describe the mechanics of African crime mystery genres.

What makes the crime investigation genre so productive is, in fact, the very continuity of ideological effects and critical preoccupations from predominantly British and American iterations of the genre, including those attached to specific subgenres, such as the police procedural or espionage adventure, as well as those attached to specific components of literary form, such as novelistic temporality or closure. I do not suggest that African writers perpetuate these ideological accruals haphazardly. Rather, African fiction writers embrace the ideological articulations of a global genre where useful, resignify them when necessary, resist them when they are counter-productive to critique, and generally transmute them for locally specific social realities. In ways analogous to how postcolonial reimaginations of the bildungsroman retain the European specter of liberal individualism to distinguish the modalities of postcolonial subject formation, African detective writers make ample use of the Western crime mystery's conceptualization of the state, citizenship, and sovereignty to assess their uniquely valanced operations in the postcolony.[23]

These transmutations and resignifications take many shapes. Some writers toy with specific narrative conventions to redirect inherited ideological imperatives. Arthur Maimane's mid-1950s serials for *Drum* magazine, for instance, scan unambiguously as detective stories. Instead of putting his investigatory prowess in the service of apartheid law, however, Maimane's protagonist utilizes his sleuthing skills to outwit the white police and the larger white settler colonial administration in ways that resist apartheid's systemic dispossession of Black selfhood. Beginning with her first police procedural in 1970, the Nigerian novelist Adaora Lily Ulasi deconstructs the crime mystery formula almost to the point of unrecognizability when she pits British presuppositions about the authority of the state and its Enlightenment-sanctioned evidentiary logic against Yoruba and Igbo conceptions of reason and justice. Her detectives routinely fail to resolve their cases in ways that reveal the epistemic limitations of Western jurisprudence in Nigeria. For other writers, changed historical contexts are enough to give new inflections to old articulations. In American and British police procedurals, for example, Dennis Porter (1981) sees little more than ideologically conservative affirmations of capitalist hegemony. Like the American and British texts that Porter analyzes, Ghanaian and Nigerian police procedurals of the 1960s affirm the sovereign power of the police, the state more broadly, and capitalist social relations but with a significant difference. They read as extensions of the counter-hegemonic discourses of decolonization that had fueled independence movements. Blackness, which under imperialist logic had been the sign of lack, comes to codify the full realization of the liberal democratic state. Some ideological continuities carry over with little variation, of course; perhaps not the fascist aesthetics that George Orwell (1944) identifies in James Hadley Chase's novels, but certainly some of Chase's misogyny. Ghana's late-1960s police procedurals, flush with female corpses and female killers, are a prime case in point. But as will be evident in the chapters that follow, Africa's writers attend regularly to the critical and thematic potentials afforded by detective fiction's narrative temporalities, its mechanics of closure and resolution, its constitution of detectives and villains, its methods of investigation and discovery, and its many other formulaic components. Through such transfigurations and resignification of inherited meanings, writers open the genre to new possibilities of representing and critiquing sovereign relations.

---

23 I am thinking in particular of Joseph Slaughter's (2007) analysis of the postcolonial bildungsroman.

Chapter Overview

Colonial domination, the euphoria and then disillusionment of self-rule, and the social-structural destabilizations of neoliberal global capitalism produce distinct varieties of crime mysteries. The same can be said for detective fiction in relation to the diverse varieties of state formations that take shape during these periods. Because of the uneven historical development of these political and literary processes, I combine a chronological and thematic approach to the material.

Part 1, 'Africanizing Detective Fiction's Un/Sovereign Subjects' traces the development of Anglophone African detective fiction from the 1940s to the early 1990s as writers responded first to the tyrannies of colonial governmentality and then to the incipient promises and perils of self-rule. Chapter 1 initiates this inquiry with an analysis of detective fiction in the vibrant urban milieus of Lagos and Sophiatown during the late years of colonial rule in West Africa and during the first escalation of apartheid law-making by South Africa's newly ascendant Afrikaner Nationalist Party. Cyprian Ekwensi, Arthur Maimane, and their contemporaries, the chapter shows, exploit the detective genre's codes of investigation and discovery and its anticipation of justice under the law to assess the carceral logics of and possibilities for resistance to colonial dispossession. Ghana's achievement of self-rule in 1957 triggered an almost immediate pivot from this dissident detective mystery to the heroic police procedural and, in the 1970s, to the counter-espionage thriller, a transformation that largely repeats itself with the achievement of full democracy in early 1990s South Africa. In Chapter 2, I explore how the cop stories and spy thrillers simultaneously celebrate sovereign self-rule and register profound anxieties about the legacies of colonial governance, the potential for authoritarian rule, and the simple day-to-day interactions between citizens and the official agents of state power. Chapter 3 looks to government corruption investigation narratives from the 1970s and '80s that focalize the economic and political crises of the period. In these novels, investigative journalists and private detectives do not so much make visible the pervasive venality perfected by the emergent kleptocratic classes – it is starkly visible to everyone in the novels – as illustrate the seeming impossibility of containing it. I argue that what emerges is a reflection on the structural fragility of a postcolonial state that is barely two decades old. By playing on the crime mystery's implicit futurity the writers of the period also question whether the nation-state is any longer the most logical or effective vehicle for reaching the anticipated future of decolonization.

In Part 2, Chapter 4 marks the beginning of a three-chapter examination of late twentieth- and early-twenty-first-century fiction that, borrowing a term from Latin American literary critic Misha Kokotovic (2006), I describe as 'neoliberal noir'. The first chapter of this section compares novels by Tony

Marinho, Unity Dow, Diale Tlholwe, and Wahome Mutahi and Wahome Karengo for how they probe the question of what happens when, as is characteristic of neoliberal governance, the power over life and death gets shifted from individual governments to international financial institutions, to global pharmaceutical, mining, and arms corporations, to economically powerful individuals, and, above all, to the self-governing citizen. Building on Chapter 4's arguments about neoliberal noir as critique and Chapter 3's focus on decolonial temporality, Chapter 5 examines mystery series by Parker Bilal and Kwei Quartey that exploit seriality itself to articulate problems associated with the increasing sovereignty of global capitalist time. One of the principal effects of their resistant seriality, I argue, is to demonstrate, in both form and content, how neoliberal time gets experienced in the postcolony as stasis and de-developmentalization, which is to say, as an obstacle to decolonization. I conclude my examination of neoliberal noir, in Chapter 6, by analyzing two detective thrillers that elucidate the significant material and ontological risks inherent to embracing the neoliberal conceit that to make one's entrepreneurial investments publicly transparent is to make oneself legible to the market. Nigeria's Rosina Umelo and South Africa's Angela Makholwa offer as protagonists paragons of neoliberal virtue who have embraced this vision of transparency but who, through investigatory efforts to clear their reputations from malicious rumors spread by economic competitors, are forced to confront fundamental tensions and contradictions of neoliberal self-governance, especially in its gendered manifestations.

The Matter of the Corpus (but most definitely not a corpse)

To write a book such as this one is to be reminded of the cultural and institutional forces at work in the constitution of archives. Like genres, archives are products of cultural intermediaries – librarians, amateur and professional scholars, critics, and the like – who group texts in ways that both assign value to them and reflect the value systems and priorities of those doing the assembling. A growing number of literary scholars, many based in institutions outside of Africa, have recently begun demarcating an archive of African detective fiction and, in the process, anointing its canon. The archive I have assembled here has been influenced by this scholarship but is distinctly my own. With Shu-mei Shih's (2004) admonition against Eurocentric modes of recognition in mind, I appreciate that I, like these other scholars, have at times brought to bear my own conceptions of what constitutes a detective story.[24] I acknowledge also that I gravitate toward novels and stories that reflect my long interest in the interplay of literary genres and political formation. But I have also remained open to

---

24 On this point, see also Adejunmobi (2017).

the intertextual currents that have generated stories and novels that deploy similar codes in ways both recognizable and unrecognizable to readers versed in American hard-boiled fiction, the British locked-room mystery, or other global mystery traditions. Cyprian Ekwensi's novel *People of the City*, which I analyze at length in Chapter 1, is perhaps the most obvious of such inclusions, but by no means the only one.

On a practical level, to assemble an archive of Anglophone African detective stories is to confront an imperialist history of taxonomic value systems. Few cataloguing systems designate the subject categories of African popular fiction with any precision. Rarely are detective plots distinguished from crime plots, and many of those are identified only as popular fiction or simply as fiction. Amaechi Nzekwe's novel *A Killer on the Loose* (1985, 2002) is a good example in that it unfolds as a formulaic murder investigation narrative but is catalogued in WorldCat as 'Nigerian Fiction'; whereas Agatha Christie's *Murder on the Orient Express* gets the subject line 'Private Investigators – England – Fiction'. Subject categories such as these reflect what has been important in a Eurocentric universe in which a text's Africanness or, say, its Nigerianness matters more than its genre or other aesthetic or thematic attributes. These facts make the basic act of identifying stories and novels with detective genre elements enormously challenging. To make the corpus of Anglophone African detective fiction visible has required no small amount of my own sleuthing: ferreting out clues, following traces and leads, and recognizing the occasional red herring.[25] I make no claims to an exhaustive accounting of either novels or periodical fiction. I trust that future scholars will fill in my gaps, looking also to the growing body of detective stories on film, video, and other screen media.

To best illustrate the evolving hermeneutic I see in my assembled archive, I have selected from the more than 200 English-language detective stories and novels about two dozen paradigmatic texts from East, West, North, and Southern Africa that engage especially acutely with the problematics of sovereignty in

---

25 Two bibliographies have been particularly helpful. Even though it makes no distinctions between crime plots and detective plots, Christine Matzke's (2012b) bibliography of African crime fiction pointed me in useful directions. The other was shorter but focused specifically on crime mysteries. It was available on the Indiana University library's website in the early 2010s, but has since disappeared. Unfortunately, I did not record the author's name or enough information to identify it now. The occasional scholarly essay or blog on individual African mystery and thriller writers pointed me to other titles. I discovered no small number of the texts by simply walking library stacks and pulling every book with a promising title and then searching for other novels by the same author or publisher or, when I was especially lucky, series name. Surveying Anglophone Africa's vast stores of newspapers and magazines for the possibility of the occasional detective story would take an enormous team of researchers so I focused my time and limited resources on a few periodicals known to have published crime mysteries.

the postcolony and that in many additional cases innovate in their interplay of form and content. Readers familiar with even a few African detective stories will no doubt question some of my choices. In the interest of analytical economy, many excellent novels have been relegated to a passing reference or endnote. In other cases, I underemphasize certain works simply because other scholars have already published such fine analyses of them that I would have little to add, and thus to highlight them at any significant length would diminish my ability to discuss works that have yet to receive due attention. Ranka Primorac's superb scholarship on Zambian and Zimbabwean thrillers come to mind, as do various studies of Mike Nicol's, Margie Orford's, and Mukoma Wa Ngugi's novels.[26]

Given my interest in the transnational constitution of an Anglophone tradition of African detective fiction, I also focus on titles that complement one another in regional comparison and emphasize those that reveal contextually induced parallels across Africa's regional and cultural borders. This comparative approach permits me to read texts from different countries and different regions of the African continent in dialogue with one another. Some chapters examine works from just two or three countries and others look broadly at crime mysteries from over a dozen. This approach allows for both microscopic analysis of specific national texts produced in any given historical moment as well as for macroscopic historicization of *African* crime mystery writing as it is represented by writing from every Anglophone country that has produced even a single crime mystery. Like all works of comparative literary analysis, my study sacrifices some of the locally contextual specificity that would come from of an extended focus on, say, Nigerian or Kenyan detective fiction. But the strength of comparative analysis is its power to elucidate textual nuances and broader patterns that might not be apparent in narrower analytical configurations. Illuminating broad patterns in Anglophone African popular fiction has been my goal from the beginning. The other impulse behind my comparatist approach has been to survey a rich body of writing that has yet to receive the synthetic overview that it deserves. While this book is not a literary history in any strict sense, I trust that its readers will discover in it the broad contours of the history of Anglophone African detective fiction that is at once a cultural history of a uniquely African critique of the ongoing problematics of sovereignty and decolonization.

---

26 Ranka Primorac's scholarship is cited elsewhere in this introduction and throughout the book. On Orford's and Nicol's detective fiction, see Comaroff and Comaroff (2016: ch. 1.3), Binder (2021: chs 1 and 2), and de Kock (2016). On Mukoma's novels, see Samuel Wambugu Wanjohi (2015), Condouriotis (2017), Pahl (2018), Ribic (2021), and Naidu (2022).

Part 1

Africanizing Detective Fiction's Un/Sovereign Subjects

Dispossession, Rescue, and the Sovereign Self in the Colonial-Era Detective Story

Anglophone Africa's first detective stories arrived in a world primed to receive them. Readers and cinema-goers from Lagos to Sophiatown were already avid consumers of locked-room whodunits and Hollywood gangster films.[1] Perhaps more importantly, the anxieties about individual autonomy, competitive social relations, urban complexity, and the availability of state-backed protections that give detective fiction its emotional weight and cultural currency were felt acutely in the fast-growing colonial cities where most potential readers resided. The urban social atomization that freed individuals from the traditional strictures of village sociability often left individuals isolated and anonymous, and vulnerable to predation. The privations of the colonial economy could force otherwise law-abiding people into the various forms of criminality required for basic economic survival. Above all, the colonial state could, and did, exert its repressive powers into even the most private spaces the city, serving as a continual reminder that the state's purpose was not to ensure the rights and security of its African population but to dispossess Africans of them. For all the city's economic opportunities, radical individual freedoms, and illicit pleasures, few places could be considered safe, few strangers or friends fully trustworthy, and no agent of the law a reassuring presence. The colonial city remained the locus of persistent menace, of perpetual risk and vulnerability, and danger of physical, social, and psychic obliteration.

With an appreciation for the detective story's unique ability to dramatize anxieties such as these, Ghana's R.E. Obeng and Nigeria's Cyprian Ekwensi wrote their first detective stories in the 1940s, and South Africa's Arthur Maimane and Mbokotwane Manqupu published theirs, in *Drum* magazine, in the 1950s. Little information remains about the style, content, or themes of Obeng's now-lost detective story collection *Issa Busanga*.[2] The same cannot be said for Maimane's *Chief* series (1953), Manqupu's 'Love Comes Deadly' (1955), or Ekwensi's short stories (1947, 1948, 1951) and novel *People of the City* (1954). For their African readers, Maimane, Manqupu, and Ekwensi craft distinctly African mysteries

---

1   See Corinne Sandwith (2018: 25, 31), Rob Nixon (1994), and Saheed Aderinto (2015).
2   For the little information there exists on Obeng's writing career, see Stephanie Newell (2002b: 184) and Kari Darko (2001).

that play on the fantasies and fears of modern urban life. Their protagonists' adventures offer tantalizing glimpses of nightclubs, high-class restaurants, fancy houses, and department stores to which so many urban Africans aspired but also of the gambling dens, hidden shebeens, and grisly murder scenes that provided their own lurid thrills. Ekwensi's, Maimane's, and Manqupu's mysteries are less Holmesian games of the intellect than they are gritty and cynical tales in which African crime reporters, private detectives, and police investigators battle those villains who are most likely to menace the readers of such stories in real life: pickpockets, con artists, black-marketeers, extortionate landlords, corrupt civil servants, and rapacious colonial constables. Rarely are culprits handed over to the police or is justice served by the state. Justice, when it comes at all, often takes the more modest form of recognition of the 'human story' of both criminal and victim, as Ekwensi's investigative crime reporter Amusa Sango puts it in *People of the City* (120).

Ekwensi's, Maimane's, and Manqupu's many critics have been unsparing in their negative assessments of the writers' crime fiction. Literary scholar Bernth Lindfors dismisses Maimane's detective stories as 'consciously, even boastfully derivative … of American short fiction' with nothing authentically South African about them (1991: 56, 57). Striking a similar note, Nigerian playwright, novelist, and cultural critic Femi Osofisan writes of Ekwensi, 'as far as form is concerned, he invents nothing; if he wrote tomorrow, it would be a Nigerian version of James Bond or of *Star Wars*' (2008: 317). Emmanuel Obiechina views Ekwensi's *People of the City* as a rich exploration of life in the colonial city, but he nevertheless levels an accusation, like Franco Moretti would about detective fiction two decades later, that 'there are in fact no characters strictly speaking but "people" and there is no intense exploration of life but a description of incidents which condition life' (1973: 153).[3]

Drum's fiction has also come under fire for its reliance on individual heroes in an era of increasingly organized collective political struggle. In his frequently cited 1991 essay 'Rediscovery of the Ordinary', South African novelist Njabulo Ndebele distinguishes *Drum*'s political writing, which he sees as successfully revealing 'much of the ugliness of economic exploitation in South Africa' (2002: 135), from its fiction, which he suggests 'simply titillated the reader' (135) and showed 'an almost total lack of interest in the directly political issues of the time' (134). The political writing Ndebele refers to includes *Drum*'s periodic 'Mr. Drum' exposés of the horrific conditions Black South Africans faced in jails and on prison labor farms, and of the hypocrisy of whites-only churches and other institutions of white supremacy. The fiction encompasses the detective stories, crime stories, romances, and moral cautionary tales that appeared in nearly every issue throughout the

---

3   In language similar to Obiechina's, Moretti declares unequivocally that 'detective fiction's characters are inert' (2006: 137).

1950s. Ndebele does not, however, dismiss *Drum*'s fiction outright. Attentive to the fiction's cultural nuance, he argues that it reflected 'the growth of sophisticated urban working and petty-bourgeois classes' (134). Among *Drum*'s roster of short story writers, Ndebele singles out Maimane in this regard. He writes, Maimane's 'Detective Morena is a self-made man, confident, fast talking, and quick thinking, playing the game of wits with his adventures. He wins. Clearly, it is the spectacle of phenomenal social change and the growing confidence of the urban African population that we see being dramatised here' (134). But, given the immediate political imperatives of the anti-apartheid struggle, such a dramatization of modern urban Black individualism was, to Ndebele, misplaced and mistimed.[4]

There is significant merit to these critiques. Ekwensi was never shy about proclaiming his love of Hollywood Westerns featuring 'Robert Taylor, Randolph Scott, Gary Cooper, and Bill Boyd' (Lindfors 2002: 122).[5] One suspects a fondness for Arthur Conan Doyle as well. Echoing Doyle's *The Hound of the Baskervilles*, Ekwensi's mystery 'The Case of the Howling Monkey' (1948) pivots on an observation about nocturnal noises from the animal world. Manqupu's murder victim in 'Love Comes Deadly' dies with an imported Peter Cheyney novel at his side, and Maimane peppers the third part of the *Chief* series, 'You Can't Buy Me', with allusions to William Keighley's 1948 noir film *The Street with No Name*, Dashiell Hammett's *The Maltese Falcon*, and Raymond Chandler's *Farewell, My Lovely*.[6] Moreover, Ekwensi and Maimane were the products of elite colonial and mission schooling. Ekwensi attended Government College in Ibadan, as would Chinua Achebe, Wole Soyinka, Femi Osofisan, and other prominent Nigerian writers. Maimane matriculated from the then St. Peter's College, the 'Black Eton' of South Africa. These schools steeped their charges in European literary classics and extolled the values of liberal individualism, influences that can be seen throughout Ekwensi's and Maimane's writing careers.[7]

---

4 Other activist-critics made much the same argument during the apartheid era. See in particular Don Dodson (1974) and N.W. Visser (1976).
5 Ekwensi was not alone in his fascination with the Western. The genre enjoyed great popularity in South Africa in the 1940s and 1950s as well. Unlike the Hollywood law and order dramas that were also popular and in which audiences overwhelmingly identified with the gangster antagonist, Black audiences often identified with the cowboy rather than the Native American. Troy Blacklaws (2014) teases out some of the reasons and implications for this fraught identification with the White representative of the law. For insightful examinations of African adaptations of the Western elsewhere, see Lily Saint (2013), Tsitsi Jaji (2014a), James Burns (2002), and Didier Gondola (2016).
6 For an explanation of these allusions see Guldimann (2009: 270). Keighley's immense influence on *Drum*'s writers and the larger Sophiatown community has been well documented. See Anthony Sampson (1957); Guldimann (2009); Fenwick (1996), Nixon (1994), and Michael Chapman (2001).
7 Ekwensi highlights his early exposure to Swift, Tennyson, Dickens, Oliver Goldsmith, and his later fascination with Steinbeck, Hemingway, Chekov, Maupassant, and Tolstoy (Lindfors 2002: 113, 126). Maimane read a similar canon at St. Peter's College.

Ekwensi's, Maimane's, and Manqupu's critics fail to recognize, however, just how innovative the writers are in their reconceptualization of the detective story's ideological articulations. As the first African writers, indeed as among the first non-Western and non-white writers globally, to take up the detective genre, Ekwensi, Maimane, and Manqupu recognized how the Anglo-American detective story's liberal figurations of theft and restoration could be deployed to illuminate and critique the illiberal logics of dispossession under colonial rule. During the century between Poe's formalization of the mystery genre and its adoption by Ekwensi, Maimane, and Manqupu, British and American detective fiction writers understood possession in much the same way that the philosophers of classical liberalism conceived it. For theorists such as Locke, private property relations anchor liberal political subjectivity. Lockean possession includes both property extrinsic to the self and the self itself. As Locke argues in *Second Treatise of Government* 'every Man has a *Property* in his own *Person*. This no Body has any Right to but himself' (qtd in Nichols 2020: 122). Through self-ownership flows individual liberty and the rights of political citizenship that inhere in it. In the classic Anglo-American whodunit, the detective thus both restores the property extrinsic to the self and shores up the idea of self-sovereignty, and does so with the sanction of the liberal democratic state and its legal frameworks. What Ekwensi and Maimane make clear – Manqupu to a lesser degree – is that in the decidedly illiberal context of colonial rule, where the colonial state's primary purpose was to dispossess indigenous populations of land, labor, freedom, and self-sovereignty, the detective, as imagined by Poe and Doyle, cannot restore property rights to an African victim who does not possess them to begin with. Nor can the detective serve the forces of law and order without ratifying the colonizer's assertion of the 'the right to demand, to force, to ban, to compel, to authorize, to punish, to reward, to be obeyed' (Mbembe 2001: 32). That is, to dispossess.

In highlighting the limits of detection to restore self-possession in the colony, Ekwensi and Maimane reveal the instability, if not impossibility, of liberal subjecthood under colonial capitalism. But for as much as Ekwensi and Maimane make their detectives increasingly aware of their inability to secure liberal subjectivity for African bodies, they never permit their detectives to abandon their generically coded responsibility to rescue or restore African self-possession. As they plunge Sango and Morena ever deeper into the carceral structures of colonial dispossession, Ekwensi and Maimane compel both their detectives and their readers to rethink the purpose of criminal investigation, the forms justice can take in the colony, and the definition of criminality itself. In short, Ekwensi and Maimane transform how the detective story might be used to articulate modes of sovereign self-possession, with a postcolonial difference, for the African subject. The result is a dissident detective fiction that sets a template for the generations of Anglophone African mystery writers to follow.

Magazines and Modernity

By no means were Africans in the 1940s and 1950s new to modernity, nor for that matter to city life. The Global South has always been constitutive of a global modernity that still too often gets referred to as 'Western'. As Matthew H. Brown elaborates, the areas that now comprise Nigeria, for example, 'supplied the material and conceptual resources on which the modern world was built' and, moreover, 'served as laboratories for juridical innovations that have sustained capitalist enterprise as well as liberal political philosophy for four centuries' (2021: 10). In economics, politics, philosophy, and culture, there is no modernity in which Africa and Africans do not play a central part. That said, the 'growing confidence' of urban Africans in the middle of the twentieth century, referenced by Ndebele, signaled a newly invigorated modern Africa committed to dictating the terms and representations of modern African life.

To appreciate the complexity of the colonial-era detective fiction writers' aesthetic and critical articulations, it is first necessary to understand that to read and write detective stories at all in the 1940s and '50s was to assert a defiant claim to modernity in the face of colonial ideologies that persisted in viewing Africans as rural tribal people. It was defiant in both its claims to the city and to a modernity that was simultaneously African and global in its constitution and outlook. Detective Morena's adventures in Johannesburg and Durban and investigative journalist Sango's in Lagos expressed this defiance and required a reading and consuming subject fluent in the idiom of modern urban life and cognizant of its leisure practices and dominant cultural forms. To gain such fluency was to read novels and peruse magazines and attend the cinema in the first place.[8] Maimane's and Manqupu's rapid-fire cultural references required hours spent in Sophiatown's or Lagos's many movie halls taking in Hollywood crime dramas. When not at the cinema but with time to spare, readers might pick up a copy of *West Africa Review* where they would first meet Cyprian Ekwensi's crime reporter Amusa Sango in 'Death on the Bus', which appeared in a 1951 issue. Above all, to be a modern reading and consuming subject was to devour *Drum* magazine. *Drum* published Arthur Maimane's twelve-month, three-part *Chief* series – 'Crime for Sale' (January–March 1953), 'Hot Diamonds' (April–July 1953) and 'You Can't Buy Me' (August–December 1953) – published under the pen name Arthur Mogale, and two years later in its January 1955 issue, Mbokotwane Manqupu's 'Love Comes Deadly'. More than any other publication of the era, *Drum* crystallized the contours of a modern urban African sensibility.

---

8   A contemporary review of Ekwensi's *People of the City* (1954) emphasized this point when it described the novel as the 'beginning of a new literature' destined to be 'of greater interest to West African readers' than stories of 'fantasy and tradition' (Bevan 1958: 53).

White-owned and white-edited but written and photographed almost exclusively by a roster of Black male authors, including Can Themba, Es'kia Mphahlele, Bloke Modisane, Henry Nxumalo, Lewis Nkosi, and Todd Matshikiza, *Drum* published a mix of sports and music news, exposé journalism, fiction, advice columns, pin-up photos of buxom young women, and other items that would appeal to urban South Africans – mostly, but not exclusively, male – and, through its international distribution networks, other African and African diasporic readers.[9] Established in 1951, *Drum* reached a peak circulation of nearly half a million by the 1960s and was available in Nigeria and Ghana within a year of its launch (Guldimann 2009: 48; Fleming and Falola 2005: 139).[10] Ekwensi himself contributed columns to the magazine (147). One of *Drum*'s most cohesive storylines was the one that celebrated, and indeed fostered to the point of mythmaking the 'dreams and fantasies of modernity' represented by the magazine's home of Sophiatown (Gready 1990: 145, 146).

With its unapologetic celebration of Sophiatown sophisticates such as Detective Morena, *Drum* also offered its readers in South Africa and across the African continent a glimpse of a potential African future after colonial rule. Racially segregated Johannesburg's Sophiatown was 'a dazzling new cosmopolitan world, relatively free from state control where all classes mixed' (Gready 1990: 145) and a cultural hotbed for writers and musicians and for its everyday residents seeking to experiment with new social identities. Bloke Modisane called it 'the most cosmopolitan of South Africa's black social igloos and perhaps the most perfect experiment in non-racial social living' (1963: 16). Sophiatown's population was comprised of Black, mixed-race, Asian, and white (primarily Jewish) South Africans, and like Harlem in the 1920s, drew whites from other parts of the city to its jazz clubs and entertainment venues. Until its razing by the apartheid government during the second half of 1950s, it remained, along with two neighboring areas, the only urban site where Black South Africans could own property, making it the most promising home for the country's Black petite bourgeoisie (Gready 1990: 145). But it was also a place of crowded slums and criminal gangs, making it, according to one historian, a community that 'lacked a geography of class … It was possible to live, or create the illusion of living, in all layers of society at once' (145). Altogether, in Sophiatown 'it was possible to believe that the state owned a little less of your soul' (145). *Drum*'s Black staff frequently bristled under the editorial limitations imposed by white management. Nevertheless, in content and style, as well as in the well-known 'forward-thinking, hard-drinking, fast-talking' (Ball 2018:

---

9   On gender and audience in *Drum*, see Dorothy Driver (2002).
10 Fleming and Falola focus primarily on *Drum*'s efforts to develop a stand-alone West African edition. Tom Odhiambo (2011) considers the broader African and diasporic cultural and political impact of the magazine.

2) biographies of its celebrated Sophiatown writing staff, Maimane included, *Drum* laid a defiant Black African claim to the future. *Drum*'s detective fiction and the African crime mysteries published elsewhere in the same period were central to this endeavor.

Africanizing the Detective Story for the Colonial City

Arthur Maimane's and Mbokotwane Manqupu's detective stories were not the first to be published by South African writers; British colonial administrators and white settlers had taken up the genre as early as 1891, producing the expected tales of colonial adventure and intrigue (le Roux 2013: 139). Apart from their shared South African setting, little connects Maimane's and Manqupu's writing to these earlier texts. In content and style their kinship is much closer to 1940s and '50s American hard-boiled detective novels and Hollywood crime films. In addition to the aforementioned intertextual references to Cheyney, Chandler, and Hammett, the two South Africans fill their stories with the alluring femmes fatales, illicit sex, fast Buicks, and wisecracking gangster anti-heroes who taunt their victims with lines like 'I'm leveling a torpedo at your spine, and if you do anything funny I'm liable to pump you so full of lead they'll need twenty guys to carry your coffin' (Manqupu 1955: 71). Hollywood and pulp references such as these were in keeping the times. Modisane devoured Leslie Charteris's detective novels so voraciously that he came to be known by the nickname 'Bloke', from Charteris's frequent use of the term (Modisane 1963: 166–167). One of Sophiatown's most infamous shebeens was called the 'Thirty-Nine Steps' (8), and 'men and boys with long records of murder' picked up names from the 'gallery of Hollywood films – Boston Blackie, Durango Kid, Lefty, Stiles, Gunner Martin' (63).

The Sophiatown writers' embrace of imported cultural forms fit with the broader pattern of resistant reading in apartheid South Africa. Government censors banned any film 'that might be interpreted as subverting white authority' (Nixon 1994: 34) but permitted most American crime films because 'the enforcers of the law routinely triumphed over the outlaws' (34). What the apartheid regime failed to anticipate was Black South Africans' lively counter-identification with gangster anti-heroes, a category expansive enough to include those hard-boiled detectives who operate in shadowy margins of legality.[11] South African audiences identified deeply with the gangster as a figure 'foreign to and in conflict with the wider state apparatus' (Fenwick 1996: 617) and celebrated him for his 'effective resistance to state control' (626). The 'American image of living outside the law thereby provided a perfect vehicle' for a community

---

11   For a detailed examination of the influences and adaptations of hard-boiled detective fiction during the era, see Tyler Scott Ball (2018).

whose very ability to live a law-abiding life was increasingly foreclosed by apartheid legislation (Guldimann 2009: 63). In much the same way that it will for Francophone African crime fiction writers later in the century, American culture in general also offered an appealing alternative to the Englishness so valorized in colonial society.[12] Writing about the appeal of James Hadley Chase novels to a slightly later generation of Black men living under apartheid rule but in terms that could just as easily have emanated from Modisane or Maimane in the 1950s, Fred Khumalo explains:

> In Chase we discovered the perfect antidote to the English Classics. While the Wordsworths of the world wrote about dales and daffodils ('What the fuck is a daffodil?' we wondered) Chase told us about fast cars, beautiful women, fast-talking well-dressed gangsters, guns and knives – stuff that resonated with us because we saw some of it in the streets, or in movies that we watched at the local community hall (which doubled as a bioscope, showing movies projected on a white sheet pinned to the wall). It also helped that Chase wrote in easy English, with lots of American slang, straight out of the Hollywood films we were familiar with. (Khumalo 2018)

For all their Hollywood veneer, the *Drum* detective stories evoked identifiable narratives about the struggles of Black and mixed-race South Africans. The lurking presence of white police in Manqupu's 'Love Comes Deadly', for example, encourages readers to view township violence in terms of racist institutions and predatory social relations. The quick discovery of the body brings the neighbors into the street. Finger-pointing ensues, but not to generate the kind of narrative tension seen in a classic whodunit. The neighborhood's anxiety is not that everyone is suddenly a suspect and no one is trustworthy, an anxiety that the detective story often alleviates through the cathartic scapegoating of an individual culprit. Instead, the consensus that emerges is that anyone could in fact have stuck the knife because, as a local teacher exhorts, criminality and immorality are environmental and their township environment, though never explicitly contextualized within apartheid's structures of dispossession, breeds violence. The teacher implores the crowd: 'It is not the fault of the boys … for how can a good potato stay good among the rotten ones? How can these boys stay good when they are surrounded by evil?' (Manqupu 1955: 68). A civil-service clerk who had not studied literature, Manqupu never quite integrates 'his own codes of realism with pulp' (Chapman 2001: 207), but the attempt to bring a sociological critique to popular genre narratives is consistent with *Drum*'s other fiction.

---

12 On Francophone African crime fiction and American culture, see Higginson (2011).

Drum staff writer Arthur Maimane takes a slightly different tack to representing Black experience in South Africa by using his detective to illuminate the impossibility of a law-abiding life under settler colonial social conditions. In 'Crime for Sale', the first sub-serial of the year-long *Chief* series, O. Chester Morena, aka the Chief, sets out to establish himself as a legitimate private detective, only to be treated by a white petty theft victim he hopes to serve with the dismissive racial condescension typical of the period. She presumes, based on the colour of his skin, that he is just another thief looking to scam upstanding white South Africans. Cut off from one avenue of respectable labor, and unable to find clients in a Black community that is conditioned to distrust anyone claiming to investigate crimes, Morena finds himself compelled to put his sleuthing expertise to the task of identifying and surreptitiously filming African and Asian pickpockets, warehouse burglars, and card sharks only to extort the perpetrators for a cut of their ill-gotten gains. As the series progresses, Maimane develops variations on this theme, blurring the distinction between the Black private detective and gangster and casting both as anti-heroes who disrupt official law and order but who never quite evade its grasp.

Ekwensi's *People of the City* paints a similarly ambivalent portrait of life in a fictional West African city that very closely resembles colonial Lagos. The greater part of the narrative is given over to loosely linked episodic sketches of Amusa Sango's encounters, both personal and professional, with bribe-taking bureaucrats, shoplifting good-time girls, penicillin black marketeers, scam artists posing as housing agents, political charlatans, and others whose meager wages and constricted labor and housing opportunities under colonial domination force them to make continual legal compromises. Sango's twinned occupations of crime reporter for the newspaper *West African Sensation* and bandleader at the cosmopolitan All Language Club make him, much like Maimane's detective Morena, the perfect vehicle to convey readers across the city's many social planes and along its economic strata. As Obiechina puts it, Ekwensi gives Sango the perfect perspective to witness 'the whole spectrum of the city's corruption' (1973: 153). But the city he illuminates is also one of freedom and possibility. Madhu Krishnan writes that Sango's city is one in which 'the varied spatial practices of its inhabitants ... remain beyond the grasp of centralised authority' (2018: 39), rendering Lagos even more alluring and threatening as a result. Ekwensi sets the action during the months between the ratification of a new political constitution, described in terms similar to the 1951 MacPherson Constitution that unintentionally set Nigeria on its path to political self-rule – it was supposed to have quelled nationalist claims for immediate independence – and the first elections in which Nigerians could stand for regional legislative office.[13] The Lagos of the novel is consequently a

---

13 Martin Lynn (2006) makes the case that the MacPherson Constitution was designed to placate Nigerian nationalists by creating a relatively powerless legislative system of

place of anticipation for the promises of African political sovereignty. In this respect, *People of the City* differs significantly from the *Chief* series and 'Love Comes Deadly', which Maimane and Manqupu wrote from a colonial space undergoing a rapid concentration of state power in the hands of a white settler minority seeking to further restrict the already limited freedoms of Black and other non-white communities. Sango's Lagos is nevertheless decidedly colonial.

Ekwensi significantly revised *People of the City* in the early 1960s for inclusion in Heinemann's then nascent African Writers Series (AWS). The AWS edition, published three years after Nigerian political independence, and later reissued by Fawcett in 1968, and New York Review of Books Classics in 2020, significantly streamlined the original 1954 version published in London by Andrew Dakers. The revised edition tightens the plotting and the novel's narrative arc, giving its bildungsroman aspect greater emphasis. However, in its greater economy it loses Sango's most direct and confrontational encounters with the agents of colonial state. Because my immediate interest is in the colonial-era detective genre writings of the 1950s, the analyses and citations that follow in this chapter focus exclusively on the 1954 edition.

Unlike Maimane's and Manqupu's detective stories, *People of the City* defies easy genre categorization. The novel's episodic structure reflects the origins of many of the chapters as radio entertainments that Ekwensi had earlier written for BBC's Africa service. It is part investigation narrative, part bildungsroman, and part picaresque. It owes more to Onitsha market literature's episodic plotting, stereotyped characterization, and moralizing than it does to any of these genres.[14] Given its hybrid generic engagements, *People of the City* does not scan initially as a normative detective story. Schemes are hatched, crimes are committed, bodies are found, and reckless self-interest disrupts the modicum of social equilibrium enjoyed by Lagosians. But there is no central crime in need of solving, no locked rooms, no forensic examinations of corpses or bloody knives, no cross-examinations of suspects. In fact, there are rarely suspects. Even Sango's investigative journalism largely bypasses the detective story's normative narrative development from crime to investigation to discovery. When his personal or professional life gives him privileged information about violations committed, Amusa Sango shows little inclination to reveal identities in the press or deliver culprits to the law. Like Eugène Sue, Vidocq, and other early crime writers, Ekwensi does appear to be interested in the sociology

---

elected Nigerian officials. The goal was, in part, to subvert the independence movement and extend the horizon for colonial rule. Instead, it galvanized calls for self-rule precisely because it gave official voice to elected legislators.

14 Elizabeth Isobel Baxter (2019: 118–119) details the novel's resonances with Onitsha market literature.

of crime, poverty, and colonial racism but, here too, *People of the City* resists classification as a crime novel more broadly defined.

Despite its protean form, I include *People of the City* as a foundational text in the canon of Anglophone African detective fiction because Ekwensi employs Sango's investigatory journalism within the larger narrative in ways that experiment with important conventions of the mystery genre and that tap the genre's recurrent ideological preoccupations. I see him as testing the possibilities of what an African detective novel might look like. Ekwensi incorporates five of Sango's news stories for *West African Sensation* into the narrative, the first ones reproduced diegetically. These are set off from the main narrative visually and read in a journalistic voice rather than in the novel's otherwise third-person narration. In these reproductions of Sango's newspaper articles, readers see the results of Sango's empirical and inferential reasoning but little of his methods or labor. It is as if the classic whodunit skipped straight to the final chapter, in which the detective lays out for an assembled audience whodunit and how. For the later journalistic pieces, Ekwensi does the opposite, depicting Sango at work gathering evidence, interviewing witnesses, piecing together clues, and drawing conclusions but leaving the final explication implied rather than verbalized. Taken together the five newspaper accounts anchor the novel's other sketches of city life, providing some sense of what the victims' lives would look like were they to merit official attention or be narratable at all in a world where so many like them remain anonymous African bodies in the colonial machine. More importantly, the journalism pieces activate the detective story's longstanding concerns about the morality of the state, the operations of sovereign power, and the presumption of individual juridical rights to make sense of colonial dispossession. Obiechina's contention that Sango's profession as a crime reporter is merely a narrative device to reveal the city's corruption misses this point. Ekwensi taps the detective genre's narrative architecture in very specific ways to make visible social problems of those members of society whose racial and economic position put them outside the protection of the state and, in many cases, make them disproportionately vulnerable to state violence. For this reason, Sango's crime investigations deserve closer scrutiny than they have received.

The Detective and Sovereign Selfhood

Given Ekwensi's and the *Drum* generation's fascination with the freedom and adventure of city life, on the one hand, and the atomized, predatory nature of urban social relations on the other, it is not surprising that they turned periodically to detective fiction. While the crime mystery has repeatedly demonstrated an accommodating elasticity in its repertoire of settings, its European and American origins in the eighteenth and nineteenth century coincide with explosive urbanization and the emergence of a capitalist middle class. For those eras' professionals and small business owners seeking to exert their hold over the city, urban life provoked no end of anxieties. The economic desperation of the poor masses put the middle class's private property at perceived risk. Bohemian countercultures called into question bourgeois sensibilities and the capitalist system of commerce on which middle class livelihoods rested. The very notion of individuality, so central to economic and political liberalism, could be difficult to sustain in the anonymizing urban crowd, the same crowd that could for the same reason easily hide thieves, scam artists, rapists, murderers, and other real or imagined predators of bourgeois life. So populous and socially complex as to become unknowable, the city also threatened the foundations of rationalism itself, the city's proliferating signs seemingly illegible to even the most astute inhabitant. The detective story expertly activated and exacerbated these anxieties to such a great extent that Walter Benjamin would come to view the detective story as a 'phantasmagoric description of the city' itself (Salzani 2007: 168). While Benjamin's proposition does not entirely account for the anxieties provoked by intimate social relations that drive the twentieth-century country house mysteries that W.H. Auden found so enjoyable or for the novels Agatha Christie sets on archaeological digs and snow-bound trains, it captures many of the energies that propelled the crime story's initial development.[15]

Ekwensi and Maimane establish analogous, though not identical, Nigerian and South African social worlds populated by characters whose fierce faith in personal freedom and boundless entrepreneurial potential is perpetually under siege in the city. Ekwensi's reader learns quickly that Sango 'was the city man – fast with women, slick with his fairy tales, dexterous with his eyes and fingers' (1954: 15). 'Every little affair' he muses, 'was a gay adventure, part of the pattern of life in the city. No sensible person who worked for six days a week expected anything but relaxation from these strange encounters' (15). The freedom he envisions is one from obligations to others and from the commitments exerted by history. 'To Sango, yesterday was past. You made a promise to a girl yesterday, but that was because you were selfish and a man who wanted her *yesterday*' (14). Moreover, 'The girl must not be allowed to remain in his memory. She must be forgotten – like the others before her' (15). And, as Sango makes clear, unfettered personal pleasure is of a piece with his individuated professional ambition 'to make a name as a musician, become editor of the *Sensation*, and settle down with some girl' (147). To achieve bourgeois ambitions such as these, it is necessary but socially acceptable, Sango knows, to be 'hard-hearted' (17) to get what you want without giving in to others' desires. This sort of freedom is not without its risks. City life is 'the game of the hunter and the hunted' (70)

---

15 Auden (1948: 406).

where the predator can easily become prey. Sango's rapacious landlord, Lajide, for example, 'was prepared to go to any length to make money and yet more money, to rob and cheat and victimise' (152). When Lajide boots Sango from his room, the crime reporter is reminded of how 'a man thrown out of his lodging in this city could be rich meat for the ruthless exploiters: the housing agents and financiers, the pimps and liars who accepted money under false pretences' (85). Despite this understanding, Sango still retains a faith in what he sees as the consensual social contract of modern social relations in the city. He presumes, and assumes that others share the presumption, that the autonomy to seek pleasure and individual professional advancement overshadows other social bonds. Annoyed by a recent city arrival with whom he enjoyed a single sexual encounter, Sango reflects, 'Aina must know that. Sango had his own life to lead, his name to make as a band-leader. All else must be subordinated to that. Nothing must be allowed to ruffle the direction of this up-hill task' (15).

When we first meet Morena, he too articulates a faith in bourgeois achievement and liberal selfhood. Addressing the reader directly, he introduces himself as the proprietor of his own detective agency. His pathway to this life, he explains, took him first through the formative middle-class institutions of school and family. But after 'they kicked me out of university during my second year, and my father kicked me out of the family' (24), Morena drifts to the margins of the law and of respectability. He becomes 'a gangster, pick-pocket, robber and all-around crook' (24). But this is only momentary. A success in the criminal underworld, Morena makes an unexpected, but decidedly entrepreneurial choice: 'after a few years, I decided the old saying "crime doesn't pay" was correct. I joined the police force in Pretoria – where I wasn't known' (24). In good liberal capitalist fashion, during his 'year's excellent service' (24), Morena puts his training and skills to legally legitimated use for the state. Morena acts on his entrepreneurial ambitions again by resigning from the force to set up shop as a private detective. Impressed with Morena's service, the Inspector 'pulled a few strings to get me a private detective licence – and one for a gun' (24). Thus, after the early setbacks and his stint as a gangster, Morena appears to redeem himself for a respectable bourgeois future. Without knowing the historical context of apartheid, a reader at this point in the series could be forgiven for mistaking the story for a conventional Hollywood treatment in which law, order, and middle-class respectability reign supreme.

For economically striving Africans in the colonial city, urban life entails significant danger not unlike those of nineteenth-century London or Paris. The detective stories from the period underscore the general illegibility of the city's signs and the risks that attend in being unable to decipher them. Lagos's residents, Amusa Sango despairs, are dangerously unreadable. In the city, 'you don't know a thief from an honest' person (27) and 'you see men riding shiny cars and taking glittery women to restaurants … and their unpaid debts! Everyone looks as if he has all the money' (32). Lagos is consequently a 'city of bubbles' (32), defined by its shiny but deceptive surfaces. In 'Love Comes Deadly', Manqupu introduces Johannesburg's Alexandra Township with a similar depiction. Comparing the starlit Black township to a 'lovely evening frock', the story's narrator laments that the darkness of night-time masks 'the filth and wickedness' of the 'slum area' (66), the gendered depiction of deception foreshadowing the male victim's inability to interpret the sinister machinations of the beautiful woman who orchestrates his murder. Maimane's urban South Africa is no more clearly legible. The Johannesburg and Durban of his series are cities where pickpockets mask themselves in respectable suits and gabardine overcoats (2001a) and where sophisticated warehouse burglars appear to the untrained eye as common bicycle deliverymen (2001b). Morena himself becomes one of the city's lurking dangers, a 'bookworm' by outward appearances, nameless in the crowd, but in reality, a cunning blackmailer and expert sleuth (2001b). In the criminal underworld, too, crime bosses pose as crime boss molls, capitalizing on gender stereotypes, to throw off both the police and rival organized crime gangs (1953b). On busy shopping thoroughfares, in warehouse districts, and in cafes, these menaces to private property and the efficient workings of capitalism are anonymous as can be.

Scholars of the so-called Golden Age Anglo-American whodunit argue that detective fiction can alleviate the anxieties provoked by modern urban life by demonstrating the enduring social utility of 'bourgeois rationalism' (Close 2008: 25) and 'specialized knowledge' (McCann 2000: 4) which the detective relies upon to identify, assess, and contain modern society's myriad risks. According to this understanding, detective stories express the notion that 'there was no strife or dissension that could not be absorbed by a healthy civil society' (4), and that the genre articulates this vision of liberal society 'by raising the prospect of its inversion' (8). Until the moment when the detective reveals the identity of the culprit,

> the traditional detective story depicts civil society as a regime of doubt and confusion – one where individual freedom results not in spontaneous order, but in an anarchic war of all against all, in which everyone schemes, acts duplicitously, and is motivated only by squalid purposes or irrational passions … only then to reverse that image by banishing a pair of scapegoats (murderer and victim) who embody the worst of those evils. (8)

The reader's relief comes from being reminded that the villain 'is not, after all, a person like you or me' (Wilson 1944: 84). Instead, the detective assures the reader that the greater mass of society is motivated by rational self-interest rather than heedless desire; that neighbors are to be trusted rather than feared; and that free association gives rise to orderliness rather than to anarchy. To sustain such a salutary vision of liberalism requires its own sleights of hand. Holmes's tidy resolutions obscure capitalism's intractable inequalities, for example, and his and Watson's insular homosocial bond frequently masks Britain's exploitative class and social divisions. Moreover, that the detective story gained its initial popularity in Britain at the height of its empire and the United States during its aggressive settler colonial expansion is both ironic and entirely in keeping with their championing of their own liberal superiority.[16] The equitable liberal social order that gets restored in any individual detective story is consequently more often myth than reality, but it is a reassuring myth for certain audiences.

In the context of colonial rule, especially in South Africa with the apartheid regime's rapidly proliferating acts regulating everything from mixed marriages to free movement by its Black and mixed-race subjects, a believable crime mystery featuring the easy restoration of liberal equitability would certainly have been challenging to execute. But for a critique of colonial dispossession, detective fiction's capacity for valorizing liberal values as the antidote to the dangers of modern living is not without its uses. For Ekwensi and Maimane, one of the chief benefits is the detective story's efficacy in illuminating the profoundly illiberal conditions of African life in the colony. By giving their readers protagonists who initially believe in the detective's powers of reason and rationality to ensure their own and other people's economic and social liberty, the two writers tempt their readers to the same belief. However, as Maimane and Ekwensi confront detectives Morena and Sango with the limits of their powers, they, and the readers along with them, will be forced to grapple with the specific valences of colonial dispossession.

Maimane and Ekwensi establish the tension between the liberal ideal and the illiberalism of the colony by holding out the generically conditioned promise that criminal aberrations to the otherwise prevailing social equilibrium are solvable through technologies of surveillance and the diligence, psychological insight, and general expertise of the detective, which is to say, through bourgeois rationalism and specialized knowledge. Like Poe's Dupin and Doyle's Holmes, Morena pursues his investigations by playing it 'scientifically' (2001a: 24). With a hidden camera, he dedicates hours to observing and recording population movements around the warehouses and the behavior patterns at the card tables in Johannesburg's illicit gambling dens (2001b: 28–29). Not unlike Hercule Poirot with whom Maimane's readers were familiar, Morena identifies the culprits of the crimes he investigates with his intellect alone, and never through the brute force or the indiscriminate sweeps conducted by the South African police

---

16 Detective fiction as a genre of empire is an altogether different discussion. Yunma Siddiqi (2008) develops an especially nuanced explication of how detective stories and thrillers by white British writers expressed the anxieties provoked by imperial rule.

throughout the apartheid era. The evidence gleaned with the hidden camera aids Morena's ratiocination, but as Mac Fenwick suggests, it also grants him a significant degree of individual authority insofar as he employs the surveillance technology as a mechanism of social control over others (1996: 628). In a context where Black bodies are intensely surveilled by the state, Morena thus asserts a significant measure of personal autonomy, making him, if not a liberal subject precisely, then something close to it.

Ekwensi and Maimane further tempt their readers to believe in the possibility of liberal subjectivity with investigation cases that reflect the liberal capitalist value system often associated with the classic Anglo-American whodunit. The second of Sango's formal investigations, for instance, details the murder of a young woman and her child by neighbors to whom the young woman had lent a gramophone. By all appearances trustworthy, the men reveal their craven greed by refusing to return the record player. When the woman insists, the two men kill her and her baby, dumping the bodies in a swampy woodlot at Lagos's outer edge. While Sango laments that such violence is too commonplace, he presents his discovery in the familiar terms of an aberrant disruption to a liberal social contract predicated on rational self-interest and trust. As told in the early pages of the novel, the men simply break what is presented as a liberal social contract. Maimane initially presents a similar scenario. The crimes Morena uncovers in the first instalments are those targeted against innocent – or at worst naïve – individuals whose carelessness in leaving purses unlatched, goods unattended, and playing cards unveiled indicates a fundamental trust in the other members of society to abide by the liberal conventions of private property, the legal system, and a shared belief in rational self-interest. The story's thieves and card sharks are savvy and impressively brazen but are merely individuals seeking to capitalize on other individuals' lapses in self-protection. In both texts, punishment would appear to re-establish a liberal status quo. That appearance turns out to be a ruse.

As their personal and professional trajectories unfold, Sango and Maimane find it increasingly difficult to sustain their belief in liberal personhood or in the detective's powers of rescue and restoration. Maimane's detective Morena is the quicker of the two to acknowledge the limits of his liberal aspirations. Immediately after Morena introduces himself to the reader as a Black bourgeois liberal subject, licensed to carry a gun and state-sanctioned to privately police thieves, he confides, 'Of course, you all know that such creatures don't exist in Johannesburg. Well I don't exist either – except on paper' (24). Colette Guldimann takes the statement as an indication of Morena's self-conscious textuality. As she points out, 'a black detective with a license and a gun was … a legal impossibility, a fiction in apartheid South Africa' (2019: 262). Even 'black police officers were not allowed to carry weapons' until the 1970s (264).[17] For sure, apartheid law made Morena's professional self an impossibility, but no less fictional is his identity as a bourgeois entrepreneurial liberal subject in possession of his own self. His intellect, his urbanity, his iconoclasm – the same attributes that cement Sherlock Holmes's bourgeois liberal selfhood – render Morena illegal under the apartheid doctrine that constituted Black Africans as rural tribal people useful for little other than manual labor or, in the case of the country's Black constables, for enforcing white property rights and white bodily security. Any appearance of self-possession therefore obscures a fundamental dispossession of self and freedom under apartheid law. As a person in possession of self, Morena can, in fact, exist only on paper.

A bleak vision of social relations and cynicism about individual freedom begins to infiltrate Ekwensi's *People of the City* with a crime investigation of Sango's that comes near the middle of the novel. After a corpse washes up in the lagoon, which the colonial police determine to be a suicide, Sango investigates the man's life history 'anxious for a more human story for his paper' (120). What he turns up, much as the typical fictive detective would, is a motive for the act of (self-inflicted) violence. Sango discovers a man of no remarkable life: married, the father of four, a clerk in a department store. But, Sango laments, 'the man had been unable to make ends meet. The city had been against him all the time. It raised prices; it made life for his wife and children a matter of hand-to-mouth, with the hand often bitten in the process' (120). By validating the man's struggles and ambitions, Sango initially narrates him as a liberal subject with a self to possess. However, the deeper Sango takes his sleuthing, he gains greater clarity about impossibility of that subjectivity in the colony.

Sango learns that as the man approached his breaking point, a colleague invited him to join a secret society that functions as a mutual aid organization for striving men like himself. The man joins and finds that his life 'became bearable' (121). He enjoys a quick raise and a promotion, with a promise of a second within a month's time – it turns out that every other employee in the department stores is a member. The man begins to acquire all the outward markers of bourgeois success, self-determination, and liberal self-possession to which he, and Sango himself, has aspired. But society membership comes with its own forms of dispossession. 'Nothing went for nothing' the secret society members tell the man and then demand the sacrifice of 'his first-born son' (121).

---

17 Guldimann's contextualization serves as a reminder of how radical Maimane's proposition was. And his use of the detective was not just radical in South Africa. As she points out, there were virtually no Black detectives in crime fiction globally at the time. Maimane was thus pioneering in refashioning the genre's racial registers to assert a place for the Black detective in a genre in which the Black body was typically coded as criminal and disruptive.

The nature of the sacrifice is never explained. Regardless, he refuses, but his only alternative is to take his own life. He knows too much to be trusted to leave the society. Sango thus concludes about the city's financially successful that '[t]hey literally sold their souls to the devil' (121).[18] It might be more accurate to suggest that financial success in the colonial city entails the loss of self-determination. Like Morena's, Sango's ultimate narrative suggests that the autonomous, self-made man is nothing more than a fiction that drives its believers further into the clutches of forces bent on exploiting them. In his reportage on the suicide for the *Sensation*, Sango does not explicitly link these forces to colonial capitalism, but the story sets the stage for his subsequent investigation reports that do.

Labor, Law, and Colonial Dispossession

In drawing attention to the seeming impossibilities of liberal selfhood for either their protagonists or victims, Ekwensi's and Maimane's texts do not represent a radical rupture from other global detective fiction traditions. Their American hard-boiled contemporaries displayed a similar skepticism of the stabilizing power of liberalism, for example. Maimane's frequent allusions to American hard-boiled fiction and film suggest that he may even have seen himself as participating in a shared global literary project. Ekwensi and Maimane do, however, propel the genre to interrogate different conditions of dispossession and unfreedom than had been examined elsewhere. This is not a simple matter of crafting new plots for African settings. The Nigerian and South African recognize that the social and psycho-subjective effects of colonial capitalism and colonial governmentality differ in fundamental ways from the industrial capitalism and concentration of corporate power, the New Deal expansion of the administrative state, the alienating bureaucratization of everyday life, and the spread of fascism that preoccupied Hammett, Chandler, and other hard-boiled writers.[19] After all, colonial power did not operate through the anonymization

---

18   Ekwensi develops this theme further in the revised 1963 edition. As in the 1954 original, when Amusa's search for new lodgings leads him into the office of a nationalist candidate for a local council position, talk turns to self-rule as a moral imperative and as an expedient to effective government. But Ekwensi adds several lines in which the candidate decries his opponent's tactic of showering cash on potential voters. His concern proves to be less that the opponent will win as a result of this tactic than that liberty itself will be undermined. 'They do not know that they are selling their freedom' he laments of the people (2020, 51). The presumption here is that there is a sovereign self to be sold. In the context of Nigeria's new democratic governance such a conception of selfhood is more easily conceivable than in the colonial-era original. But it also evidences a new pessimism; the dispossession of colonialism would appear to be taking new form in the emergent political culture of an independent Nigeria.

19   McCann (2000) lays out this history in his introduction.

of the liberal subject in the modern city as Walter Benjamin contends in his assessment of detective fiction, or of the depersonalization of the worker in Taylorist industry as Gramsci postulates in his. For both Benjamin and Gramsci, writing about European and American crime mysteries, there remains a self in possession of itself to lose.[20] Colonial domination relied instead on a more fundamental dispossession of the legal selfhood that could claim such rights in the first place.

As the 'camera obscura image' of the liberal nation-state as it emerged in Europe (Comaroff and Comaroff 2016: 17), the colonial state brooked no presumption of the 'political or civil equality' inherent to political liberalism (Mbembe 2001: 35). Nor was it under 'social obligation to the colonized … this latter is owed nothing by the state but that which the state, in its infinite goodness, has deigned to grant and reserves the right to revoke at any moment' (35). This is not to suggest that the colonial state ruled exclusively through coercive violence. Colonial governance was organized through and relied on an ever-proliferating series of laws, acts, codes, rules, licensures, and ordinances that governed nearly every aspect of African life. These varied regionally and over time and were, moreover, implemented differently from colony to colony. Indirect Rule as it was practiced in Ekwensi's Nigeria, for example, put the colonized subject in a different relation to state power than did more direct applications of governance that were being developed by South Africa's Afrikaner Nationalist Party during Maimane's 1950s. But in no case did these regulations function to protect 'contractual freedom and juridical equality as [the] two primal norms of liberalism' (Ince 2020: 24). Rather, they

---

20 For Benjamin, the nineteenth-century anxiety about loss of the self in the crowds of the city was particularly acute in the context of the period's broader understanding of the liberal self – that there was a self-possessed self to lose. Consequently, for Benjamin, 'the detective's work can … be read as a reassuring rescue of individual traces from the anonymity of the masses' (Salzani 2007: 172). Antonio Gramsci postulates an analogous rescuing function for the detective but in slightly different terms. The appeal of detective stories in the Taylorist, highly bureaucratized, and increasingly fascist 1930s, Gramsci argues, is a function of how the 'coercive rationalization of existence is increasingly striking the middle and intellectual classes to an unprecedented degree' (1985: 374). What the detective provides, in Gramsci's thinking, is a substitute for 'the precariousness and involuntary adventure of modern life with that of the controlled and aesthetically beautiful life of the detective' (374). While there may be an element of escapist fantasy in turning to the detective story in this context, Gramsci suggests that the genre nevertheless helps the reader retain a measure of belief in individual agency. Gramsci explains, 'people aspire to the adventure which is "beautiful" and interesting because it is the readers' assertion of their own free initiative' in a society organized against individual autonomy (374). Ernest Mandel makes a similar point about the detective story, arguing that it serves as an escape 'from the monotony of daily life into vicariously enjoyed adventures' (1985: 71).

regulated a bureaucracy of dispossession for all but a small comprador class, who, nevertheless, could not claim the identical liberal freedoms as their white counterparts in the United Kingdom.

The way that colonial rule prioritized the policing of labor over that of property further distinguished the quality of dispossession in the colony. Jean and John Comaroff point out that, in Europe, 'with the rise of the bourgeois state, law-making and law-breaking ... hinged primarily on the protection of property and the (self-possessed) persons who owned it from variously criminalized others' (2016: 16). The control and disciplining of labor, while also a central function of policing (of vagrants, the indigent, communists, the merely poor), remained secondary to that of securing private property (17). In the colonies, including the settler colonies in the Americas and elsewhere, they argue, the relation was reversed. As extractive monopolies whose first task was to dispossess indigenes of their land, colonial administrations viewed local populations as 'a reserve army awaiting deployment' on plantations, in mines, on road construction crews, and other work sites organized to enrich the metropole (17). Therefore, law 'enforcement was primarily invested, for the state, in labor relations; labor relations, here, broadly defined to include the insurrectionary violence, vandalism, and petty theft, especially directed against Europeans, that arose out of the refusal to work under prevailing conditions and could, therefore, be read as political' (17). Perhaps no fact better illustrates this aspect of colonial rule than South Africa's infamous pass laws, which regulated all movement of non-white bodies based on labor needs of the white state. Such influx controls were not isolated to South Africa; Ekwensi highlights similar, though less draconianly enforced, policies in Nigeria when he has a court registrar divulge to Sango the details of a bribery scheme to bypass Labor Department residency regulations designed to limit the size of the urban Black population (39).[21]

---

21 Ekwensi attributes a great deal of the colony's proliferating pressures, crises, and illegalities to these residential labor influx controls. After Sango witnesses Lajide taking Fento, the registrar, aside, Fento explains that Lajide offered a bribe in exchange for a false declaration for a relative seeking a job. Having neither been born in the city nor having worked in it for the previous five years the relative would not, legally, meet labor department influx control regulations designed 'to keep the over-crowding down' and to discourage people 'coming here to work' (39). Far from preventing over-crowding and housing and employment pressures, the policy simply exacerbates a culture of corruption and turns large swaths of the population into criminals. Where, in a putatively liberal society, social and political institutions would be designed to contain the heedless excesses of individual desire, Sango finds, much as do Dashiell Hammett's Sam Spade or Raymond Chandler's Philip Marlowe, only extortionate financiers, with police both crooked and indifferent to actively hostile bureaucrats. Ever sanguine, Fento explains 'bribery is like prostitution, a private thing between giver and taker. Nobody knows about it, nobody can prove it, nobody is hurt' (40). Sango's counterargument, couched

Colonizers worked hard to convince everyone, themselves included, of the civilizing mission of disciplining 'natives' to their labor schema.[22] And labor, in the colonizer's imaginary, 'is supposed to make possible the creation of utilities, and to produce value and wealth by putting an end to scarcity and poverty', thereby 'raising the native to where he/she can contemplate the recovery of his/her rights' (Mbembe 2001: 35). To be sure, the rights to be recovered through European understandings of labor were the Eurocentric conceptions of selfhood and citizenship that the colonizer denied to the colonized in the first place. Prime among them was that Lockean notion that to own something is to retain rights over it. Thus, if selfhood exists as a property, the individual enjoys the rights to dispense with it as he or she pleases. Conversely, where there is no self-possession, there is neither individual freedom nor individual sovereignty. Colonial law's primary focus on labor rather than on property does not so much reconfigure the primacy of self-possession as concentrate the law's logic of dispossession.

The Comaroffs make the case that the colony – settler and administrative alike – thus needs to be viewed as a carceral state. 'For those employed in the mines, plantations, and industries of Africa, South Asia, and the New World', they write 'the workplace *was* a prison: the labor, liberty, and civil rights of entire, racially marked populations were annexed under legally sanctioned arrangements of indenture and enslavement' (2016: 17). The Comaroffs perhaps overstate the point insofar as indenture and enslavement do not cover every colonial labor situation. Their larger argument is nevertheless valuable for understanding Maimane's and Ekwensi's texts. In the act of being reduced, through the scaffolding of colonial law, to a being that labors for the sovereign, the colonized is, as an object of the law, dispossessed of the self that could sell its labor. Precisely this happens to Morena, for instance, when he is denied the legal authority to utilize his powers of ratiocination in any way that Locke would recognize as self-ownership. In fact, the South African state imprisons him just as soon as it catches on to his attempts to sell his labor freely. His body, like every other African body, becomes the de facto if not de jure property of the colonial state.

At the midpoints of *People of the City* and the *Chief* series, after having hinted at the effects of colonial dispossession, Ekwensi and Maimane bring their detective protagonists face to face with its mechanics at their most brutal. It is

---

in the language of imminent 'self-government' and personal 'responsibility' (41), falls on deaf ears. Sango admits that this line of reasoning cannot stand up to 'competition … scarcity. If everybody had enough food to buy, houses to rent, a fair chance into jobs by merit and not "on recommendation", then the vampires would pack up. Their merciless extortion would end because no one would need to pay extortion money' (42).

22 See also Frederick Cooper (1996) and Onur Ince (2020).

in the pivotal moments when Amusa Sango and O. Chester Morena confront the most explicitly carceral examples of colonized labor – the militarized coal mine and the prison labor camp, respectively – that their detective labors most effectively illuminate the structural logic of colonial dispossession and, through this act of illumination, rescue, if only to a limited degree, the freedom and rights of the individual for the collective African body politic.

Detecting Dispossession, Detection as Repossession

In the second of Maimane's three-part *Chief* series, 'Hot Diamonds', Morena is forced to confront the realities of how the settler colonial state captures and deploys his detective labor, and the resistant freedom he derives from it, even in the putative spaces of freedom outside the prison walls. *Drum* published 'Hot Diamonds' in four instalments. The full narrative sees Morena infiltrate and break a sophisticated diamond smuggling ring run out of Durban by 'non-Europeans' (1953a: 30). The operation had 'trebled the amount of uncut diamonds being smuggled out of the country' and, in another of Maimane's jabs at the apartheid regime, had successfully eluded the Special Criminal Branch's most skilled officers (30). The story features no shortage of gun play, sexual intrigue, car chases, or other physical action, but Morena conducts the larger part of his investigation with the same combination of intellect, patient observation, and ratiocination that served him so well in 'Crime for Sale'. His sleuthing eventually leads him to Moollah, an old Johannesburg nemesis, and Diamond Lil, aka the White Dahlia, whom he initially mistakes to be Moollah's moll but turns out to be the gang's actual boss. In the end, Morena outwits both and hands them over to the police, but not before pocketing enough uncut stones to fund a comfortable retirement.[23]

A crucial detail in 'Hot Diamonds' is that Morena does not work the case of his own volition. Unlike his blackmail operation in 'Crime for Sale', in which he put his sleuthing acumen to the project exploiting petty crime rings for

---

23 Dorothy Driver makes the case that could just as easily be leveled at Ekwensi, not to mention Dashiell Hammett or Raymond Chandler, that *Drum* consistently relegated women to the domestic sphere of the nuclear family where they would fulfill their duties as mothers and housewives – and punished those such as Diamond Lil who did not – this despite the fact that apartheid labor controls had left Black 'community and family structures … in disarray' (2002: 156). Maimane's femmes fatales, like many of the magazine's pin-ups, are presented as sexually alluring objects of the male gaze – and certainly as sexually available to the male protagonists – and punished for defying what Driver sees as *Drum*'s overwhelming 'European and American constructions of gender' (156). Ekwensi displays more sympathy for the limited economic opportunities faced by women, but his detective narratives too are complicated by their vilification of city femmes fatales.

personal pecuniary gain, Morena's investigation of the diamond smugglers is at the behest of the South African Police's Special Criminal Branch. In the story, as in apartheid-era South Africa, the Special Branch's twinned goals are to protect white property and government tax revenue. These goals reflect the reality of policing at the time. As Bloke Modisane writes, when it came to the Black townships, the police were 'only interested in Passes and liquor ... kill a white man ... then you'll see the police turning the place upside down' (1963: 53). Given Morena's expressed antipathy to the police and to white law and order – he vows in the second instalment of 'Crime for Sale', for instance, to never again show his papers to the police – Morena assumes this assignment might surprise his readers. 'I reckon you must be wondering', he asks in the first instalment, 'what I'm doing here when the last time you heard from me I was doing compulsory labor on some prison farm' (1953a: 30). Morena answers his own question by explaining that the police see him as their only remaining hope for identifying and infiltrating the gang's ranks. In exchange for a successful investigation, they offer him a full pardon for the blackmail activities he committed in 'Crime for Sale'. Morena sees no option but to take the offer but manages to additionally bargain for the return of his private detective and gun licenses and, for the period of the investigation, the command of police resources, including officers and cars, and a generous budget. The additional concessions by the prison warden and the police notwithstanding, Morena 'still thought [he] was doing them a favor', suggesting that he understands full well the profound power asymmetry in the compensation for his labor (30).

Throughout Morena's escapade to infiltrate Diamond Lil's smuggling ring, he appears to retain the markers of independence and authority central to the image of the liberal self he presents in 'Crime for Sale'. But it is essential to view Morena's investigation of the diamond smugglers as another manifestation of his compulsory labor on the prison farm. Many of *Drum*'s readers would have been familiar with the brutal and exploitative conditions of farm labor either from personal or second-hand experience or from *Drum* itself. Henry Nxumalo's undercover exposé on farm working conditions in Bethel in the March 1952 issue secured the trust of a Black readership for the white-owned magazine and serves a good example of how *Drum*'s fiction gleaned political heft from its nonfiction, Njabulo Ndebele's argument to the contrary notwithstanding. Throughout the investigation Morena labors under the authority of the prison warden and his Special Branch minders. The simple difference from his prison farm life is that the state demands the work of his intellect rather than of his physical body. The state's surveillance is not as totalizing as in the prison – a fact that Morena will exploit – but he still remains an object of direct surveillance insofar as his minders attempt to keep tabs on his progress. His unrestricted mobility and his power to command a small platoon of police officers spread across Natal and the Orange Free State – a mischievously ironic choice of settings – thereby mask a distinctly carceral aspect of his existence. To refuse to protect white property would return him to the physical space of the prison but would not transform his status under the law. Whether on the prison farm or on Durban's streets, Morena remains the de jure property of the apartheid state. From the being that cannot exist whom we encounter at the beginning of the series, Morena has become the being that *can* exist because, by virtue of his dispossession under the logic of settler colonial law, his labor and his selfhood have been coerced into the service of white private property. While Maimane gets the reader to cheer Morena's blackmail scheme in 'Crime for Sale', one is almost disappointed that he hands over Moollah and Diamond Lil to the Special Branch officers in the final instalment of 'Hot Diamonds'. It seems a capitulation to his own dispossessed legal status.

Ekwensi also propels his detective toward the recognition of his own dispossession. Whereas Morena possesses a politicized consciousness of dispossession from the beginning, Sango only begins to come to a similar political consciousness during his investigation of the colonial regime's brutal suppression of a coal miners' strike. On the heels of his story about the department store clerk's suicide, Sango's white editor sends him to the country's 'Eastern Greens' where a mass labor action by coal miners has triggered a brutal response by the colonial police and military. Sango's investigation of the government's killing of twenty-one workers in its brutal crackdown is the most fully fleshed out and methodical of all his investigations in the novel. The reader sees him interviewing witnesses, family members, and union leaders. Sango stakes out the airfield for evidence that the government is flying troop reinforcements from England under the cover of darkness. He goes down into the mines to observe the punishing working conditions.

> In his report he was loud in praise and caustic in comment. His youthful fire knew no restraint and he wrote about the bleeding and dying, the widowed and the homeless; the necessity to compensate these men who sacrificed so much that the country's trains might run, its power-houses function, its industries flourish. (125)

As the sovereign power, the colonial state cannot be criminal in any legal sense, of course, and neither the editor nor Sango calls the colonial regime's violence a crime. But Ekwensi's decision to have the paper send its ace crime reporter is suggestive that the government's violence ought to be viewed as criminal and Sango's investigatory work as a form of criminal detection. More to the point, Sango's discoveries make explicit that the colonial state's power is predicated precisely on the theft of freedom and of life of the African subjects under its authority. In fact, the colonial conditions in the Eastern Greens are more carceral than any Sango has experienced. 'While they drove through the unmade roads, Sango had the cold chill one experiences in a town under the iron boot. Policemen were everywhere. Not the friendly unarmed men he had been used to in the western city, but aggressive boot-stamping men who carried short guns, rifles or teargas equipment. There were African police and white officers and they all had that stern killer-look on their faces' (124). Targeted by this show of raw state power are the 'peasants who had been lured from their farms to work in the white man's mines for money; and now only to be confronted with death' (123). In this 'state of emergency' (124), Sango discovers that 'only the able bodied men remained to face the terror' (125). Conscripts to colonial capitalist resource extraction, the African men work under distinctly carceral and necropolitical conditions.

On its own, Sango's detective work does not rescue the miners from complete dispossession. Their workplace action in the face of overwhelming state force stands as its own powerful assertion of collective selfhood. Awed, Sango thinks to himself, 'unified intervention from their own people had prevailed: not force … Inwardly he determined to do his best for these trusting people' (126). And indeed, Sango's investigative news reports help mobilize the country against the colonial regime. In that regard Sango fulfills an expectation conditioned by the crime mystery: that the detective, through securing the rights of the victim, helps recover human self-possession from the social forces that seek to obliterate it. While there are echoes of Gramsci's emphasis on Taylorist production in Sango's depictions of the coldly rationalist industrial mining operation, the rescue produced by Sango's detective work conforms with neither the heroic adventure envisioned by the Italian theorist nor the recovery of the liberal individual from the anonymizing urban crowd described by Benjamin. In place of Benjamin's and Gramsci's focus on the individual, Ekwensi reconceives the detective's power of rescue in distinctly collectivist and nationalist anticolonial terms. 'It had taken a catastrophe, the shooting and killing of twenty-one miners', Ekwensi has Sango reflect, 'to bring together as one man the North, East and West, to make the country realise as never before where its destiny lay' (128). This is the story of collective selfhood that Sango's investigation helps make visible. And by making it visible, his labors of detection help give form to the body of the nation as a political self in possession of itself. Through African labor thus emerges the African nation-state.

Sango himself is initially only dimly aware of the full import of his journalism, especially for his individual self as a colonially dispossessed subject. With the union president's exhortation to 'keep up the struggle' in the back of his mind (127), Sango vows again on the long bus ride back to Lagos 'to spend the rest of his life doing good' (128). But even as his own detective labors catalyze the formation of a cohesive nation, he still views the miners' carceral existence under colonial capitalism and their vehement assertion of collective selfhood as external to his personal situation. 'What catastrophe, Sango wondered, would crystallise for him the direction of his own life?' (128). To Sango's Lagos friends, the strike *has* already begun to crystallize something in him. 'Nearly everyone', we learn, 'had something to say about how different Sango looked after nearly two weeks' absence' (133). Sango himself chalks the difference up to his disillusionment in his own capacity to live up to the miners' example (133). He can see no personal future that does not result in retreat to the rapacious individuated social relations of the colonial city. Indeed, the loss of his band's standing engagement at the All Language Club, the eventual dissolution of the band itself, Aina's claim to be pregnant with his child, his best friend Bayo's murder, the deaths of a female friend and his mother, his firing from the *West African Sensation*, and a reckless act of physical brutality – all of which follow on the heels of his time with the striking mine workers – reduce Sango to a condition of bare life in the colonial city. It will take not one, but this series of catastrophes to make the crime-reporter band leader comprehend not only the degree to which his own dispossession under colonial capitalism matches that of the miners, but also that his investigative labor contains the seeds of his personal rescue from that dispossession.

Central among the catastrophes is his sacking from his job as a crime reporter. The ostensible reason for his firing is that one of his stories decried the 'Syrian and Lebanese menace' (186). The piece had reported the double murder of his friend Bayo and Bayo's Lebanese girlfriend at the hand of the young woman's wealthy and well-connected brother. Because of his friendship with the victims, Sango enjoyed insider knowledge of the affair and was at the scene at the time of the shooting. His first-hand evidence sends the killer to the gallows and gives the *Sensation* the city's best stories on the scandal (186). After the fact, Sango's editor, McMaster, reminds Sango that colonial law banned the provocation of intracommunal antagonisms (186). Presumably, McMaster bears significant responsibility for the legal fallout from the article's publication, but Ekwensi leaves unanswered the question of why the editor let the story run in the first place. McMaster's overarching reason for sacking Sango, however, appears to be his anger at what he views as Sango's turn from 'objective observer to partisan reporter' (185). The editor identifies the shift as beginning with Sango's investigation of the miners' strike and notes that it became more pronounced in a non-crime piece Sango published on the death of the country's greatest anticolonial nationalist, an article which Sango himself viewed as 'injecting his own despondency into that of the nation' (170, 185). In other words, Sango's crime is in expressing an unacceptable subjectivity as an African living under British colonization. Sango's punishment, then, is the silencing, which is to say the dispossession, of his personal voice.

The exchange with McMaster also forces Sango, and the reader along with him, to confront his illusion that he ever enjoyed full ownership of his self in the first place. Up to the point when he loses his job at the paper, Sango has viewed himself as an uncompromising and fearless voice for the people. Reflecting on the impact of his first piece of investigative journalism in the novel, for example, Sango thinks proudly that 'people would speak of it as their paper – the fearless paper that attacked the Government. This tonic was needed for a paper which had often been accused of not declaring a definite stand' (33). The declaration makes clear that Sango perceives himself to be in possession of an autonomous voice, existing under but independent from the mechanisms of colonial power. With only a blush of hyperbole, McMaster himself concedes, that Sango's 'original' writing, with its 'fresh viewpoint' (184) is powerful enough to precipitate 'armed uprisings, tear-gas, troop reinforcements' (186). But what the reader learns in the moment when Sango loses his job is not just that McMaster seeks to silence Sango's potent critique of the colonial government, but that Sango's voice was never as powerful or autonomous as Sango thought it was. In his paternalistic explanation of how Sango went wrong, the white editor reminds Sango that the *Sensation* is widely regarded 'as the voice of the British Government' (186). If this is not news to Sango, it certainly is to the reader, who has been guided by Sango's conception of himself as a champion of the city's African communities and thorn in the colonial government's side. But if the *Sensation* truly voices the imperatives of the colonial regime, then Sango's voice has long been co-opted and contained by the colonial state. He has, however unwittingly, served colonial power all along. Simply put, his labor as a crime investigator is not his own any more than Morena's is. His existence cannot be described as carceral in the literal sense, but neither can he be said to be in free possession of his self. Thus, his detective work, from which he derived so much sense of freedom, would appear to be a critical mechanism of his unfreedom.

But of course, it is precisely Sango's detective work more than any other factor, including his music, that leads him to his moment of self-rescue from the dispossessing forces of colonial capitalism. McMaster would not need to silence him otherwise. Central to his transformation is his development of a collective consciousness, a collective 'I'. The transformation gathers momentum from the instant he illuminates the miners' example of individual self-sacrifice for the collective good. Even as Sango is stripped of the markers of self – his home, his band, his closest friend, his newspaper job – his sense of self evolves, and his voice grows more distinct and emphatic. The subsequent death of the country's most prominent advocate for self-rule, for example, prompts Sango to contemplate 'what he had missed by not being an active nationalist' (164). At the elder statesman's funeral, attended by

> overflowing crowds ... Sango was seeing a new city: not just a collection of landlords and tenants, but something with spirit and feeling. The madness communicated itself to him, and in the heart of the moment he forgot his worldly desires, and threw himself with fervour into the heat of the moment. (165)

In the crush of the crowd, Sango bends to help a woman who has fallen and is in risk of being trampled. As he did when he followed the workers into the mines and when he staked out the airfield, Sango acts for another without concern for self-gain or for immediate physical pleasure. The young woman, whom Sango will eventually marry, dreams not of financial accumulation at the expense of others nor of fleeting sexual gratification, but of training as a nurse to help those most in need of medical attention. To Sango's initial objection that she 'won't make much money', she affirms her collectivist commitment to the 'thousands [who] are dying for want of medical aid' (169). Confronted with another example of the miners' spirit of self-possession, Sango is further transformed. 'If you could win her', he thinks, 'you would find a new foothold in this city and all your desires will focus on a new inspiration' (170). Newly inspired, he writes his passionate articles on the nationalist leader's death and on Bayo's murder. The stories get him fired, of course, but they also affirm that no matter how co-opted his voice had been, it is in fact his to be cultivated, but only in the first-person plural.

As the novel closes, with Sango and his new wife en route to Ghana where imminent political self-rule affords the opportunity to develop their talents until Nigeria gains its own independence, Ekwensi leaves the reader with the promise of unbounded cultivation – of voice, subjectivity, agency – on the same horizon as political self-rule. What the coal miners teach Sango, more than the facts of their shared dispossession, is the redemptive power of the collective 'we' over the pleasure-seeking 'I', a lesson that reverberates backward to give his past investigations new meaning and forward to those he will write. By remaking, with a postcolonial difference, the detective story's recovery of the individual from the anonymizing forces of modernity, Ekwensi mobilizes the genre's thematic registers to restore the sovereignty of the collective self in possession of itself in resistance to the colonial cultures from which the genre first emerged.

Maimane's *Chief* series traces a similar narrative arc from dispossession to self-possession. Morena draws 'Hot Diamonds' to its close with a self-congratulatory salute: 'A real made-in-America double-double-cross we made, wasn't it?' (1953c: 29). The immediate and most obvious reference is to his success in tricking Moollah and Diamond Lil to betray each other to the police while he quietly walks off with their gems. The double-double-cross can also refer to how Morena gets an upper hand on his white Special Branch minders. He fulfills his contractual obligation by handing them Moollah and Diamond Lil, letting the white authorities believe that they have successfully extracted his full value as a laboring Black body in the service of white property and state revenue. By grabbing the gems and removing his underworld rivals, Morena thus retains enough self-possession within his carceral position to continue selling his illegality as he did in 'Crime for Sale'. In other words, he denies the apartheid state its property claim to his body and self, thereby rescuing himself as an autonomous, albeit legally circumscribed, individual agent. Like the nineteenth-century detective who rescues the bourgeois individual from the anonymizing urban crowd, Maimane's detective rescues the colonized individual – himself – from the dehumanizing forces of colonial dispossession. Moreover, in tricking the white authorities, Morena makes visible to the reader the structural mechanics of colonial dispossession on which white authority rests. That he can so cleverly circumvent that authority suggests furthermore that the assertion of sovereign authority by South Africa's settler colonial state is little more than a delusion on the part of its perpetrators.

Conclusion

In early 1950s South Africa and Nigeria, a fully self-possessed Black individual would have been just as much a legal impossibility as the Black private eye with a license to carry a gun, each a fiction that could exist only on the printed page. But by articulating the conditions of that impossibility, Ekwensi's *People of the City* and Maimane's *Chief* series assert a claim to liberal self-possession. The texts are radical not so much for undoing the Eurocentric liberal logic that itself was part and parcel of epistemological colonization – Maimane largely preserves its fundamental premises; Ekwensi tweaks it to accommodate a collective self – than for claiming it for Nigerians and Black South Africans. By taking up a narrative genre deeply rooted in liberal culture and remaking it for illiberal colonial contexts, Ekwensi and Maimane re-animate the long-standing anticolonial and anti-slavery imperative to affirm self-possession as the foundation for liberty. Through the act of detection and through the act of being a detective, Sango and Maimane rescue and restore the possibility of self-possession for their African communities. Ekwensi and Maimane do not explicitly acknowledge the long-standing anticolonial and antislavery critique that the self could not be owned. This aspect of colonial domination generated significant dilemmas for anticolonial and anti-slavery movements because it left them in a position of having to assert self-ownership as the condition of their right to freedom even as they questioned the premise that a self can be property.[24] But Ekwensi's and Maimane's focus on labor, property, and alienation is not altogether discrepant from the larger anticolonial struggle in its challenge to the legal logics of dispossession. Add to this the fact that their Africanization of an imported genre directly defied colonial legislation of racial and cultural purity – most fully realized in South Africa under apartheid governmentality – their detective fiction is much more radical than it has been given credit for.

---

24 On this point, see Robert Nichols (2020).

That radicalism notwithstanding, few Black or white South African writers would publish crime mysteries again until the 1990s.[25] Politics, more than literary taste, dictated the interruption. The bulldozing of Sophiatown and the militarized resettlement of its residents to Black townships and rural 'homelands', the broader intensification of apartheid repression (including, but by no means limited to the 1963 Publications and Entertainments Act that outlawed *Drum*'s brand of crime and cheesecake in the name of public morality), the forced exile of *Drum*'s core staff, and the increasing militancy of anti-apartheid movements conspired to supplant crime mysteries with the protest novel. By contrast, nearly every other country on the African continent would achieve self-rule within a decade of Ekwensi's and Maimane's first crime mysteries. With independence came a slow trickle of detective stories, novellas, and newspaper serials in the 1960s. These texts, primarily from Ghana and Nigeria, begat a minor flood of detective stories in the 1970s and 1980s by writers from West, East, and southern Africa. For a brief period, the euphoria of self-rule elicited a very different type of detective story from the kinds told by Ekwensi and Maimane in the 1950s, one in which trustworthy honorable police preserve the peace of fundamentally just societies or in which secret agents defend independent nation-states from neocolonial conspirators. It is to those celebratory texts that we now turn.

---

25 The notable South African writers producing detective fiction between 1960 and 1990 include James McClure, Wessel Ebersohn, and Gillian Slovo. George Sabelo published his Skip Dlamini thriller during this time as well. For a comprehensive list of South African crime writing, not just detective fiction, see Le Roux (2013).

Sovereign States: Police Investigators, Secret Agents, and Sleuthing Citizens after Independence

2

In 1960, the prolific Ghanaian fiction writer Gilbert A. Sam self-published what is possibly the first Anglophone detective story to appear in print in a politically independent African nation-state. The novella, *Who Killed Inspector Kwasi Minta?*, is set in Accra in the late 1940s and traces the police inquiry into the murder of a fellow police investigator. Tasked with the case, Sergeants Oduro and Ahia pursue the investigation with little fanfare and a great deal of the drudgery that defines routine criminal detection in both the police procedural and real life. Sam's cops are never less than methodical, practicing what Sergeant Oduro describes proudly as 'practical criminology' (9). The novella's main plot twist comes when Minta's love interest Georgina beats the cops to the big reveal, eliciting the killer's confession while the police can merely listen from the wings, present only to make the formal arrest. From the moment of Oduro and Ahia's introduction, however, there is never a question that with or without Georgina's private sleuthing they will prevail over the killer. Set as it is during the colonial era, Sam misses no opportunity for his African protagonists to show up their white British superiors, demonstrating again and again Ghana's superior claim to self-government. Even the plot resolution, with the private citizen dedicating herself to the public good, suggests the primacy of popular sovereignty for effective and democratic governance. For its post-independence readership *Who Killed Kwasi Minta?* dramatizes the socially beneficent power of a civic-minded citizenry working in tandem with an equally civic-minded African police force. In every respect, Sam's vision of the state as a guarantor of the rights and protections of citizenship contrasts radically with the assessment of state power laid out in the colonial-era texts encountered in the previous chapter.

As it would turn out, in Nigeria, too, the first detective story to appear after independence, Cyprian Ekwensi's *Yaba Round-about Murder* (1962), was a police procedural with a similarly salutary vision for the state. Other West African writers would follow, steadily producing police investigation narratives throughout the 1960s and early 1970s. The announcement of fully participatory democracy in South Africa in 1990 ushered in the quick publication of two Black South African-authored police investigation novels there as well. When police procedurals fall out of favor in West Africa, civic-minded constables give almost immediate way to their close kin, counter-espionage experts. Between the two, police procedurals and espionage thrillers constitute a significant portion of the detective genre stories and novels written well into the 1980s by Anglophone African writers from not only Ghana and Nigeria, but also Kenya and Zimbabwe.[1] Unfailingly, the diligent cops, military hotshots, secret agents of MI6-like Pan-African defense agencies, and the occasional private citizen in these texts heroically protect Africa, its independent nation-states, and their citizens from threats domestic and international. In Sam's wake, these two sub-genres narrate nationalist tales in which law enforcement agencies, the military, and civil society carry on the task of liberation initiated by political independence. But in crucial ways, they also register the profound anxieties about the colonial legacies of the police and military and, more importantly, about the state's capacity to sustain the liberation project.

After Cyprian Ekwensi's and *Drum* magazine's dissident detective fictions of the 1950s, the immediate and widespread embrace of the police procedural and the espionage thriller might not have been an obvious choice for many writers. As the 1950s stories make clear, the colonial police and military enjoyed no favor from the general African public. The British established the first formal police corps in West Africa in the in 1830s as paramilitary forces deployed primarily to quash resistance to missionaries, European traders, and colonial administrative institutions as well as to extend the territorial reach of the colonial state.[2] Not surprising, 'colonial policing relied heavily on the ability to project and deploy force and violence, rather than to cultivate popular support and consent' (Tankebe 2013: 580). Periodic efforts by colonial administrations in the twentieth century to elicit popular support for law enforcement and military agencies did little to sway public perception of them as the brutally repressive arms of an illegitimate colonial cartel (581). The South African government, especially that of the Afrikaner-led Nationalist Party after its ascension to power in 1948, did not even pretend to attract the support of the country's majority non-white population. It amplified both the rhetoric and display of overt force, with South African Police Service (SAPS) regulars and Security Branch officers deployed as frontline troops against all threats to the white supremacist social order.

---

1   Tanzania saw a similar phenomenon in Swahili-language writing. See Bernth Lindfors (1994) and Emily Callaci (2017).
2   Africanist historical scholarship on law enforcement institutions and practices is more extensive than I can highlight here. The works that I found most helpful for my immediate purposes include Philip T. Ahire (1990), Etannibi E.O. Alemika (1993), Otwin Marenin (1982 and 1985), Adoyi Onoja (2013), Wycliffe Nyachoti Otiso and Ruth Joyce Kaguta (2016), Tekena N. Tamuno (1970), Justice Tankebe (2013), and Justin Willis (2015).

Accordingly, the African forces in the colonial- and apartheid-era constabularies and military were viewed with a special derision by the communities they ruled. In 1905, a Gold Coast Police Commissioner declared about the African police corps, 'more disgrace is attached to the calling of a Policeman than to the fact that a man is a convict or ex-convict ... everyone's hand is against a Policeman who is looked upon as a traitor to his race' (qtd in Tankebe 2013: 580). Quite often, African recruits within the various constabularies and rifle guards were ethnic outsiders where they were stationed, and their authority could be more ruthless for its tenuousness. Wole Soyinka captures this dynamic in *Death and the King's Horseman*'s most humorous set piece in which a group of schoolgirls trains its derision at the Hausa constables policing the local Yoruba community (2003). As indicated in the previous chapter, the African police officers depicted in Ekwensi's and Maimane's colonial-era African detective stories are by turns indifferent, cruel, or outrightly crooked, demanding monetary or sexual favors in return for investigating complaints by common citizens of the colony. At best, the police, paramilitary or otherwise, were to be avoided, but they were also likely to be actively resisted, especially during the later years of apartheid domination in South Africa, when dissidence to the law defined so much of the struggle for freedom and democracy.

Following political independence in West Africa, beginning with Ghana in 1957, and the announcement of negotiations to end apartheid rule in South Africa in 1990, a reconceptualization of social function of the state's repressive apparatus was in order. At the very least, self-rule generated a significant shift in rhetoric, especially in terms of the function of the police. Take, for instance, the 1959 address of Ghana's first president, Kwame Nkrumah, to the first graduating class of Ghana's newly formed Police College:

> There are colonial police forces, which exist to enforce authority of a foreign power on a colonial people. In such forces, this will be demonstrated by the fact that the police will be peremptory and even brutal in their dealings with the inhabitants of the colony while they will be ingratiating and subservient to those in authority. In a free and independent country, the conduct of the police must be the exact reverse of this. They must demonstrate to the people at large that the country is free and independent by behaving towards the ordinary man in the street with exactly the same politeness as they would behave towards those in superior positions. (qtd in Tankebe 2013: 583–84)

Nkrumah's exhortation to treat the man in the street with civility links the deportment of the police directly to the legitimacy of the state. Where colonial-era constables enacted, in their daily dealings with the African public, the colonial state's right to demand and to be obeyed (Mbembe 2001: 32), the police in self-ruled Ghana had an imperative to reflect the values inherent to constitutional liberal democracy. To treat all people with respect, Nkrumah asserts, is central to ensuring their new liberty and equality as citizens of an independent nation-state. Nkrumah thereby implores the police to transform themselves from agents of colonial dispossession into guarantors of rights and, when necessary, the administrators of fair sanction. In the end, Nkrumah implies that the moral legitimacy of the state itself is contingent on the actions of individual police officers and on the organizational approach to policing. Insofar as Nkrumah demarcates the appropriate parameters of police behavior in a self-ruled state, his remarks could be viewed as addressing the public, too, signaling the new, respectful, and philanthropic treatment they should expect from state agents and institutions.

The postcolonial state in Africa came into being with the anticipation that it would function as the primary vehicle for decolonization. Tremendous affective investments were consequently placed in governing institutions for their potential to deliver the promises of economic development and redistribution as well as to decolonize state-citizen relations more generally. Africa's independent nation-states inherited no shortage of obstacles to achieving those ideals, however. Where law enforcement institutions were concerned, self-rule brought little change in policing methods or abuse. Ghana's police, for example, inherited colonial institutions and deeply entrenched professional cultures and thus failed to gain the kind of legitimacy that Nkrumah implored they seek. Regarding the Ghana Police Service, Ghana's National Reconciliation Commission concluded in 2005 that from independence in 1957 to 1992 'all the regimes during that period failed to translate rhetoric into substantive policy reforms' (Tankebe 2013: 583). The commission asserted: 'by their actions, the police confirmed, in the minds of the public, the view that they were agents of the government for suppressing the populace and violating their human rights' (National Reconciliation Commission 2005: par. 4.1.2.1.3).[3] In other words, the country's law enforcement had decolonized only insofar as it had Africanized its leadership. In nearly every other way, Ghana's police service appeared to perpetuate the capricious methods and abuses carried over from the colonial era. Much the same could be said about Nigeria, Kenya, and other African countries that had achieved political independence. So too, the military's respect for rule of law during that same period, at least in Ghana and Nigeria, was never less than inconsistent.

South Africa faced the additional complications of the end of apartheid rule. For the country's white population, which had enjoyed the disproportionate

---

3   For some specific examples of conflicts between the police and citizenry, see Abena Ampofoa Asare (2018: ch. 5).

protection of the state's security apparatus until the early 1990s, the redistribution of policing after the African National Congress's electoral victory generated a broad-scale panic about crime and disorder.[4] Similarly, the population as a whole found itself navigating inchoate, thus hazardous, social relations after their sharp – and violently policed – legibility during apartheid. Not least, after decades of advocating a dissident relationship to the law, the new ANC government confronted the delicate task of redefining as civil crime those actions it and other militant organizations had previously defined as political resistance during the freedom struggle.

If self-rule was experienced as a state of jubilation, it was thus also experienced as a state of anxiety about the discrepancy between the ideals of decolonization and the realities of governing through legacy colonial institutions, about the persistent authoritarian potential of governments and their leaders, and about the daily interaction between citizens and the police and military agents charged with enforcing state power. By the 1970s, when the police procedural gives way to counter-espionage tale, the disproportionately debilitating iniquities of the global capitalist system and the transnational forms of disorder that it produces only compounded those tensions. The reconceptualization of law enforcement – and, by extension, of the military – outlined by Nkrumah would thus be challenging in the best of circumstances. It would demand a transformation of both policing method and the public perception of the police and armed forces. In the euphoria of independence, both seemed possible – but tenuously so.

In the police procedural and espionage thriller Anglophone African writers find a pair of detective fiction variants especially well-suited to the emotional and political tenor of the era. For all their typological differences, the police procedural and espionage thriller dramatize an interconnected assemblage of anxieties about the state's monopoly on violence and its means of law enforcement to secure its sovereign dominion and social order within that dominion. Where stories involving police detectives typically probe weaknesses in the local or national social contract and in the state's disciplinary powers to sustain itself in the face of those weaknesses, those featuring counter-espionage experts commonly shift that focus to the state's vulnerability to threats external to itself. The one can be read as a narrativization of the state's ability to project sovereignty inward and the other about the capacity to project it outward. But both register profoundly domestic anxieties about the viability of the state and its institutions. Moreover, like all genres, the police procedural and espionage story blur at their margins and share an expansive repertoire of preoccupations. *Who Killed Inspector Kwasi Minta?* is as much about the persistent external

---

4   See, among others, de Kock (2016), Comaroff and Comaroff (2006), and Rita Barnard (2008).

specter of colonial intrusion, for example, as John le Carré's espionage novels are about the internal corruption of Britain's state institutions. The promises and perils of nation-state sovereignty mobilize them both.

With their earnest constables and eager secret agents, Anglophone Africa's police procedurals and espionage thrillers re-articulate the shared dreams of a state-led decolonization. By degrees implicit and explicit, the short stories and novels mobilize the two subgenres' overlapping critical capabilities to articulate anxieties about the fragility of the postcolonial state as a vehicle to deliver on its promises of development, equality, and security. What emerges in the body of texts, and what makes them so evocative for the study of African cultural critique of the problems of sovereignty and the state, is their provocative engagement with the discrepancy between the ideals of African sovereignty and the realities of state power in the first decades after independence. This chapter traces that story. The first part of the chapter outlines the broad aesthetic and thematic contours of the two subgenres. The second part assesses their critical engagement with these anxieties.

Rather than perform close textual readings of a few paradigmatic examples as I do in the other chapters, I map the themes and ideological contours of the post-independence police procedural and spy thriller across dozens of texts, detailing their generic continuities and discontinuities with each other and with the detective story broadly and examining the larger patterns that emerge. Close readings of a smaller number of police procedurals or spy novels from specific places and times might reveal different inflections than those I outline here. Nigeria was a different place in 1983 than it was in 1975 or 1962, obviously, and both were different from Kenya or Zimbabwe during the same periods. One would thus expect to find contextual aesthetic and thematic differences. There is, nevertheless, a remarkable consistency in the narrative preoccupations from place to place and time to time. This chapter illuminates these larger transcontinental and transtemporal patterns.

Compassionate Cops and the Beneficent State

Beginning almost immediately after political independence in West Africa and after the end of apartheid rule in South Africa, African writers of detective fiction captured the optimism of the period with the police procedural. Ghana's Gilbert A. Sam was the first out of the gate with *Who Killed Inspector Kwasi Minta?* Cyprian Ekwensi followed shortly after with *Yaba Round-about Murder*. Ghanaian readers also enjoyed regular serialized police procedurals in two of the country's major weekend newspapers, *The Mirror* and *The Weekly Spectator*. During South Africa's transition to fully participatory democracy, Thabo Nkosinathi Masemola published his procedural *Mixed Signals* (1993) and Gomolemo Mokae produced his take on the subgenre, *The Secret in My*

Bosom (1995). In both 1960s West Africa and 1990s South Africa, the interest in criminal investigation stories was intense but brief. Apart from a small number of white South African and Zimbabwean writers who worked sporadically in the subgenre from the 1960s onwards, police procedurals disappear from African writing until Kwei Quartey and Adimchinma Ibe resuscitate them in the 2010s, and even then the two writers are isolated cases.[5] Because police procedural writing is so concentrated in the years following self-rule and because so few other subgenres appeared during those same years, the police procedural remains very much a genre of the early independence era.

The texts from 1960s West Africa and early 1990s South Africa initially stand out for how different they are from Nigerian and South African crime mysteries of the 1950s. Absent are criminal antiheroes and the hardworking Africans forced into legal compromises by colonial society's restricted economic opportunities. The milieu is instead the decidedly middle- and upper middle-class world of traders, clerks, lawyers, and medical professionals who typically rely the most on the police for property and bodily security. The mysteries pivot on interpersonal crimes, typically prompted by acts of unchecked individuated desire. Homicide features prominently. *Who Killed Inspector Kwasi Minta?*, *Yaba Round-about Murder*, and George Kofi Nfojoh's 'Clue to the Unsolved Problem' (1972) open with the murders of young men by sexual rivals. In Carlton Ashun's 'Who Killed Rosi?' (1967), F.A. Owusu-Ansah's 'The Tragedy of Essie' (1971), and P.D. Anuah's 'The Lost Corpse' (1973), it is the female object of affection who ends up dead, killed by spurned paramours. Less common but still prevalent are stories of property crime. S.O. Duodu's 'Subversion at Poso' (1967), 'Adventures of Annan-Clay' (1968), and 'Hot Money' (1967) and A.K. Awuah's 'Tobacco Trap' (1968) unfold from acts of theft. Similarly, Ellis Ayitey Komey's 1966 serial 'The Iron Box' crafts a mystery out of questions about the ownership of an ancient locked trunk. Mokae's and Masemola's South African novels mix sexual and financial intrigue, as does Ghanaian short story writer Constable E.J. Thompson in his story 'Point of No Return' (1966).

Missing too are corrupt or indifferent police figures who engender only distrust and contempt for their application of colonial law. Instead, the texts depict the police as the able agents of the modernist, bureaucratic state. After generations of overtly abusive colonial policing, Sam, Ekwensi, and the other writers present their readers with mentally dexterous investigators who devote their individual expertise to the rational and fair application of the rule of law. Supported by well-equipped forensics labs, their approach is never less than

---

5   With the exception of Zimbabwe's Rodwell Musekiwa Machingauta, police procedural writing between the early 1970s and 2000s was produced by white novelists, a group that includes James McClure, from South Africa, and Pauline Henson and C.M. Elliot, transplants from Britain to Zimbabwe.

methodical, scientific, and above all impartial.⁶ The interactions between the public and the police are predictably mutually civil, very much as Nkrumah charged in his address to the Police College graduates. The police-public encounters in Sam's *Who Killed Inspector Kwasi Minta?* are more saccharine than they are in the procedurals that follow, but are in their underlying tenor representative of the new citizen-state relationship that the procedurals depict. An upstanding taxi driver, for instance, goes out of his way to volunteer information to Detective Oduro because 'the late Inspector Minta was very helpful to [him]' following a motor accident (17). When Oduro first confronts Minta's love interest Georgina, still a suspect for having fled the crime scene – and doubly suspicious for her 'perfect beauty of face and form' (22) – he remains respectful (22). No less courteous to the investigating officer, Georgina asserts, with no trace of sarcasm, that she is 'ever prepared to assist the police in all possible ways' (22).

Given the genteel quality of encounters such as these, a reader might be forgiven for suspecting the hand of the police or a propaganda arm of the state in the production of these texts. In the case of the Ghanaian newspaper fiction, all of which appeared in government-controlled media during or in the years immediately following the three-year period when the joint military-police National Liberation Council held political power, the suspicion would not be far off the mark.⁷ But even in the absence of direct government intervention, as in

---

6 To wit, Ekwensi repeatedly highlights Faolu's meticulous report writing, and Sam's detective protagonists are exacting in their compliance with bureaucratic procedure. In Thompson's 'Point of No Return', Owusu-Ansah's 'The Tragedy of Essie', and Anuah's 'The Lost Corpse', detectives regularly call on professional state forensics experts to analyze crime scenes and to send evidence to crime labs, the results of which typically confirm the investigators' prior hypotheses. Chief Inspector Ambrose in 'Point of No Return' adheres to due process principles even when it means he must release his prime suspect only to re-arrest him later on the basis of additional evidence. These bureaucratic and technological activities get mirrored in the investigators own methodical, rationalized labor of investigation. Oduro and Faolu solicit witnesses, for instance, by taking out ads in newspapers or by crafting press releases in ways that draw out sources. Ahia expertly turns idle chit-chat into a promising lead. Ambrose, search warrant in hand, combs a suspect's residential compound inch by inch, eventually identifying a patch of loose soil that conceals a blood-covered cloth, which the efficient government chemistry lab confirms as the victim's. As already indicated, Oduro dismisses modern policing theories for what he describes as 'practical criminology' (Sam 1960: 9), but his emphasis on building cases through painstaking witness identification, repeated interviews, and the other unglamorous old-fashioned tasks of investigative police work paints him as no less a capable, scientifically impartial agent of the administrative state than his counterparts in the other detective stories.
7 *The Mirror* served as the weekend edition of the government-run *Daily Graphic*, and the *Weekly Spectator* was put out by the publishing arm of Nkrumah's party until 1966 when it was taken over by the military government. The first of its stories appeared shortly after.

the publication of Sam's and Ekwensi's novellas, the subgenre globally has, since its inception, shifted 'reader identification from the criminal element to the state apparatus' (Winston and Mellerski 1992: 2). Whereas in the classic whodunit, the law and the state are assumed but typically relegated to the shadows to let the private sleuth's iconoclastic genius shine, in the police procedural, the state's sovereign authority and its monopoly over the means to assert its authority are made directly visible through its proxy, the police investigator. Backed by the full force of state's monopoly on violence, the police officer enjoys an extensive arsenal of powers of surveillance, coercion, and social control. The private detective might stand in symbolically for the surveillant panoptic eye of the modern state, à la Foucault (1977), but, following Derrida (2009), the police officer, in fiction as in real life, is the eye as well as the strong arm of the law.[8] Put differently, 'Police behaviour is state power; the police make real, by what they do or fail to do, the intentions and interests of the state and those groups that attempt to control the state' (Marenin 1982: 379). In the liberal bourgeois tradition of the mystery genre, these powers to enforce law and order against society's miscreants often make the police investigator and, by extension, the state itself salutary and heroic. Or, as Winston and Mellerski put it, the procedural presents a 'utopian vision of cooperation between the police and society' (1992: 7).

For nation-states just emerging from colonialism, the police procedural thus offers the narrative means to dramatize – and celebrate – the sovereign authority of newly independent states whose legitimacy and capacity are by no means assured. The police's rationality, impartiality, meticulous adherence to the rule of law, and above all, efficient resolution of criminal mysteries ratify the independent African state as the most appropriate vehicle of collective liberation. Even *Who Killed Inspector Kwasi Minta?*, which is set during the colonial era, enacts this utopian vision of the police and state, insofar as it is only the Africans within the racially hierarchical police service who are capable of smoothing over social conflict and ensuring societal equilibrium. In fact, by contrasting ace detectives Oduro and Ahia to their inept British superiors,

---

Without exception, the police characters in the two papers always outwit the culprits, no matter how ingenious, well organized, or wealthy they are. In the one story that depicts a corrupt government employee, 'Subversion at Poso' by S.O. Duodu, published in two instalments in *The Weekly Spectator* in June 1967, the official is duly caught by a diligent cop and punished to the full extent of the law for his crimes against the state. A similar dynamic is evident in Zimbabwean writer Rodwell Musekiwa Machingauta's novel *Detective Ridgemore Riva* (1994), a relative latecomer to the African police procedural. Equal parts secret police and secret agent, his protagonist employs brutally coercive means to elicit information from and to punish enemies of the Zimbabwean state. For an incisive reading of Machingauta's novel, see Primorac (2012).

8   On panopticism and the detective novel, see Porter (1981: ch. 6).

Sam emphasizes the point; as does Ekwensi. The setting of his novella *Yaba Round-about Murder* is vague but appears to take place during the last years of colonial rule or shortly after independence.⁹ Sergeant Faolu reports to a commanding officer whose name, Winston Brews, codes, if ambiguously, as British. Like Oduro and Ahia, Ekwensi's protagonist John Faolu demonstrates greater intellectual acumen. In a play on a longstanding trope of the procedural, the rigidly bureaucratic and short-sighted Brews dismisses Faolu's proposed scheme to trap the suspect as mere 'theory' and gets annoyed 'to have to listen to such un-heard of ideas' (50). Predictably, Faolu's methods prove superior. In African hands, the state ensures the rights and security of Nigeria's legally upstanding citizens in ways that the colonizer cannot.¹⁰

Another way that the police procedural affirms the structures of state power is in its animation of the disciplinary regimes of modern governance. The procedural, broadly speaking, focalizes the panoptic authority of the state. In the detective subgenre as in real life, surveillance, not physical force, functions as a primary technology of social control. No misdeed goes undiscovered by law enforcement agents, no act of malfeasance remains invisible to officers of the law, no subterfuge escapes the interpretative mastery of attentive criminal investigators. The methodical, by-the-books investigatory regimen of report-writing, evidence-labeling, and confession-recording that typically prevails in the police procedural, even when the common-sensical everyman cop bristles against ponderous bureaucratic processes, further emphasizes the primacy of surveillance and the forms of population statistics that support it. As Foucault (1977) famously points out, panoptic power directs and shapes public and private behavior because it internalizes coercion in the form of self-governance and reduces the necessity of public spectacles of bodily punishment. In their study of the police procedural, Winston and Mellerski contend that by affirming the salutary effects of surveillance the police procedural reinforces this disciplinary regime of governance (1992: 7).

---

9   The novella has received very little critical attention despite the extensive attention given to Ekwensi's other writings. One possible reason for this is the difficulty of categorizing the story he tells in this procedural. Ernest Emenyonu (1974), for example, includes *Yaba Round-about Murder* in his list of Ekwensi's writing for children but concedes that the novella's graphic depiction of violence and its sexualized descriptions of the female body make it inappropriate for young readers (60).

10 Ekwensi brought out a significantly revised edition of *People of the City* a year after the publication of *Yaba Round-about Murder*. As explained in the previous chapter, the novel's original 1954 version depicts the police and civil servants as indifferent at best and corrupt at worst. The post-independence edition recasts African leaders and bureaucrats in a more flattering light and scrubs entirely the character of a bribe-soliciting African employee of the judicial system.

Fig. 1. *Yaba Round-about Murder* by Cyprian Ekwensi (1962). Published by Tortoise Books, Lagos.

The police officers depicted in the post-independence and post-apartheid police procedurals remain formidable figures of authority who project state force when necessary. But in place of the aggressive and armed law enforcers that Ekwensi describes in the 1954 edition of *People of the City*, Faolu, Oduro and Ahia, Chief Inspector Ambrose from 'Point of No Return', Constable Protus Sishi in *Mixed Signals*, and the many others primarily conduct their work through patient observation followed by scientific ratiocination. The better part of the action of S.O. Duodu's 'Subversion at Poso', in fact, takes place from Sergeant Dromo's perch in a public park as he stakes out the suspicious movement of goods across the street. The reader does little more than witness Dromo surveil illegal dealings; capture and arrest are almost afterthoughts and the use of force barely necessary. *Mixed Signals* devotes fewer pages to the physical act of observation than Duodo's story and, in contrast to the other texts, includes a scene in which the late-apartheid-era South African Police Service deploy at a township funeral in a display of raw state power, but resolution ultimately comes from Sishi's expert ability to reconstruct the carefully hidden movements of the killer during the hours leading up to his crime. Ekwensi's *Yaba Round-about*

Murder is the rare title among the procedurals in which a police officer resorts to physical force, but Faolu does so only after making visible the culprit's actions leading up to, during, and following the murder. Ambrose's crack surveillance powers are such that he uncovers crimes and criminals *beyond* the case of the young woman's murder that is his immediate charge. In every one of the procedurals, the all-seeing eye of law enforcement leaves no culprit unidentified, no suspicious activity unexamined, no weapon or bloody cloth undiscovered.

In no instances are the omnipotent surveillant powers of the state depicted as the oppressive menace they were during colonial rule. The all-seeing investigators are not the same as those, for example, in charge of South Africa's apartheid-era racial registries, statistics bureaus, pass laws, and informant networks. What makes the surveillance powers of the post-independence state as depicted in the procedural different, which is to say, as liberatory rather than oppressive, is in how they are shown to advance the modernizing and redistributionist developmentalist paradigms of the decolonizing state. As the examples above suggest, the transformation of the police from enforcers of the 'colonial commandant' (Mbembe 2001) into the all-seeing impartial, scientific, and civic-minded figures that populate these stories is precisely what makes the nation-states they represent modern.[11] Modern policing as depicted in these stories guarantees the conditions for individual citizens such as the murdered pharmacist-in-training Michael Chuma in *Yaba Round-about Murder* to pursue their professional ambitions. Chuma's aid comes too late, but the larger part of the populace enjoys the comfort of knowing that few would-be killers will risk the almost-certainty of capture by a modern professionalized police force. The story's police investigators periodically flex their monopoly on violence but always as a reminder that force is the exception, not the rule, and that self-governance is the most just form of governance. When Ekwensi's Inspector Faolu threatens – not particularly vehemently – an elderly couple with arrest, he does so to remind them of their civic duty to the nation, not to intimidate them into submission as Ekwensi had depicted the police doing a decade earlier in *People of the City*. The same goes for Sam's Inspector Oduro in an almost identical encounter with a taxi driver who turns out to be a willing font of information even without Oduro's authoritative bluster. And, writing in the twilight of apartheid rule, Masemola contrasts repeatedly the superior results of Sishi's gentle surveillance techniques with the strong-arm tactics of his white commander. To govern without force, the stories suggest, is govern as a modern state with the liberty, dignity, and development of its citizens at the forefront of its mission.

---

11 See Mbembe (2001: ch. 1).

In its broadest outlines, the police procedural of the early years of self-rule thus paints a rosy, and certainly idealized, vision of postcolonial society. This is not to suggest that the writers of the period shy away from the social anxieties which the genre in its longer global history has voiced. Nor is it to suggest that postcolonial police procedural writers do not rework the genre's inherited ideological preoccupations to engage the specific crises and challenges of the postcolony. As we will soon see, they do both. But before exploring this other side of the procedural's cultural labors, it is first necessary to trace certain continuities from the police procedural to the spy thrillers that follow it in the 1970s and 1980s.

Secret Agents and Special-Ops: The Anticolonial Hero Remade

By the time of the publication of the last of the West African police procedurals in 1973, stories about kind cops and beneficent law enforcement agencies had become difficult to sustain. Like the state itself, the police had decolonized only insofar as Africans helmed the leadership ranks. In most other ways, their tactics, abuses, and uneven application of sanction recalled the colonial era. Moreover, Ghanaians had lived through Nkrumah's increasing autocratic rule, the exile and imprisonment of his critics, and two military coups, all of which tested public faith in the liberal democratic model of postcolonial governance laid out in Ghana's first constitution. The police, in particular, had failed to gain the kind of legitimacy Nkrumah had, in 1959, implored they seek. Similarly, in Nigeria a civil war (1966–1970), the beginning of military rule, internecine battles over control of the country's petroleum wealth, and the persistent challenges of professionalizing the country's police forces put significant pressure on the liberal democratic ideals outlined in the country's own initial constitution. Public perception that there was 'little pressure on the police to act legally' (Marenin 1985: 79), combined with the militarization and capture of state institutions by self-dealing politicians seeking to tap revenue streams from petroleum extraction, further undermined the state's ethical authority. Consequently, like their regional neighbors in Ghana, Nigerians confronted a widening chasm between the ideals of a state-directed nationalist decolonization and the actual functioning of the state, with the police, as the public's primary interface with state power, symbolizing much of the resulting instability.

Despite these conditions, the ideal of the state as a decolonizing force retained its purchase. Even the political culture, otherwise engulfed by the battles for the spoils of office, remained influenced by the nationalist developmentalist paradigms of the early independence-era. As Andrew Apter notes, for Nigeria those developmentalist paradigms were fueled by the vast oil reserves discovered in the early 1970s, which permitted the government to pump 'oil revenues into the expanding public sector' (2000: 269). The investments were reflected throughout the 1970s in the development of schools and universities, infrastructure, and state-subsidized publishing ventures. There consequently remained significant affective investments in the developmentalist paradigms through which independent nation-states would catch up economically, politically, and socially to developed nations of the Global North (Ferguson 2006: 178).

As the realities of the state's dissipated ability to deliver on the promises of independence tested people's faith in the nation-state ideal, a new generation of popular fiction writers who came of age in the 1960s and 1970s abandoned the police procedural but not its basic faith in the heroic potential of official agents of the developmentalist nation-state. A large subset of these novelists looked to the detective story's close kin, the espionage thriller, to extend the idealism and optimism of the police procedurals. Like the crime investigation stories that precede them, the Anglophone African spy thrillers put the security, stability, and future prosperity of the nation-state in the hands of dedicated, able, and civic minded governmental employees. The protagonists come more often from elite military units or secretive government intelligence agencies than from the mid-level ranks of the police, and they are more likely to battle foreign enemies than domestic traitors, but the result is a similar reaffirmation of the sovereign ideal. And while the spy thriller might appear to be more distantly related than the police procedural to the other detective stories discussed in this book, it shares with them a reliance on related codes of investigation and discovery, often in the form of uncovering international conspiracies, foreign agents, and their hidden bases of operation. The procedurals and spy thrillers are not without their differences. Whereas the police procedurals interrogate the state's capacity to manage intimate interpersonal violence and domestic strife, Anglophone African espionage tales typically explore the state's capacity to quell external threats. What interests me here is how this difference gives writers a narrative framework for thinking more expansively about the promises and perils of sovereign self-rule that were initially dramatized in the police procedurals, but also another way of getting at many of their same ideals and anxieties.

Within a year of the last of the Ghanaian police procedurals, Nigeria's Ethiope Publishers, one of the presses that benefitted from oil-boom-era state support, published the first and most paradigmatic of these novels, Kole Omotoso's action thriller *Fella's Choice*. Omotoso's protagonist is the dashing Pan-Africanist Fella Dandogo, who serves 'the Force', an MI6-like agency operated by a multinational African governing body that is responsible for fending off neocolonial threats to the self-determination of independent African countries and the Black world globally. The novel's opening pages depict Nigeria's new oil wealth as the source of the country's tremendous potential domestic and Africa-wide geopolitical power, especially as a counterweight to white-ruled South Africa's regional and global political heft (10–11). No longer are state officials the benevolent, civic-minded public servants that they are in the police

Fig. 2. *Benni Kamba 009 in the Equatorial Assignment* (1980). Reproduced with permission of Springer Nature Limited through PLSclear.

procedurals, however. Privately, Fella castigates Nigeria's police officers for their bribe-taking and dismisses its politicians as a self-interested bunch who, though not criminal per se, are mediocrities incapable of securing the country's sovereign dominion (81). While the domestic strife they generate impedes full decolonization, the real danger is presented as external and neocolonial and exceeds the scope of any single African nation-state to counter it; hence, Fella's service in the multinational Force. Fella's covert operations take him first to Abidjan and then back to Lagos. By the end of the novel, Fella has subverted a plot by white neocolonial apologists, operating covertly for South Africa's apartheid regime, to undermine Nigeria's currency and with it the power of its petroleum-fueled international influence. As one would expect, the South Africa-backed operatives prove to be no match for Fella. The novel comes to its spectacular climax with a shoot-out in an abandoned cocoa-smuggling station on the Benin side of the Nigerian border. With his superior intellect, sleuthing acumen, and hand-to-hand combat prowess, Fella secures Nigerian, African, and African diasporic independence for another day.

Omotoso's template remained popular in Kenya, Nigeria, and Zimbabwe through the late 1980s, with a few additional titles arriving in the mid-1990s. David G. Maillu's *Benni Kamba 009 in the Equatorial Assignment* (1980), for instance, pits a secret agent of the National Integrity Service of Africa, headquartered in a sprawling bunker beneath the Sahara desert, against a stealth European-funded agency tasked with fostering puppet dictatorships in countries still working to secure their political and economic footing. The cop-turned-crime reporter-turned-private detective-turned-secret agent in Kalu Okpi's *The Smugglers* (1977) mobilizes his preternatural sleuthing skills and military know-how to take on the local agents of American drug runners seeking to turn Nigeria into their own fiefdom. Likewise, in *The Bushtrackers* (1979), Kenya's Meja Mwangi pits a pair of dutiful conservation rangers against an American mafia family out to take control of Kenya's smuggling industries. And in Monica Genya's *Links of a Chain* (1996), a later entry into the subgenre, Kenyan governmental agent Susan Juma uncovers an international plot by Texas oil barons, French financiers, and a host of Kenyan leaders to commandeer newfound oil reserves. Along similar lines, Kenya's national security is threatened in Mwangi Ruheni's *The Mystery Smugglers* (1975) when covert South African agents working on the apartheid regime's nuclear weapons program discover uranium in the country. Indeed, the most frequently recurring external menace in these novels comes from the apartheid government. Omotoso's *Fella's Choice*, Hilary Ng'weno's *The Men from Pretoria* (1975), Kalu Okpi's *The South African Affair* (1982), Tony Marinho's *Deadly Cargo* (1987), and Zimbabwean Hope Dube's *State Secret* (1981) all feature ever more nefarious plots hatched against independent African governments by BOSS, South Africa's Bureau of State Security. With great glee, the protagonists of these novels shame their South African foes in spectacular fashion, whether handily capturing their advanced military hardware, as they do in *The South African Affair*, or breezily uncovering their assiduously planned subterfuges, as they do in *The Men from Pretoria* and *The Mystery Smugglers*.

As a form of home-grown African pulp fiction, the novels reflect both the evolution of literary culture in the 1970s and the expansive freedom that writers felt to appropriate and adapt a wide range of global cultural influences. Hilary Ng'weno, author of *The Men from Pretoria*, explained that he targeted his thriller to young readers looking for nothing more than 'light entertainment' (1979: 159). Ng'weno was not alone in identifying a growing audience for easy-reading books with African settings and characters. He published *The Men from*

Pretoria as the first (and, as it would turn out, last) title in Longman Books' Longman Crime Series. Soon after, Longman launched the Drumbeats series, Macmillan introduced its Pacesetters series, Heinemann came out with the Spear and Heartbeats series, and a long list of Nigerian publishers initiated their own popular genre imprints to provide growing populations of civil servants, office workers, and newly literate tradespeople with inexpensive, quick-reading paperbacks by African writers. Longman, Macmillan, and Heinemann cast wide nets with crime novels, romances, and adventures. The Nigerian presses focused heavily on crime and detection narratives, counting among their crime series Northern Nigeria Publishing Company's Pioneers, Fagbamigbe Publishers' Eagle Crime, Spectrum Books' Panti Street Crime, De-Atman Press's Forest Crime, and Soorg Books' Soorg Espionage.[12] Few of the novels exceeded 150 pages, many featured illustrated covers of gun-wielding young men and buxom women, and nearly all narrated the adventures of heroic male detectives who

---

12 In his role as a publisher and an advocate for African writers, Kole Omotoso publicly criticized the asymmetrical economic conditions that made it so difficult for local presses to compete with the likes of Macmillan, Heinemann, and Longman. Writing in *Afriscope* in 1974, Omotoso listed the formidable economic challenges facing local publishers – import duties that made books published in Europe cheaper than those published in neighboring countries, distribution systems that paled in comparison to those of the established British publishing powerhouses, and limited resources to attract away from foreign publishers the big name authors such as Achebe or Soyinka whose sales and international publishing rights could fund development costs of other books – challenges, he emphasizes, that the market alone cannot solve (1974: 10). At the same 1973 international conference on publishing and book development in Africa that prompted Omotoso's lamentations, Abiola Irele argued that the 'growth of a national publishing industry can be considered, therefore, an important aspect of our development' (1975: 164). Irele, who was involved with the state-owned Ethiope Publishing Corporation based in Benin City, Nigeria, articulates the national development benefits of a robust book trade that are as cultural as they are practical. The publication of high-quality books, he explains, would be a potential economic driver of an extensive creation, production, and distribution chain with the added cultural dividend 'of the growth of awareness among our population, and the creation of new channels of self-reflection and of expression which represent the necessary condition for meaningful action upon the conditions of our contemporary existence' (165). To this end, Ethiope sought to capture a mix of the lucrative textbook market, which Macmillan, Longman, Heinemann, and Oxford University Press dominated, non-fiction trade publications, literary fiction, and popular genre texts such as Omotoso's *Fella's Choice*, which it published. Hilary Ng'weno echoes these points three years later when he conjoins issues of the economic viability of local publishing and editorial independence: 'one must admit that popular writing is the only avenue for sustaining indigenous publishing. So long as you don't have authors writing in a popular style, local publishers are never going to get off the ground. There is always going to be someone in London making the final decision on what is to be published' (1979: 159). For Macmillan's defense against charges of profiting from these dynamics, see Paren (1978).

capture their criminal antagonists and get their girl. Readers could also find crime and other forms of genre fiction in a wide range of new magazines.[13]

Unsurprisingly, considering the global popularity of the James Bond film franchise during the period, Ian Fleming's iconic Agent 007 casts a large shadow over these novels. Omotoso explains that *Fella's Choice* was 'a deliberate attempt to write an African James Bond' (1979: 10). Nigeria's Dan Fulani gives his readers Agent 005 and Maillu's protagonist Benni Kamba earns the designation 009, in part because 007 'is already used by the Western Secret Service' (1980: 54) and because 'nine', per some humorous numerological gymnastics on the part of Kamba's commanding officer, 'is the number of the black man, Africa' (55). With the exception of Monica Genya's protagonist Susan Juma, the Kenyan, Nigerian, and Zimbabwean secret agents most explicitly in the Bond mold demonstrate a bit more swagger than their Bond counterpart, but are likewise dashing ladies' men, sophisticated and cosmopolitan, wry, semi-detached, and tongue-in-cheek.[14]

While the most visible, Bond is far from the only influence. In an interview discussing *The Men from Pretoria*, Ng'weno notes:

> There has been a new batch of films which have been very influential – especially black American films featuring black American actors, the kind of people that youngsters here can relate to. Things which were once thought impossible these youngsters now think may be possible because they have seen such films as *Shaft* and so on. For the first time they have seen black men do things which previously only white men were supposed to be able to do. You may have a black

---

13 Among the most famous of the magazines is *Joe*, the Kenyan humor magazine founded by Ng'weno and Terry Hirst. Hirst illustrated *Joe*'s recurring Western/crime mystery mash-up 'The Good, the Bad, and the Ugali'. Among the other periodicals of the era that published crime and mystery stories are the short-lived Kenyan magazine, *Criminal* (referenced in Hirst 1979: 90), and *Pleasure: Ghana's Sunshine Magazine*, which serialized 'The Copper Wire Conspiracy' by Cofi Quaye and Ali Yemoh's graphic crime mystery narrative 'Oko & Ebo in Slaves of the Lens'. Occasional *Joe* artist Frank Odoi produced a much-celebrated superhero comic strip, *Akokhan*, that ran at different times in all three of Nairobi's major newspapers (Omanga 2016: 263). In addition to its detective fiction, *The Daily Graphic*'s weekend edition *The Mirror* ran a months-long serialized crime mystery cartoon, 'Kwame', in 1973–74. For more on Ghana's magazine culture of the period, see Esther de Bruijn (2017).

14 Explicit Bond references also appear in Marjorie Oludhe Macgoye's 1972 political thriller *Murder in Majengo* and Ng'weno's *The Men from Pretoria*. However, neither of these texts rely on the 007 template per se. Bond is important to Ng'weno's protagonist Scoop Nelson, an investigative journalist, for example, only insofar as Scoop comes to an important realization about the covert machinations of BOSS operatives in Kenya while watching a 007 film in a Nairobi cinema. The villain's actions on screen mirror, if not precisely, those of the South African agents Scoop has discovered.

detective busting a gang of white hoodlums – this sort of thing …
Also the Chinese Kung Fu films are very popular here. (1979: 159).

Evidence of these additional influences appears frequently. As noted in a previous chapter, Meja Mwangi's published *The Bushtrackers* in Longman's Drumbeat series as a novelization of Gary Stricker's script for a never-completed film by the famed Blaxploitation director Gordon Parks, Jr.[15] Nigerian novelist Chris Abani describes Drum Publications' Lance Spearman, not unfondly, as a 'low-rent Richard Roundtree' of *Shaft* fame (2018a: 19). A henchman 'carefully coached in the martial arts' protects the Asian villain of Fulani's *Flight 800* (1983: 51); Machingauta's Detective Ridgemore Riva includes martial artistry in his arsenal against Zimbabwe's foes; and, in Valentine Alily's *Mark of the Cobra*, Jack Ebony, 'Africa's Number One Kill-Master' and 'sixth dan black belt' (1980: 2), is as likely to outmaneuver foes with expert karate moves as with his quick draw.[16]

It is also important to note the potential influence of Africa's own Lance Spearman on the Anglophone African spy thriller. From 1968 to 1972, South Africa's Drum Publications' monthly photonovel *African Film* charted the exploits of fedora-wearing, cigar-smoking, scotch-and-soda drinking Lance Spearman (a.k.a. The Spear) and his band of crime fighters. Each issue included thirty-one pages of black-and-white captioned photographs storyboarded like American comic books and edited in a sophisticated cinematic fashion (Krings 2015: 60). To circumvent the economic boycott against South Africa, Drum Publications had the scripts written by Lesotho university students, the photomontages shot in Swaziland, and the magazine printed in London, Lagos, and Nairobi (60). With circulation topping 100,000 a year in West Africa alone, the magazine reached large readerships in Anglophone East, West, and Southern Africa (61). Month after month, Spearman found himself pitted against all manner of caricatured villains, often maniacal geniuses helming fanciful weapons and driven by visions of global domination. As Omotoso's Fella

15   See Roland S. Jefferson (1984: 63).
16   Attesting to the popularity of martial arts films in Ghana at this time, Muftau Ganiyu (1974) notes in his terrifically titled news story, 'Children picking up bad practice "Karate" Films Blamed', that at least 129 different karate films were circulating in the country as of the article's November publication. For cultural histories of Blaxploitation and martial arts circulations and influences in specific African contexts, see Laura Fair (2018), Vijay Prashad (2002), and May Joseph (1999). In 1972, South Africa's National Party began providing special subsidies for 'Bantu films' in African languages made by white filmmakers that would provide moral entertainments. Crime never paid in the films and separate development ideologies reigned supreme. Drawing heavily on Blaxploitation and kung fu film aesthetics, but not on detective mystery or spy thriller plots per se, the films nevertheless offered Black South African audiences parallel entertainments to those enjoyed in the same period by their compatriots in other parts of Africa. See Gairoonisa Paleker (2010) and Keyan Tomaselli (1988).

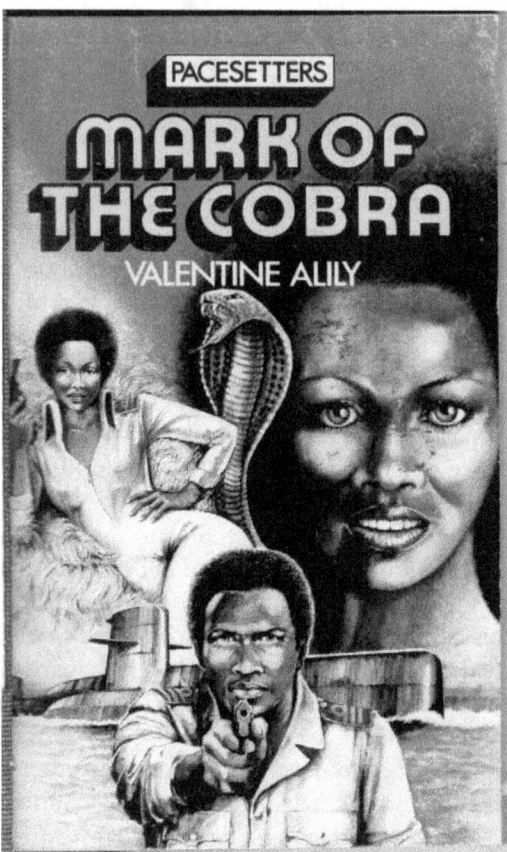

Fig. 3. *Mark of the Cobra* by Valentine Alily (1980). Reproduced with permission of Springer Nature Limited through PLSclear.

Dandogo and Maillu's Benni Kamba 009 would a decade later, The Spear battles his foes with high-tech gadgetry, submarines, and other real and imagined military hardware as often as he employs his fists and intellect. And like his successors, Spear never lacks for the attention of beautiful women. So popular was the magazine that it begat many other African photonovels.[17] While there is no documentation of *African Film*'s direct influence on future novelists, it is difficult to imagine that the spy thriller writers were not at least aware of it and of the potential opportunities in replicating its plots and style.

Like Spearman, Fella Dandogo, Onyex Halla, Jack Ebony, Benni Kamba, and most of the other protagonists of the spy thrillers that appeared throughout the 1970s and 1980s are fantastical figures more than they are the hard-edged realist

---

17 The detective novelist F. Katalambulla edited the Swahili-language *Film Tanzania* for East African readers, for example, and Nigerian novelist Chris Abani lists another half dozen look-reads that were widely available in Nigeria in the 1970s (2018a: 19).

characters of the earlier police procedurals. Unlike the everyman cops who perform so methodically the rationalist surveillance functions of the modern state, they are action heroes whose exploits to secure African sovereignty unfold as spectacle and fantasy. For this reason, Bernth Lindfors dismisses the tales of globetrotting, gadget-wielding secret agents as 'escape literature pure and simple' (1991: 137). Indeed, it is difficult to read any of the counter-espionage novels as taking themselves or their plots too seriously. Even the most sober of them lack the earnestness of *Who Killed Inspector Kwasi Minta?*.[18] Real-life counterparts to fictional journalists such as Ng'weno's protagonist Scoop Nelson or Mohamed Tukur Garba's newspaper owner Tahir Hussein in *Stop Press: Murder* (1983) could, for sure, realistically uncover covert foreign plots like Nelson and Hussein are made to do. The existence of a Pan-African MI6-like defense agency as well equipped and effective as Maillu's multinational National Integrity Service of Africa, on the other hand, reads as pure daydream. For Nigerian readers living through the reality of self-dealing kleptocrats torching entire ministry buildings to destroy evidence of their misdeeds, as occurred repeatedly between 1977 and 1983, the discrepancy between the fictional depiction of cash-flush, bureaucratically efficient, purely civic-minded governments and those realities would have been vast. Equally discrepant are the novels' representations of essentially discord-free nations, whose seemingly worst threats come from without. The then-fresh Nigerian memories of the war over Biafra's secession, for instance, are nowhere evident in the novels, despite the fact that at least two of the spy thriller authors also wrote Biafra war novels.[19]

I view the shift away from the mundane realism of *Yaba Round-about Murder* and other police investigation narratives as less of a departure from the procedurals' socio-political engagements than as a reconfiguration and expansion of them for changed historical circumstances. For a readership soured on police officers but not on the ideals of the modern state, the novels' protagonists provide what police inspectors could no longer offer in terms of

---

18 Spectacle and humor are certainly central. In Okpi's 1982 *The South African Affair*, for example, Wing Commander Onyex Halla, an ace fighter pilot in Nigeria's Air Force, builds a decoy oil refinery over which he vanquishes his white South African foes in a climactic fighter jet battle and then flies off into the sunset with a beautiful female television producer. From the earliest of the novels, humor and satire play as important a role as action heroics. Ng'weno begins his 1975 novel *The Men from Pretoria* in the office of Petrus van der Huizen with a satirical depiction of the white South African BOSS headman gazing uneasily upon a portrait of apartheid architect Jan Smuts, feeling 'uneasy under the stare of the portrait – a sense of inadequacy perhaps' (1). The same year, Ng'weno's fellow Kenyan, Mwangi Ruheni, proffered in his novel *The Mystery Smugglers* the comically bumptious villager rather than the supremely talented urbane detective as the unwitting foil to an international smuggling ring.

19 See Okpi (1982) and Alily (2022).

celebrating African sovereignty. Because most of these fantastical figures are so far removed from the reader's daily experience of policing, secret agents and counter-espionage experts can consequently represent postcolonial statist ideals even in an era when law enforcement is deeply discredited. Moreover, by placing responsibility for governmental fragility on foreign agents, writers minimize the risk of running afoul of governmental censors. Omotoso's Fella Dandogo grumbles about inept civil servants, for example, but Omotoso is politically astute enough to emphasize that Nigeria's real problems stem from colonial nostalgists and covert South African operatives.

The spy thrillers' expansion of the procedural's framework for understanding sovereignty is equally a function of the period's geopolitical imperatives. To read the police procedurals of the 1960s is to get the impression that successful self-determination is merely matter of managing domestic social relations. Nowhere are internal conflicts linked to global geopolitical or economic asymmetries. By contrast, the spy thrillers of the 1970s and 1980s dramatize the African state's very real vulnerability to global political, economic, and social inequities. As caricatured as their depictions of geopolitically disadvantaged African states are, the spy thrillers tap the era's common fears about neocolonial threat to African autonomy. In these novels, sovereign self-rule demands vigilance against those institutions and non-state actors unwilling to relinquish white Europe's territorial claim to African soil. That level of vigilance, many of the novels suggest, requires more resources than any one African nation-state can muster. It calls instead for a Pan-African world-building that Adom Getachew (2019) argues was as important in the 1960s and 1970s as nation-building. About the real-world institutions and alliances built by Kwame Nkrumah, Julius Nyerere, Michael Manley, Sukarno, and their contemporaries, Getachew explains that 'nationalists argued that in the absence of legal, political, and economic institutions that realized an international principle of nondomination, the domestic politics of postcolonial states were constantly vulnerable to external encroachment and intervention. Worldmaking was thus envisioned as the correlate to nation-building, and self-determination stood at the nexus' (2019: 4). A new global infrastructure would, in short, help assure the viability, security, and sovereignty of individual African, Caribbean, and Asian nation-states. In their own way, the spy thrillers articulate a similar vision.

One of the primary ways that Omotoso, Maillu, and the other espionage novelists craft their Pan-African anti-neocolonial politics is through an ironic reimagining of the genre's long British history as a cultural defense of imperial power. Birmingham-school cultural critic Michael Denning asserts that at its root the British spy story narrates the collective fantasy of the white English-speaking world, which above all is the collective fantasy of Empire. Denning explains:

It is no accident that the genre first appears at the beginning of the twentieth century, in the imperialist stage of capitalism when the existence of rival imperialist states and a capitalist world system made it increasingly difficult to envision the totality of social relations as embedded in any single 'knowable community'. The novel of espionage is the tale of the boundary between nations and cultures and the spy acts as a defender or subverter of the nation in the face of the other, the alien. (1987: 13)

Denning further explains that the genre arose and developed as an expression of the will to national and imperial dominance in face of threats to that dominance, and by extension in the face of threats to the very viability of Britain itself (13).[20] The early twentieth-century spy novel's narrative imperatives were all the more necessary because Great Britain's dominance was, in the eyes of its beneficiaries at least, under threat, especially by rival empire-builders whose spies were presumed to be anywhere and everywhere in Britain's global domain. By contrast, the Nigerian, Kenyan, and Zimbabwean spy thrillers revel in turning the British spy thriller's assertion of imperial might against itself. If Bulldog Drummond, John Buchan, and Ian Fleming put their British spies in the service of protecting Britain against the threat of rival empire-builders, then Mwangi Ruheni, Tony Marinho, Hope Dube, and the others set their protagonists to the crucial task of protecting Kenya, Nigeria, and Zimbabwe from the new empire builders of the 1970s and 1980s. These include South Africa's apartheid regime and international drug, game, and mineral smuggling cartels whose efforts to build global financial regimes disarticulated from the nation-state threaten to undermine the concept of the sovereign nation-state altogether.

An Africanized 007 suits the Pan-Africanist inflection of these texts unexpectedly well insofar as Bond is a British hero who serves a larger international community. Appearing at the tail end of Britain's empire, James Bond, unlike many of his fictional predecessors, does not actually protect Britain from the direct threats to its imperial dominance. In their study of the political lives of James Bond, Tony Bennett and Janet Woollacott clarify that Bond 'is a hero of the NATO alliance' (1987: 99), fighting the battles of the Cold War rather than those of the British empire per se. However, they argue, Bond was 'first and foremost an English hero. Indeed, the system of NATO alliances ... typically functions as a means of placing Bond – and thereby England – imaginarily at the centre of the world stage' (99–100). It is thus through a multinational NATO, but unambiguously from Britain, that Bond secures a Cold War global order mastered by that country. The Empire might have faded but, in effect, Britain's

20 On this point, see also John G. Cawelti and Bruce A. Rosenberg (1987).

imperial might persists and, because of Bond, persists untarnished. As John le Carré's novels about the corruption of the British secret services attest, the spy thriller has never been monolithic, of course.[21] Yet when 007 appears in the 1950s, as a super-agent in the waning years of the British imperium, when Englishness had become especially unstable, Ian Fleming fashions a hero to place Britain back at the center of world affairs and to revel in a nostalgia for its global might.

The Anglophone African spy novels re-orient 007 British-centered internationalism to suggest that the African state worth protecting is the state that is part of a larger global community. If anything, the global Pan-African community is even more essential to the Anglophone African spy novels than the NATO alliance to in the Bond adventures. Fella Dandogo is reminded of this imperative when his superiors explain that the attack on Nigeria puts the survival of 'the black man' worldwide under severe threat (Omotoso 1974: 15–16). Benni Kamba's commanding officer spurs him to action by reminding him that the 'history of the black man is full of suffering. For decades, centuries, he has remained the hunted monkey, the source of labour, the servant, the slave, the despised, the underdog and the child of pains. 009, you will now be the star of the black man' (Maillu 1980: 52). When Wing Commander Onyex Halla fends off Nigeria's white South African enemies in *The South African Affair*, he too fights simultaneously for Nigeria and other struggling African nations, in particular Angola, to whose SWAPO liberation fighters he delivers a captured South African military plane. In these novels, Bond's imperative to protect the NATO alliance gets refigured as an imperative to protect 'Africa', Africa as both a racially figured idea and as a collection of sovereign nation-states each of whose individual security remains contingent on the collective viability of every other individual nation-state.[22] Fella Dandogo, Benni Kamba, and Onyex Halla thus take shape as Pan-Africanist heroes who bring glory to individual countries but whose efforts serve to restore honor and dignity to all Africans on the continent and in the diaspora. In the process, they secure the sovereignty of every politically independent sub-Saharan African nation-state. If Britain could not envision itself as a viable nation without its empire, neither Kenya, Nigeria, nor Zimbabwe can imagine themselves as sovereign nation-states without Africa remaining free from colonial and neocolonial shackles. In the spy thriller as in real life, to make a postcolonial state is thus to make a new kind of world.

---

21 The British spy thriller of the 1930s and 40s, for instance, paralleled the hard-boiled detective story of the era, in which the morality of power and the complicity of the individual secret agent with the abuses of institutional authority came under scrutiny. But even these works were not, as Denning narrates it, anti-empire per se.
22 Peter Ribic employs Getachew's framework to make a similar argument about Maillu's Benni Kamba 009 novels (2021: 9).

Crime, Control, and the Anxieties of Self-Rule

There is more to the police procedurals and spy novels than a simple, uncritical affirmation of state power. Both subgenres have long grappled with the tensions inherent to the viability, legitimacy, and functionality of the nation-state. This fact is no less true for the Anglophone African texts than for the *policiers* or espionage tales of any other linguistic tradition.[23] In the context of 1960s West Africa and 1990s South Africa, the police procedural and spy thriller frequently articulate, if not manage, as Fredric Jameson (1979) would have it, an interrelated set of anxieties about economic development, democratic governance, and the workings of state institutions. These anxieties would not be unfamiliar to readers of police procedurals from other parts of the world, nor would their resolutions, which often follow conventional American and British generic pathways wherein 'the spectre of absolute state control' (Winston and Mellerski 1992: 7) contains threats both domestic and foreign. But context is everything, and in the African postcolony, even these similarities take on distinct inflections.

One need look no further than to the register of characters in the Anglophone African police procedurals to identify an anxious preoccupation with the emergent class relations and economic productivity of the new nation-states. The protagonists, whether villain or victim, fall into one of two categories. The first comprises the would-be drivers of national development: the promising young police inspector and a successful cocoa broker in *Who Killed Inspector Kwasi Minta?*; a medical trainee and a building contractor in *Yaba Round-about Murder*; an esteemed doctor and a young lawyer in *Mixed Signals*; an anti-apartheid movement lawyer in Mokae's *The Secret in My Bosom*; a tourist hotel manager in 'Subversion at Poso'; and a timber dealer in 'Who Killed Rosi?'. The other category includes men and women unwilling to commit themselves to the 'honest work' of productive capitalist labor. Heedless to the point of personal and social recklessness, these characters undermine the emergent nation-state not only by committing crimes that lead them to jail and out of the productive workforce but also by taking the lives of the lawyers, pharmacists, and other striving professionals who are equally important for future economic and social development. The good-time girls who populate several of the texts effect a similar outcome by driving otherwise upstanding, hardworking, family men to murderous rage with their insatiable appetites for ever-more expensive material goods. One can certainly read the frequency with which the women end up

---

23 For a survey of European, American, and South African examples of procedurals that turn the genre's focus to the illegitimacy and structural violence of the modern police state, see Winston and Mellerski (1992). For a comparative analysis of global espionage fiction from a period similar to that of the African novels addressed in this chapter, see Allan Hepburn (2020).

murdered by these men as a moral punishment for their defiance of patriarchal sexual norms.[24] At the same time, the morgue as the women's recurrent fate must also be seen as a narrative punishment for intemperate consumption in the absence of productive labor. The young nation-state, these stories suggest, cannot afford citizens who consume more than what they contribute. In story after story, the police heroically step in to mitigate any threat to this bourgeois patriarchal developmentalist ideal, but not before they vocalize significant anxieties about domestic obstacles to national economic development.

West Africa's police procedurals of the 1960s and South Africa's of the early 1990s also register an apprehension about the residual traces of colonial policing and unchecked governmental power. Ekwensi's Inspector Faolu struggles periodically against a conditioned distrust of the police. To a woman reluctant to provide the whereabouts of someone he hopes can shed light on his primary suspect, Faolu admits: 'So many people think the police are their enemies and are very reluctant to help' (1962: 23). Despite this assurance, the woman withholds information, leaving Faolu with the impression that: 'It was not the first time that people had lied to him because they guessed he was a detective' (24). The novella actually generates much of its narrative tension from the question of whether Faolu can overcome this legacy of public mistrust of the police.[25] While Ekwensi only obliquely links this mistrust to Nigerians' historical experience of colonial policing, South Africa's Thabo Nkosinathi Masemola makes the relation explicit.[26] Charged with investigating the murder of a township lawyer, 'Bantu Detective Constable' Protus Sishi cleverly uncovers private motivations for what higher-ranking, racially prejudiced white criminal investigators and the news media treat as political crimes, committed by rival Black political movements. Like Faolu, Sishi finds himself thwarted at every turn by fear of and resistance to

---

24 Stephanie Newell's *Ghanaian Popular Fiction: 'Thrilling Discoveries in Conjugal Life'* (2000) remains the authoritative text on the complex gender dynamics represented in and through Ghana's rich tradition of pamphlet, newspaper, magazine, and other popular fictions. For a psychoanalytic analysis of the narrative punishments meted to female bodies in European and American film, see Joan Copjec (1993). For a comparative study that takes in the United Kingdom, Spain, the United States, and Latin America, see Glen S. Close (2018).

25 A Tanzanian school reader from 1968, Fortunatus Kawegere's *Inspector Rajabu Investigates, and other stories*, traces a similar passage from mistrust to confidence.

26 Masemola's *Mixed Signals* and Mokae's *The Secret in My Bosom* deserve far more attention than I can give them here, particularly *Mixed Signals* for its treatment of the competing discourses of law, order, obedience, and dissidence in a transitional South Africa. In addition to the South African Police Service, an Inkahta-like conservative African organization, an evangelical Christian church, and a resurgent Zulu cosmological belief system battle individually and occasionally in concert for authority over township social life. For a more extensive analysis of the novels, see Lindy Stiebel (2002).

the police, in large part because of the historical complicity of Black police officers in maintaining white supremacy. In one exchange, Sishi's sister, a feminist anti-apartheid proponent, goads him into repeating apartheid-era Boer homilies that the police must kill 'radical elements ... in the interests of peace and state security' and that without the Boers Africans would 'still be killing each other' (61). An important subplot sees Sishi shed these white ideologies as his investigation turns up truths about power, policing, and race beyond those related to his murder case. However, the fact that he, the African constable who proves to be the ideal police detective for a post-apartheid future, struggles to decolonize his individual conception of law and order calls attention to the immense task of decolonizing the institutions of law enforcement whose primary purpose had been to enforce racial apartheid. In the end Ekwensi and Masemola quell anxieties about policing by anticipating futures in which crime is principally private rather than political and the police, ever polite as imagined by Nkrumah, exist as the institution of last resort for ensuring the social equilibrium of liberal society.[27] The anxiety haunts the texts nevertheless.

In the spy novels, the principal tension stems the precariousness of state institutions more generally. Omotoso's Fella Dandogo and Maillu's Benni Kamba 009 make clear that their expertise is necessary precisely because the postcolonial state remains unstable and vulnerable to external predation. Dan Fulani's satirical novel *Flight 800*, published by Nigeria's Spectrum Books in 1983 and reprinted in 1986, turns the chasm between the ideals of the decolonizing state and the realities of early-1980s Nigerian institutions into tragicomic farce. Charged with infiltrating and destroying an international drug smuggling operation being run through Nigeria's porous borders, Agent 005 Pius Shale cannot get from northern Nigeria to Lagos and from Lagos to his seat on an international flight without confronting every cliché of corruption, favoritism, entitlement, fraud, armed violence, technical incompetence, and infrastructural failing, not least of which comes when his domestic flight makes an emergency landing in Ibadan because 'an error of judgement' on the ground left the fuel level unchecked (15). Whose error – ground crew, flight staff, safety inspector,

---

[27] The Black post-apartheid writers were not the first to attempt such a move. With his seven Kramer and Zondi police procedurals, published between 1971 and 1984, James McClure offered a liberal vision of multiracial brotherhood within the South African Police Service and of criminal investigation as a purely apolitical act of the intellect. It would be unfair to characterize McClure's novels as apologetic for apartheid. Rather, they reside comfortably within the body of South African white liberal writing, critical but accommodationist of white rule. At a time of collective struggle to dismantle the apartheid state, McClure's fiction marginalizes 'collective black action against the system and replaces it with a purely personal, "hopeful" vision of individual cooperation' (Winston and Mellerski 1992: 88).

or the regulatory officers charged with overseeing each of the previous – is left unremarked. And all this before he can begin his actual investigation. Stephen Atalebe takes related problems of state efficacy into philosophical territory in his 2014 novel *The Hour of Death in Harare*. While stationed in Prague, his secret agent uncovers a foreign plot to assassinate President Robert Mugabe. Before acting on the information, the agent contemplates the many crises suffered by everyday Zimbabweans under Mugabe's rule and the question of whether the country would be better off with his murder.

The spy thrillers' response to these crises is typically to reaffirm the imperative of the nation-state as a political form. In the face of institutional ineffectiveness, Fulani's protagonist, for example, persists in his adventure to save Nigeria from its external predators and, indeed, to preserve the very idea of 'Nigeria' as the statist vehicle for collective liberation. What Fulani's novel suggests, however satirically, is that Nigeria requires for its viability precisely that which is absent in Shale's adventure to initiate his investigation: a professionalized police force such as the one depicted in the police procedurals, more technologies of surveillance, robust border controls, and efficient and authoritative regulatory agencies. In other words, the institutions of the modernist nation-state remain the most effective vehicles to save the postcolonial nation-state. Indeed, as if to emphasize this point, critical surveillance information that helps Shale uncover the well-masked drug smuggling operation comes from the Nigerian High Commissioner in London. As state agents, Shale and the High Commission officer represent the power of the state to secure its sovereign dominion for the protection of its citizens.[28] Insofar as Shale and the commissioner are far removed from the lives of average Nigerians, the novel skirts the problematic reality of the corrupt, high-handed, and poorly trained state agents that even Shale must deal with daily. But much the same could be said about the James Bond franchise as well.

---

28 Novelist Kalu Okpi stakes a similar claim to the modernist liberal democratic state. In *The South African Affair*, Nigeria's government, military, and civil society join forces efficiently and effectively to fend off white South African saboteurs seeking to destabilize the country's oil industry. That said, with *The South African Affair*'s flattering portrayal of the Nigerian military and its depiction of an unfailingly civic-minded and economically solvent government, the novel deflects broader questions about morally legitimate and politically efficacious forms of militarized and anti-democratic governance that a story about apartheid South African interference might otherwise raise about Nigeria itself. Which is to say, in the context of Nigeria's intermittent military rule during the period of the novel's publication, *The South African Affair*'s valorization of government security agencies and the armed forces might trouble some readers for whom the text could read as an ideological cover story for antidemocratic military domination.

Interrogating the Law

What is missing in these calls for robust governing institutions is the recognition of the profound problematics of real-life state-making. Fulani laments the impotence of Nigeria's regulatory agencies and Maillu castigates Africa's feckless leaders, but neither they nor any of the other spy novelists make more than passing reference to the institutional precarity that confronted the elected officials and civil servants in the 1960s and 1970s as they sought to make sense of and decolonize the governing institutions that they had inherited from their colonial rulers. Historically, such interrogations have not been a strength of police procedurals or spy novels, or of detective fiction more broadly. The law as enforced by the police and its execution in the courts is routinely left unexamined. The tendency in the stories is to take the law itself, as well as the modern bureaucratic state in general, at least in its idealized American or British forms, for granted.[29]

Despite this tendency, the detective story contains the narrative tools for interrogating the tensions inherent not just to the institutions of the postcolonial state, but also to the underlying process of postcolonial state-making. This is because practices of jurisprudence, legal doctrine, conceptions of property ownership and bodily integrity, methods of investigation, boundaries of sovereign right, and practices for establishing proof all shape the contours of detection genre narratives. What constitutes a crime, the methods by which the culprit is identified, and how the wheels of justice turn are the detective story's fundamental building blocks. And they are all culturally and historically specific.[30] Moreover, they are in a constant state of flux, rarely more so than in the years that immediately follow the end of colonial rule. For new-born nation-states still deep in the complicated process of writing law, interpreting constitutional doctrine, and establishing legal precedent, the practices of jurisprudence were by no means securely established. By way of concluding this chapter, it is worth pausing at some length to consider Ellis Ayitey Komey's

---

29 See Porter (1981: 121) on this point.
30 On the issue of popular understandings of state sovereignty as they shape detective mystery narratives, consider an example from the inception of the mystery genre, Poe's 'The Purloined Letter' (1845). The horror (or glee, depending on one's attitude toward monarchy) in seeing the patriarchal sovereign's authority rendered impotent by a mere courtier has few direct contemporary equivalents, but for its nineteenth-century readers, to show the king at the mercy of an inferior is to put an entire cosmological conception of the state in crisis. That critical debate over 'The Purloined Letter' now revolves largely around the missing letter's function in the chain of signification rather than on its political-ideological function should give some sense of how the immediacy of royal sovereignty and its crises for Poe's nineteenth-century readers has lost its salience for readers in the twentieth and twenty-first centuries.

1966 serial, 'The Iron Box', a courtroom drama whose suspense is predicated on the early independence problems of jurisdiction, legal interpretation, and precedent, which is to say, on Ghana's struggles to form the kinds of robust institutions for which Fulani and so many of the others call.

Komey is better known as a poet, and 'The Iron Box' might be his only published mystery fiction.[31] The story ran in Ghana's *Sunday Mirror* newspaper beginning 19 June 1966, four months after the National Liberation Council toppled Nkrumah's government. It was one of the newspaper's first mystery fiction serials. At the story's center are two interrelated mysteries: the contents of an ancient iron crate and the identity of its rightful owner. How Komey resolves the two mysteries is itself a mystery; library holdings for the *Sunday Mirror* are incomplete, and I have been able to locate only the first instalment. Yet, for the story's richly complex and unusual exposition, the first instalment deserves attention even without an understanding of the ultimate plot resolution.

Several aspects of Komey's story stand out from other Anglophone African detective stories and are crucial to its critical articulations. First is that the story's central mysteries are innocuous. The reader learns promptly that there was likely no crime committed at all. The story's protagonists are provincials and fundamentally honest farmers instead of cosmopolitan urbanites on the make. In fact, the neighbors contesting ownership of the box want what is theirs but seem to be happy to concede the property in question to its rightful owner. Another unique aspect is that the investigation unfolds as a courtroom drama under the purview of a small-town chief instead of police officers or big city journalists. As in other courtroom mysteries, the work of investigation and discovery is carried out by lawyers and judges in the place of police detectives or counter-espionage experts, but as with the other two subgenres discussed in this chapter, the power over investigation and discovery remains firmly in the hands of the state. The narrator in this case is an anthropologist, Ghanaian by nationality, who takes a professional interest in the twin mysteries and in the broader national implications of the legal case that results. Anthropology, like policing, is deeply rooted in histories of colonial knowledge production and social control. By making his narrator a professional anthropologist, Komey appropriates that power for Africans themselves. But what is most fascinating about the story is the way Komey's opening paragraphs turn a defining tension of the two-tiered legal system adopted for Ghanaian jurisprudence at independence into an evocative generic problem. If the detective genre first

---

31 Some of Komey's poems appear in *Messages: Poems from Ghana* (1971), edited by Kofi Awoonor and Geormbeeyi Adale-Mortty. Komey also played an important role in editing and promoting other African writers. With Ezekiel Mphalele, he edited the collection *Modern African Stories* (1964), published by Faber and Faber and worked on the magazine *Flamingo*, which covered Black British life and culture in the 1960s.

developed to reflect and reproduce American and British criminal law, Komey points to the complications facing African writers attempting to reconcile the genre with local legal realities.

'The Iron Box' begins with Kodjo Boateng unearthing the ancient metal trunk while uprooting a palm tree on his cocoa farm. In what turns out to be an important detail, the tree's roots enwrap the box, and Boateng is forced to hack them off to liberate the object. Once he frees the heavy trunk, Boateng finds the lock to be too complicated and box's construction too solid to open. Boateng's inability to open the trunk sets the initial mystery in motion: what treasures, if any, are trapped inside? The second and greater mystery is the question of who can claim ownership of the trunk, Boateng or his neighbor Kwaku Barnor, whose family has long held possession of a large rusty key that appears as if it could fit the trunk's lock. As the narrator suggests in the opening instalment, it might surprise readers that anyone would entertain Barnor's claim. 'You may wonder', the narrator questions, 'how a man who could not prove ownership of the land could claim ownership of treasure found on it' (12). The narrator goes on to explain that the reason why readers might question the property claim is because of the difference 'between our customary law and the English law that we have now adopted' (12). Which is to say the question's central importance is a function of the thorny distinction between how the Ghanaian Constitution defines the difference between customary and common law as well as of the inconsistent and conflictual ways that customary law gets applied in practice.

With political self-rule, the Ghanaian Constitution enshrined the distinction between customary law and common law, the former consisting of the 'rules of law which by customs are applicable to particular communities in Ghana' (Asante 1965: 848). But over the course of a century of British colonial jurisprudence, which was predicated on the doctrine of Indirect Rule, and several years of political independence, the Ghanaian courts had universalized a singular nationwide set of customary legal principles out of the multiple doctrines and practices of Ghana's diversely constituted communities (848). As a result, what was taken as customary law in the Ghanaian national courts could, and often did, look quite different from what was understood as customary law in any given Ga or Ashanti town. Asante writes that, 'Nowhere is this cleavage between textbook law and social reality more glaring than in the customary land law of Ghana' (849). Barnor, the neighbor with the key, makes his claim based on the generalized principle of customary land law that, to use Asante's description, 'drew a sharp distinction between soil or earth and the tangible fruits of man's endeavor thereon' (851). Under this doctrine, Boateng owns the soil but does not necessarily own the trees or buildings on it if they were planted or built before his tenure. The palm tree encasing the mysterious box predates Boateng's ownership and may date to the days when Barnor's ancestors are said in local oral histories to have farmed the land. Under customary law, Barnor's legal petition for the box would thus be legally justified.

But if the story's readers were still surprised by Barnor's claim to ownership, it might have been because the Ghana Interpretation Act of 1960 had rejected the customary distinction between soil and the fruits of human labor in favor of 'broad English definitions of land' (Asante 1965: 851). Theoretically, at the time of the story's 1966 publication, Barnor's assertion of ownership consequently no longer enjoys legal force. But the matter had hardly been settled. In 1961, Ghana's Supreme Court ignored the Interpretation Act to apply the customary definition of land in a major decision, and in any case, local application did not necessarily conform with the nation-state-level rule of law (851). Asking a local chief to adjudicate, for example, could potentially limit the likelihood of the 1960 legislative standard from being applied to the case. Which is precisely why Barnor jockeys to get the case in front of the chief. As the anthropologist narrator explains: 'Our chief always insisted that our customary law was better and saner than the new laws' (1966: 12).

Mahmood Mamdani (1996) argues that this bifurcation between customary authority and civil law gives rise in the subsequent decades to the crises and fragility of the postcolonial African state. Among other consequences, Mamdani contends that the patrimonialism endemic to chieftaincy rule filtered into the liberal democratic institutions of the central state, leading to conflict-laden, winner-take-all ethnicity-based competition for the spoils of state power (ch. 4). Despite his depiction of the chief's antidemocratic high-handed manner, Komey appears less interested in despotism than in jurisprudence. Neither does the first instalment of Komey's serial suggest a preoccupation with the national-level political consequences of the split between customary and civil law that interests Mamdani. The story's frame of reference is never wider than the farming community in which it is set. Instead, Komey poses a simpler but no less significant problem arising from the inchoate status of the existing law and imperfectly aligned structures of power.

Far from taking the law and the state for granted as, say, Ekwensi does in *Yaba Round-about Murder*, Komey's story hints at the fragility of institutional authority and legitimacy in the early years of postcolonial state-making. The Ghanaian legal system is presented as dynamic, distinct and, much to the delight of Komey's anthropologist narrator, still under formation. Komey's choice of an anthropologist is especially interesting in this regard for it depicts Ghanaians not only asserting sovereign authority over the process of state formation but also over the social scientific reflection on that process. One of the facets of the case that especially intrigues the anthropologist is that there remains no clear protocol to determine customary or civil court jurisdiction. The problem of which court will hear the case under which doctrine becomes as much a point of suspense as the story's other mysteries. And even when the mystery of jurisdiction is resolved, confusion remains about due process. The chief admonishes Boateng, for example, for failing to distinguish the procedure of civil courts from customary courts (12). Significantly disadvantaged by the customary court's land tenure doctrine, Boateng had attempted to object to a point of order as would be his right in the civil courts, taking an adversarial stance to the judge and the other litigant and hoping to gain at least some legal footing.

Komey's focus on the ambiguities inherent to the adjudication of property rights and on the bifurcation of the rule of law illuminates two additional substantial tensions inherent to the structure of Ghana's political system. First, competing property rights doctrines elicit anxieties about economic productivity and bourgeois class relations. How, after all, can commerce be securely transacted where basic questions about ownership are so unsettled? In this regard, Komey's story is not so different from the other post-independence and post-apartheid police procedurals. Second, the story's focus on uncertainty where rule of law is concerned also highlights the tenuousness of the rule of law as a foundational principle of governance in a bifurcated postcolony such as Ghana. In this split form, the rule of law becomes a source of social conflict and antagonism, as Boateng's increasingly adversarial stance toward the customary court suggests. And where it generates conflict, it can erode faith in the state itself, even more so when the application of the law appears capricious, as the chief's highly subjective attitudes toward 'the new laws' would make it appear.

By establishing this set of tensions in the opening paragraphs of his story, Komey's courtroom drama illustrates fundamental structural challenges for the postcolonial state. It is, of course, very possible that the later instalments of 'The Iron Box' resolve these tensions in such a way as to suggest that they were never a real threat to the smooth functioning of society. Regardless, the initial questions Komey raises about the rule of law and the state's sovereign dominion highlight the novel uses of the police procedural and its variants to engage the unique problematics of the postcolonial state. Even texts such as Masemola's, Ekwensi's, or Sam's, which leave the police procedural's narrative architecture intact, transmute the procedural's normative Anglo-American valorization of the police. For sure, the African procedurals generate consent for the state's repressive apparatus and, at times, for the class and gender interests of the bourgeoisie that helmed the institutions of the state at independence. In this way, they can appear to conform to Foucauldian understandings of the disciplinarily coercive effects of the police procedural. But simultaneously, to affirm the moral authority of the state in the historical moments that they do is to sustain the dream of decolonization in which the state would serve as the vehicle for collective liberation. Moreover, in keeping sight of the vulnerabilities facing Africa's newly independent countries, the police procedurals of the immediate post-independence and post-apartheid moments sought to rethink the very function of the state and sovereign power as they had been shaped by imperial Europe. Fulani's satirical spy novel, coming nearly twenty years after Komey's courtroom drama, highlights just how important but dauntingly monumental that project would remain.

Conclusion

Despite their rich engagement with the nation- and world-building projects of the first decades of self-rule, the police procedural and spy thriller largely drop out of the Anglophone African crime mystery archive by the mid-1980s, not to reappear until the 2010s. The problematics of sovereign rule that they sought to comprehend, however, continued to animate the continent's detective fiction writers. As early as the appearance of the last serialized Ghanaian police procedural, in 1973, plots about the domestic dramas of political corruption and lawlessness had begun appearing in East and West African crime mysteries. By the mid-1980s, the detective-novel-as-anti-imperialist adventure tale gave way most fully to narratives investigating what Jean and John Comaroff (2006) have described as the 'metaphysics of disorder' in the postcolony. That is to say, writers began experimenting with the genre's conventional treatment of law and order to assess the perceived escalation of domestic economic crimes and violence, on the one hand, and the incapacities of the postcolonial state to deliver the order, security, and economic well-being promised by the nationalist meta-narratives of decolonization, on the other. We turn now to the first of these textual interrogations.

Decolonization Arrested   3

During the first decades of self-rule, decolonization was commonly understood as a telos predicated on state-driven socio-economic development and progress. Through collective endeavor, national agricultural, industrial, and economic planning, and the simple fact of political autonomy on the world stage, newly independent African nation-states would attain over time a similar standard of living as the former colonial powers and other economic leaders of the Global North. As anthropologist James Ferguson puts it: 'If "backward nations" were not modern, in this picture, it was because they were not *yet* modern. Modernity figured as a universal telos' (2006: 178). This modernizing ideal propelled governments to pump revenue into 'ambitious national development plan[s]' and to invest 'in parastatal industries, education, hospitals, and mass media', as well as in the 'sports stadiums, national monuments, bridges, highways, and palatial hotels' that would visibly signify these efforts (Apter 2005: 22). The euphoric anticipation of a quickly achieved modernization proved difficult to sustain. For one, it had become impossible to mask the vast quantities of revenue that were being siphoned off into the private bank accounts of government officials and their business-world cronies. Additionally, the global recessions of the 1970s and precipitous drops in commodities prices left vastly insufficient revenue to feed the voracious appetites of a corrupt leadership and fuel further construction and investment or even, for that matter, to fund the basic operations of the state bureaucracy.

As the foreclosure of the developmentalist telos became increasingly apparent, the criminal doings of the emergent kleptocracy proved irresistible to African detective fiction writers. In Amaeche Nzekwe's 1985 novel *A Killer on the Loose*, for example, Nigeria's Home Secretary hires Ken Whisky, a hard-drinking and hard-living private detective and security consultant, to find his wife's killer and keep the story out of the press. For reasons that become clear later, the Home Secretary also hires the private detective to keep the police at arm's length. As it will turn out, the crime itself is commonplace. The wife was killed by a resentful ex-lover whom she had left for the greater material luxury of marriage to the Home Secretary. But what Whisky's investigation uncovers is that this seemingly private crime, in which the Home Secretary appears to be a secondary victim, illuminates a history of the minister's abuse of public office, which in turn, implicates a much wider array of public officials in various forms of coercion, blackmail, and embezzlement. While the spectacular violence of the woman's murder initiates the investigation narrative, that narrative evolves to trace the story of the accumulating criminal practices that characterize Nigerian political life in the 1980s. As the weight of his responsibility as a detective-citizen becomes clear, Whisky wills himself to action by declaring 'Nigeria! Oh Nigeria my country, your democracy must survive' (95). There is more than a hint of tongue-in-cheek humor in Whisky's phrasing, but his anxiety about Nigeria's future as a political formation that serves its population equitably comes across as sincere. He fears for both the ability of the democratic electoral process to survive its hijacking by kleptocrats like the Home Secretary and for the petroleum-rich Nigerian state's ability to fulfill its promise of national economic and social development.

Other novels in this vein include Marjorie Oludhe Macgoye's *Murder in Majengo* (1972), Chukwuemeka Ike's *Expo '77* (1980), Louis Omotayo Johnson's *Murder at Dawn* (1981), Sola Oloyede's *I Profess This Crime* (1981), Dickson Ighavini's *Thief of State* (1982), Mohamed Tukur Garba's *Stop Press: Murder* (1983), James Irungu's *Circle of Betrayal* (1987), Chuma Nwokolo's *Dangerous Inheritance* (1988), and Akosua Gyamfaa-Fofie's *Murder at Sunset* (1991). Read in tandem these mysteries paint a vivid portrait of Kenya's, Nigeria's, and Ghana's heedlessly self-interested classes. Like Ken Whisky, the private investigators, investigative journalists, and upright civil servant-detectives in these works battle heroically, though not always successfully, to save their countries from the villains whose treachery jeopardizes the promised future of decolonization.

While setting and plot provide these authors mechanisms for critical reflection on the telos of decolonization, the detective story's own narrative temporalities offer additional material for nuanced critique. In the simplest terms, the crime mystery reconstructs destabilizing events in the past with a view to achieving future justice, thereby measuring social life as depicted in any given text against the teleological promises of decolonization narratives. Narratologists have identified three specific temporal characteristics of crime mysteries that make the detective genre useful for such acts of reflection. First is the mystery's doubled storyline: that of the investigation, which moves progressively forward in time, and of the crime, which retreats recursively in time (Todorov 1977: 44, 46). Second is the 'delay of exposition' that suspends readers in a nearly static present, holding them in abeyance and subjected to a seemingly infinite array of possible outcomes, until the arrival of the anticipated narrative future (Sternberg 1978: 180). Third is detective fiction's reliance on the story of 'what will have happened' (Champigny 1977: 14), a narrative grammar in which the future perfect operates as the genre's privileged hermeneutic structure. 'The narrated process', Robert Champigny explains, 'is oriented toward a retroactive denouement that should transfigure the whole sequence' (14). In other words, the detective reconstructs, as a historical determination, the sequence of decisions, actions, and events that will have to have occurred for the crime to have been committed.

Individually and in combination, the bifurcated chronologies of crime and investigation, delayed exposition, and a future perfect narrative grammar make the detective story available for a nuanced exploration of the multi-layered and dynamic conditions leading to the arrested time of decolonization and, significantly, of the effects of this arrestation on commonly accepted conceptions of development, collectivity, and sovereignty. For Anglophone African writers, these temporal mechanisms prove to be especially useful for reassessing dominant teleological understandings of decolonization in which the colonially inherited nation-state form operates as the primary vehicle to a future collective liberation. This chapter traces three such explorations in Nigerian novels spanning the late 1970s to the late 1980s. I begin with Chuma Nwokolo's experiments with temporal suspension and future perfect hermeneutics in his 1988 novel *Dangerous Inheritance*, which, like *A Killer on the Loose*, reconstructs the 'what will have happened' to arrest Nigeria's developmentalist projects. I turn next to Chukwuemeka Ike's 1980 procedural *Expo '77* wherein Ike strands his detective in a state of temporal suspension where he can accomplish nothing more than to solve the same crime ad infinitum, a stasis that symbolizes Nigeria's own developmentalist paralysis. I conclude with Adaora Lily Ulasi's twinned deconstruction of the narrative times of detection and decolonization in her 1978 mystery *The Man from Sagamu*. By putting the colonial Enlightenment temporality of the investigation in conflict with the Yoruba cosmological temporality of the crime, Ulasi deconstructs the episteme of the postcolonial state itself. Working chronologically backward like this reveals how these three novelists deploy and transfigure the mystery genre's temporal forms to illustrate the nation-state's fragility as a teleological vehicle for future liberation.

My departure from the Africa-wide comparative framework of my other chapters is a function of the dynamics in Nigerian literature and political life that make Nigeria an especially illuminating case study. During this period Nigerian writers produced some of the most innovative detective fiction focused on domestic crises. Moreover, if Nigeria enjoyed a heightened 'expectation of modernity' (Ferguson 1999) because of its outsized oil wealth, it also confronted in spectacular fashion its disastrous collapse. Which is to say, the telos that interests me here was under intensified stress.

The Future Perfect and the Thwarted Perfect Future

Chuma Nwokolo's *Dangerous Inheritance* deploys with unusual clarity the whodunit's future perfect grammar to consider the foreclosure of Nigerian nationalism in light of the country's relative resource wealth. Published three years into the military regime headed by Ibrahim Babangida, Nwokolo's detective thriller imaginatively explores the world of criminal malfeasance behind the real life fires that consumed over a dozen Nigerian governmental buildings in the early 1980s. The blazes were presumed to be acts of arson carried out to cover up evidence of embezzlement or impede corruption investigations.[1] The true-crime aspect makes the novel something of an outlier in Macmillan's otherwise politics-averse Pacesetters series but its themes of corporate and governmental corruption are consistent with Nwokolo's nine other books.[2] Nwokolo establishes in the first chapters a contrast between the narratives of what should have happened and what will have happened to the institutions of Nigerian governance. In the novel, the National Bureau of Allocations (NBA) headquarters burns in what initially appears to be an accidental electrical blaze. The fictionalized NBA holds responsibility for allocating mining and other resource extraction concessions, most notably uranium, which in the world of the text, is depicted as enjoying an export surge akin to Nigeria's oil boom of the previous decade (13, 34–35). As the reader learns from the novel's protagonist, the investigative reporter Biodun Beckley, the agency had been carefully structured with multiple safeguards to ensure broad domestic benefit from the country's natural resources and to prevent elected officials and government employees from using their influence to trade concessions for personal profit (14). As Beckley points out, the NBA enjoys a solid reputation for taking a hard-line stance against violators. From every outward measure, the NBA stands as model of sovereign state authority in the service of the citizenry, endeavoring to advance the developmentalist teleology on which so many African postcolonial nationalisms were crafted. It is against the backdrop of a model of what *should* have happened – the NBA metonymically standing in for the postcolonial state as a whole – that Nwokolo crafts a future perfect narrative of what *will* have happened. Which is to say, Biodun Beckley will reconstruct the story of the criminalization of the Nigerian state and do so in a manner that illuminates the arrested teleology of its would-be decolonization.

Working with the codes of the detective thriller, as opposed to the locked-room whodunit, Nwokolo gives readers privileged knowledge that Bakare's gang set the fire at Senator Chitoom's request to destroy incriminating evidence. The novel's suspense derives from two sources, which, when combined, shape the novel's critical engagements. First, suspense flows from the tension generated by the race against time typical of the thriller: can Beckley uncover the culprits' identities before they discover and destroy a duplicate set of NBA files? In its signaling of intense urgency, Nwokolo's use of thriller aesthetics registers the imminence of complete state criminalization and the necessity for immediate triage. But Nwokolo's introduction of a broader array of characters representing

---

1   *The Washington Post* reported on 27 February 1983 that at least twelve fires had destroyed federal and state government buildings between 1979 and 1983. The presumed cause in every instance was arson with the intent of destroying incriminating accounting records. See Leon Dash (1983).
2   Nwokolo (2015) discusses his literary interests in an interview with Adaobi Nkeokelonye.

the primary sectors of economic, political, and juridical life presents the second and more productive source of suspense employed in the novel and the form that creates the conditions for considering the fuller foreclosure of postcolonial nationalist teleologies. In alternating chapters, the novel develops five parallel stories that focus not only on the expected parties – Beckley, representing the press, Chitoom from the government, and Bakare's criminal gang – but also on Fola Davies, an overly leveraged conglomerate boss who has made unprofitable bets on solar energy production and is now in need of quick cash, and a corrupt police sergeant stationed in the main mining region. Nwokolo thereby asks his readers not simply to identify the culprit nor to enjoy only the game of wits between Chitoom and Bakare on one side and Beckley on the other, but instead to unravel the tangle of the interrelationships among government, police, business, and organized crime.

Holding the reader in suspenseful abeyance until the moment of anticipated resolution, *Dangerous Inheritance* confronts it audience with an important question, the answer to which is central to both the novel's suspense and to its interrogation of Nigeria's political predicament. Is the reader witnessing the random isolated actions of several individuals seeking the same ill-gotten gains, or is the illegal appropriation of mining resources symptomatic of a broader systemic breakdown of the nationalist-developmentalist ideals signified by the National Bureau of Allocations? Little by little, Beckley's dogged investigation points to the latter cause. Self-dealing within ranks of government is suggested to be so endemic as to be normalized – Beckley's half-brother quips about his fellow civil servants that a successful corruption inquiry requires only an angry wife seeking matrimonial revenge to turn up damning evidence (16). But it is the corporate tycoon Fola Davis, Beckley discovers, who turns out to have assembled a network of lieutenants and enforcers including Bakare and his thugs, Senator Chitoom, and the police sergeant. What will have happened, Biodun Beckley eventually explains, is that a well-capitalized and well-connected individual exploited institutional vulnerabilities and mobilized the individual greed of politicians and police for personal gain. In *Dangerous Inheritance*'s final accounting, the teleological imperatives of institutions such as the National Bureau of Allocations, crafted so carefully to put a sovereign governing apparatus to work to advance the decolonizing developmentalist goals of the postcolonial nation-state, fail to stand up under these conditions. Consequently, decolonial time gets arrested.

Nwokolo is not alone in developing a critique of the postcolonial Nigerian state as being vulnerable to such forces. Published just a year prior to *Dangerous Inheritance*, Chinua Achebe's *Anthills of the Savannah* (1987), for instance, depicts a fictionalized Nigeria named Kangan in which, as one critic puts it, 'the real actors of state power are … a cult of business magnates among whom Kangan's apparatuses and business interests are partitioned and privatized' (Amoke 2018:

41). As in *Dangerous Inheritance*, putatively democratic institutions such as those symbolized by Nwokolo's Bureau of Allocations are shown to be easy targets for a powerful elite looking to enrich itself at the expense of the general population. And like Nwokolo's novel, *Anthills of the Savannah* suggests that this vulnerability calls into question the viability of the nation-state as the most logical political form for achieving the collective liberation that at least two of the novel's protagonists – both journalists as well – still idealize. 'Frozen time' is the phrase that Achebe voices in an interview when describing how people viewed Nigeria in the 1980s (1989: 343). *Anthills* gives a fuller accounting of 'the complexity of the African crisis and its many sources' (Gikandi 1991: 133) than do either *Dangerous Inheritance* or Nzekwe's *A Killer on the Loose*. For Achebe, the problem of the postcolonial nation-state is more complex than simply its susceptibility to capture by magnates such as Nwokolo's Fola Davis or Nzekwe's Home Secretary. Periodic military coups, regional and sectarian competition for the spoils of office and resource wealth, ongoing social divisions from past conflicts, and extraordinary economic inequality further complicate any belief in the decolonial state. Moreover, Neil ten Kortenaar sees in *Anthills* a meditation on the seemingly fundamental impossibility of realizing the conjunction of 'nation' and 'state', both colonial impositions, that would be necessary for the kind of nation-building presupposed by discourses of decolonization (1993: 60). Simon Gikandi suggests similarly that, 'this is particularly the case within the context of the independent African nation and the function of the new state as an instrument that represses rather than succors human freedom' (1991: 128). Gikandi also reads Achebe's novel as a metacommentary on narrative itself:

> Within the complexities and reversals of the postcolonial situation, Achebe's novel is plagued by doubts about its own relevance. This may appear strange, especially in view of Achebe's affirmative declarations on the power of art to rewrite history and to evacuate the self from the events that entrap it in frozen time. (1991: 129)

Nwokolo's detective story offers its readers a less complex diagnosis of Nigeria's arrested decolonization and less metacommentary on nation and narration than Achebe's novel, but it asks its readers to reflect on many of the same fundamental questions about the role of the state in overseeing the postcolonial liberation project. That it does so with a literary genre that might reach readers disinclined or unable to work their way through Achebe's aesthetically experimental novel is not inconsequential. It also bears noting that neither Achebe nor Nwokolo is so pessimistic as to intimate that the Nigerian nation-state is entirely beyond rescue. *Anthills*' ending suggests the possibility of 'renewal and rebirth', asserts Gikandi (1991: 125). And in *Dangerous Inheritance*, craven individuals like Fola Davis might be able to interrupt Nigeria's march toward a future in which its resource wealth is shared equally by all, but they are no match for a robust civil society, represented in the novel by the journalist-detective. When civil society takes responsibility for protecting the body politic from those who are avaricious enough to put their personal desires ahead of collective needs, Nigeria and its citizens will be freed once again to pursue their promised future. What *will have happened* is not, in the end, inevitable or irreversible. Nwokolo thus preserves the cathartic resolution that typically inheres to the detective story's future perfect narrative grammar. The ability of his detective to restore faith in the Nigerian nation-state depends upon it.

Suspended States

Taking a different tack from his compatriot Nwokolo, Chukwuemeka Ike undermines the crime mystery's future perfect structure in a way that makes the detective genre available for an investigation of the social-structural conditions required for a nationalist developmentalist logic to operate in the first place. In Ike's 1980 novel *Expo '77*, Nigeria's Registrar of the National Examinations Board hires Mora, a private detective, to trace the source of leaked secondary school examination questions. Mora fulfills his duties as charged to reveal that students at Nigeria's most elite mission school had broken into the principal's office to steal the exam materials. In the process of breaking this case, however, his investigation uncovers multifarious cheating schemes all over the country. Like *Dangerous Inheritance*, *Expo '77* reads as a quasi-true-crime novel. The narrative is based loosely on the 1977 cheating scandal that implicated over 77,000 students nationwide. At the time, Ike was the chief executive of the West African Examinations Council, and the novel can read at times like a pedantic vindication of his efforts to combat academic malfeasance during his tenure. Ike himself graduated from one of Nigeria's elite secondary schools, Government College Umuahia, where he formed part of a tight circle of future literary luminaries, including Achebe and Christopher Okigbo.[3] Apart from Ike's personal stake in this particular history, his choice of scandals – there were many to choose from in Nigeria at the time – registers key crises in the narrative of decolonization as the country confronted the boom-and-bust cycles of global capitalism and the increasing incursion of late capitalist rationalities into everyday life.

Andrew Apter points out that as Nigeria pursued the developmentalist models of modernization, professional credentials, including secondary school diplomas, escalated in importance for Nigerian job seekers. For Apter, the actual late-1970s cheating and counterfeiting scandals on which Ike bases his mystery

---

3   For more on Ike's schooling and literary aspirations, see Terry Ochiagha (2015).

were propelled less by a generalized moral corruption than by the increased urgency in a highly competitive employment market of attaining visible markers of self-optimization, meritocratic achievement, and entrepreneurial ambition (2000: 275). If exam theft, plagiarism, and collusion undermined the value of credentials and put other public markers of self-improvement in crisis, Apter argues that the students nevertheless acted according to the new rules of a neoliberal market rationality. For Ike, the resulting disregard for the collective consequences of the new rationality threatens to 'ruin the country' (54). The danger is not simply that Nigeria will become a population of incompetent and untrained cheats, but that 'Nigeria' as a telos will become unsustainable.

Ike registers the threat Apter describes by undermining crime mystery's common narrative progression in ways that root Detective Mora in a static present, his stasis standing in metonymically for the paralysis of the de-developmentalized state and nation. *Expo '77* maintains the pretence of the forward propulsion of investigation and discovery. Mora reads clues, maps the movement of suspects in space and time, dismisses false leads, and eventually identifies the perpetrators at the elite mission school. But instead of piecing the clues, movements, and false leads into a unitary progressive unfolding of what will have happened, *Expo '77* fractures and multiplies the future perfect narrative. Mora's investigation reveals that the theft at the elite mission school is just one isolated instance of corruption among dozens in the educational system. Mora turns up collusion by teachers and school administrators to manipulate test results (ch. 4), sexual exploitation of female students under the threat of failing or with the promise of advance access to the questions (ch. 4), the manufacture of fake exams by scam artists seeking to capitalize on student anxiety (ch. 5), complicated schemes to smuggle answers into test rooms (ch. 6), efforts to bribe education ministry employees (ch. 11), and the hiring of professional test-takers (ch. 12). The structure of *Expo '77* is counter-formulaic insofar as none of the crimes are directly connected to any other, nor do they lead to the final discovery of the perpetrators of the theft at the mission school. Mora perpetually hopes that each scheme he turns up will help him unravel an interconnected web that leads to the culprit whose arrest would end all cheating completely. Instead, every chapter functions as a semi-autonomous mystery narrative, yielding its own isolated schemes and culprits. The final arrest of the elite mission school students is thus shown to be almost meaningless because the scandal is depicted as having become cancerous, metastasizing across the body politic. Arresting one set of perpetrators in no way helps halt the crime's damage or further proliferation.

The only unifying force Mora identifies to link all the violations is the motivation to manipulate the test results, which have become so consequential for Nigerian students that cheating has become culturally endemic. This insight is matched by the realization that the schools have perverted their function as a training ground for civic life, producing instead 'future bandits' (12) and a 'nation of seasoned, irredeemable criminals' (93). A schoolgirl's mother reinforces these points when she protests her daughter's punishment by asserting that 'all the big men are cheating in this country' (66). Ike links this failure directly to the decolonizing developmentalist ideals of Nigerian nationalism when, upon being confronted with the full scope of the academic fraud schemes, the Acting Registrar of the National Examinations Board exclaims, 'we cannot continue waiting for that elusive date when society will suddenly be transformed' (190). In the final paragraphs, he issues a series of reforms to the exams system that amounts to a call to action to save the state, the nation, and the ideals of decolonization from the disproportionately powerful epistemic blow inflicted by the relatively minor violence of falsifying credentials. In other words, he seeks to reignite Nigeria's movement toward a collectively imagined future. In this respect, the detective's investigation would appear to function as a catalyst for committed nationalist action as it does in Nwokolo's novel. However, because of the metastatic quality of the central crime, the Acting Registrar's promises come across as noble but hollow. Were he to continue in his task of discovering every perpetrator of exams corruption after the implementation of the reforms, Mora would be left solving the same crime ad infinitum. Under these conditions, there can be no narrative progression for either the story of the crime or of the investigation. Narrative time comes to a standstill, signifying the seeming impossibility of societal transformation over time.

Read together like this, Chukwuemeka Ike's and Chuma Nwokolo's mystery thrillers measure the disorder and violence of everyday Nigerian life in the late 1970s and 1980s against the nationalist liberation rhetoric in which the developmentalist and collectivist ethos of decolonization still hold significant purchase. In this regard, they call to mind Jennifer Wenzel's study of South African literature about the nineteenth-century Xhosa cattle killing movement, in which she proposes that 'what survives anticolonial movements is an imagined but as yet unrealized future, not merely memories of fallen heroes or of some primordial past' (2009: 7). By decoding the historical determinants that have impeded decolonization's realization, the future perfect grammar of detective mysteries gives the writers a framework for similarly sustaining the 'imagined but as yet unrealized future' of political, social, and cultural independence.

Modern States and Sovereign Time

While Ike and Nwokolo highlight the arrested time of postcolonial Nigerian nationalism, they leave the postcolonial nationalist chronotope itself unexamined. Development, progress, the bureaucratic imperatives of mining concession lotteries and exam calendars – each rooted to some degree in European Enlightenment figurations of the state and political economy – go unremarked. Given the detective genre's long-standing entanglement with the anxieties and contradictions of liberalism, colonialism, and capitalism, this elision should not come as a surprise. The deflection of questions about postcolonial temporality is also consistent with the ways in which the postcolonial nation-state is so deeply embedded, as Simon Gikandi puts it, in 'the hegemony of European modernity' (2001: 641). For these reasons, the novelists' embrace of a developmentalist teleology points to a deeper problem of postcolonial temporal sovereignty. Gikandi explains, 'The truth is, we cannot speak of a new global culture without at the same time accounting for the forms of time consciousness associated with its genesis in modernity, a modern temporality that cannot be conceived outside colonial governmentality' (642). Neither the postcolonial nation nor state can, in Gikandi's view, escape entirely the hegemonic European Enlightenment rationalities out of which both modern nationhood and modern states emerged. This is because they are vehicles for time as much as they are spatial forms for collective identification. But Gikandi adds the crucial qualification that 'the new time of postcoloniality cannot be imprisoned in the politics of modern time and the teleology of modernization for as the *post* in the term suggests, postcolonialism is a condition that must be contained both within and beyond the causality of colonial modernity' (641).

For the novelist Adaora Lily Ulasi, the resulting epistemological problem of how to imagine and thereby generate a temporally sovereign postcoloniality within and against the hegemony of a modernity disproportionately shaped by colonial governmentality informs a broader literary engagement with the legitimacy of state power, justice, and popular sovereignty. Situating most of her novels in Nigeria's colonial past, Ulasi illuminates the detective genre's reliance on modes of investigation that are rooted in the institutions and temporal imperatives of colonial rule. She then deconstructs the temporal structures of the normative detective story in ways that underscore the problematic Gikandi describes while simultaneously envisioning a postcolonial state that is sovereign both politically and temporally. This articulation finds its clearest expression in Ulasi's third and most fully realized mystery, the 1978 novel *The Man from Sagamu*. What follows is an extended close reading of the novel. Its status as an early and important woman-authored text in what remains a male-dominated Anglophone African detective fiction tradition is sufficient in itself to justify the disproportionate focus on this one book. However, I devote more attention to it than I do to Nwokolo's and Ike's mysteries – and to many of the texts featured in my other chapters – because of the politically significant narrative complexity of Ulasi's undertaking. Only Cyprian Ekwensi before her and only very few Anglophone African writers after her subject the literary-cultural form of the detective story to so much pressure to ask such provocative questions.

Born in 1931 in the eastern Nigerian town of Aba, Ulasi attended university in the United States, where she studied journalism, a career that she would take up in Lagos upon completion of her degree. Published between 1970 and 1978, her five novels span the final months of the Biafra war, the peak of the oil boom, and much of the military dictatorship of Yakubu Gowon. While she was not the first Anglophone African writer to take up the crime mystery, she was, in 1970, one of the first to explore the possibilities of novel-length narratives when most others were still producing short stories and novellas. And she did so in unexpected ways. Unlike nearly every subsequent Anglophone African detective novel, all but one of Ulasi's novels are set in the colonial past. Also making them distinct is that they typically feature as detective-protagonists passably competent British colonial administrators working to solve crimes committed by Africans against the colonial state. Ulasi also breaks periodically from the detective genre's implicit realism by incapacitating her British detectives through supernatural forces. Even in relation to the Victorian-era British detective fiction that features supernatural plots, she shies away from that era's conventions that give the detectives themselves occult powers or those such as Rudyard Kipling's Strickland stories that see the colonial police officer untangle supernatural mysteries.[4] In her stories, the supernatural always prevails. Moreover, Ulasi's narratives rarely culminate with either the identification or punishment of any sort of criminal by the colonial police or colonial administrators. This has led at least one critic to suggest that Ulasi leaves readers with 'reservations as to the detective quality of her novels' (Moyola 1989: 178).

For other scholarly readers, the politics, more than the aesthetics, of Ulasi's texts are suspect. With her white British investigators and Black Nigerian criminals, Ulasi's fiction conforms to neither the conventions of the heroic detective adventures nor the gritty social realism typical of the Anglophone writing of the 1970s. While one critic reads her novels as 'a satire on the inefficiency of British administrators in Nigeria during the colonial era' (Umeh 2001: 328), other scholars suggest that the colonial-era settings and central preoccupations of her texts seem to come from an earlier time and to rehash outdated themes. Mannfred Loimeier (2012) contends, for instance, that Ulasi's crime and detective plotting should be viewed as secondary to her larger preoccupation with the cultural conflicts and mistranslations between colonial and traditional cultures and mores. As he sees it, the novels consistently stage 'the conflict between the colonial order and the local order' more typical of writing from the 1950s and 1960s (144). Jane Bryce similarly posits that the central tension in Ulasi's novels results from the 'confrontation between two, differing, mutually uncomprehending value systems' (1988: 9). Describing Ulasi

---

4   Of Kipling's six Strickland detective stories, 'Mark of the Beast' (1890) and 'The Return of Imray' (1891) see police inspector Strickland reveal the occult sources of otherwise inexplicable crimes. The others rely on the realism more often associated with the crime mystery.

as 'deracinated' and not 'sufficiently in touch with her roots to attempt a *Things Fall Apart* novel of tradition' (6), Bryce further suggests that Ulasi's fiction 'lacks [political] commitment' (21). Critical frustration with Ulasi's oeuvre is also exacerbated by occasional lapses in historical and cultural accuracy, such as her incorrect attribution of the Oshun cult to the town of Sagamu in *The Man from Sagamu* (Moyola 1989: 179).

In a welcome reappraisal of Ulasi's fiction, Chikwenye Okonjo Ogunyemi (1996) argues for both the subversive Nigerian feminism of Ulasi's white-male-centered texts and for the contemporaneity of her historical fiction. Ogunyemi reads Ulasi's privileging of mediocre male British protagonists and their male Nigerian underlings not as a marginalization of African women's struggles but instead as a narrative tactic to unsettle dominant structures of gendered authority (188). Furthermore, Ogunyemi contends that, far from being anachronistic, Ulasi's narrative interrogation of the tyranny of colonial power and insecurities of both colonial administrators and their Nigerian agents must be read as an allegorical critique of the 1966–1975 military regime under which Ulasi lived and wrote most of her novels (187). The real conflict of the novels, Ogunyemi thus insists, is not between colonizer and colonized but between the usurpers of Nigerian sovereignty, which can include the country's own African rulers, and the usurped. In this light, Ulasi's British colonial administration functions as a safe stand-in for any government predicated on extractive exploitation, an especially cogent concern as oil revenues were at the time increasingly enriching Nigeria's military dictatorship. Other critics mirror this point, noting that all but one of her novels reflect thematically on the failures of Nigeria's twentieth-century leadership to 'uphold the dignity of traditional life' or to respect, let alone foster, a strong civil society (Taiwo 1984: 86; Loimeier 2012: 145).

Ogunyemi also insists that Ulasi's novels should not be dismissed as failed detective novels. In fact, she claims, they are not detective novels at all. She argues instead that they dismantle the broader mystery genre and reassemble it as part of a new Nigerianized genre of 'juju fiction'. Ogunyemi defines juju fiction as a 'bewitched crossroads, where many literary aspects intersect: juju, the mystery novel, fantasy, the ghost story, the tall tale, the gothic, etc., are grounded on a cultural imaginary that thrives on such inventiveness' (1996: 184). Ogunyemi argues, as Jane Bryce eventually does, that by infusing the mythic and mystical that are for many Nigerians part of everyday life into the materialist realism of normative detective fiction, Ulasi radically transfigures the crime mystery to reflect Nigerian, rather than European or American, social realities.

While I am compelled by Ogunyemi's categorization of Ulasi's novels as juju fiction and am committed to the project of identifying genre formations that reflect local cultural realities, I want to retain a focus on the identifiable crime mystery aspects of Ulasi's writing. As one of the very first Anglophone African writers to write novel-length mysteries, she was clearly experimenting with and expanding a familiar genre, testing its reliance on an Enlightenment-conceived realism and questioning whether the genre can hold up under the conditions of postcoloniality. By retaining recognizable generic codes from the mystery, she preserves her authority to register the detective story's longstanding ideological articulations while simultaneously making them available for transfiguration and for the social and cultural critique that such transfiguration generates. All of which is to say that I want to take Ogunyemi's assertion that Ulasi makes genre central to her literary project a step further and argue that Ulasi does not so much abandon the crime mystery's basic formula as she does to reconceptualize it. A primary effect is a deconstruction of the Enlightenment temporalities that structure both the normative detective novel and the postcolonial nation-state. By holding those temporalities up for scrutiny within the framework of a familiar literary genre, Ulasi turns her reader's attention to the temporal precepts of decolonization. Thus, decolonization becomes a problem not of how to achieve developmentalist ideals but of implementing the temporal sovereignty from which those ideals can be achieved.

The Man from Sagamu reads as a police procedural with shadings of the detective thriller and antihero crime tale. The novel opens with a common enough narrative device, the mysterious disappearance of a forty-year-old vagrant from the town of Sagamu, in Nigeria's Yoruba-speaking South West. Had Olu Agege's disappearance not come just a week before Sagamu's famous Oshun festival and had Agege not been born under spiritually conspicuous circumstances – 'It was said that a cock crew at noon on top of his mother's thatch-roofed home on the day he was born' (6) – the townspeople and the authorities might have paid little attention to the disappearance of a man few trusted and fewer wanted as a neighbor. However, because of widespread fear that Agege's disappearance could be linked to a plot to undermine the Oshun rituals, both the colonial regime and the Oba, Sagamu's traditional ruler, put the full force of the colonial and traditional state into deciphering the mystery. As the narrative unfolds, the colonial police, the British Resident Officer, a Nigerian magistrate in the colonial assize court, the Oba, and the Oba's most trusted seer employ their respective tools of the trade to solve the mystery. To this extent, Ulasi abides by the police procedural's narrative norms. That she provides the reader privileged information about Agege's supernatural powers of invisibility in the opening chapter does little to trouble this narrative conformity, as the reader remains unaware of Agege's motives and expects the police investigation to reveal them. Moreover, this knowledge adds an element of the thriller's cat-and-mouse narrative tension. Ulasi's fidelity to genre expectations stops there, however. Even though the greater part of the novel details the procedural investigation, only the seer manages to turn up a viable clue and none of the detectives succeed in solving the mystery. In the end, contrary to all formulas, Agege provides the resolution to his own mystery.

If, as Porter (1981) argues, detective novels often generate consent for the state's repressive apparatus, *The Man from Sagamu* stands out initially for the way that it employs the form to lay bare the vanity of individual rulers and the compromised morality of state power. In both content and form, the novel reverses Porter's ideological formula, most notably by critiquing the governing apparatus for existing only to reproduce and extend its reach and for punishing any individual who illuminates its ruses. With no other evidence than the witness accounts that Agege simply vanished into thin air, the colonial police and the Oba's representatives are initially unable to determine whether there is a crime committed, let alone a criminal to be pursued. But as time passes, the British Resident Officer and his constables repeatedly lament that the colonial police had never arrested Agege on charges of vagrancy and, as time passes, both the colonial and traditional states begin to recast Agege as the prime criminal suspect in his own disappearance (17, 28, 39). Because Agege's spectacular escape from their reach magnifies their failures to bring him under their disciplinary authority, the British Resident Officer and the Oba grow increasingly anxious, and therefore tenacious, in their desire to punish him. That he lived beyond the reach of the state is criminal enough; that he has made his successful resistance to state subjugation and interpellation so visible – ironically, by publicly turning himself invisible – is intolerable. Thus, Agege's crime is no more or less substantial than perforating the carefully stage-crafted performance of the state's sovereign domination. Moreover, by denying the colonial or traditional authorities the ability to capture or punish Agege for this violation, Ulasi refuses to let her police procedural ratify raw assertions of this power. What begins as an investigation narrative ends as a story of investigatory failure that for Nigerians is a tale of triumph over an unjust and illegitimate government.

It is important to pause here to emphasize that, while the novel is set in 1950s Nigeria, its references to the new political parties (32) and its conspicuous description of the symbolically Pan-African red, gold, and green caps worn by a group of chiefs during the Oshun festival make Nigeria's imminent political independence an explicit subtext. Moreover, for readers taking up the novel at the time of its publication in the late 1970s – after the Biafra war, the three military coups that followed it, and the capture of the state by ever more professionalized autocrats – the novel's thematic focus on the state's criminalization of citizens who expose the ethical lapses and self-interested machinations of individual leaders might have come across as more presentist than historical. In other words, *The Man from Sagamu* frequently reads as a commentary on the contemporary Nigeria of its era. In that Nigeria, as in Ike's, developmentalist time has become unstable. The state, as represented by its law enforcement authorities, struggles to lead its public to the anticipated decolonial future. For Ulasi, the problem is not that time is merely suspended. In her accounting, the temporal suspension of decolonization is symptomatic of a deeper failure of imagination to envision a modernizing nationalist time not beholden to Western temporal constructs.

In content, *The Man from Sagamu* is saturated with temporal obsessions. In fact, time serves as a central motif. Each character, the physical setting, and the plot are dictated by matters of time. The greater part of the novel details the thoughts and actions of the British Resident Officer, Roy Whitticar, and depicts him as a man governed more by bureaucratic time-labor sequencing than by the imperatives of the civilizing mission. In nearly every scene his thoughts drift to the hour of the day, to the scheduled times for work, lunch, and recreation, or to the differential between the expected and actual duration of various tasks. Even Whitticar's anxiety about Agege's disappearance stems less from the nature of the mystery than from the pace of the investigation. Similarly, when a visiting assize court judge takes ill, Whitticar's distress stems not from any concern about the Nigerian's health but from the possibility that the court will fail to get through its case log before the judge leaves for his next posting (85). The Nigerians under Whitticar's authority are no less creatures of the clock. 'As though by telepathy', constables raise their eyes to the clock at the end of their shift (10–11). By habit and for no apparent reason, the court custodian checks the time on the watch given to him by a retired magistrate (109). Ulasi similarly depicts Whitticar's driver, secretary, steward, and household staff acting according to the rhythms and dictates of the British clock and calendar. So too, those individuals working outside the British bureaucracy articulate anxieties and reassurances in terms of time. The 'respected and very well-known citizen' (113) Duro Segun, for instance, reassures the public in the awkward English that Ulasi employs to represent Nigerian Pidgin, '"We see the thing for broad daylight, even though", he paused to look at his watch, "it be half past eight for morning-time"' (113–114). For the local population, too, time, in particular the temporality defined by Yoruba cosmology, shapes their self-conceptualization: 'Considering the vastness of Nigeria, the length and breadth of Sagamu is tiny. To its citizens, it was not the size of their town that mattered as much as its traditions, which were rigidly held, and its rituals, which were observed without fail' (44). With faint echoes of Achebe's *Arrow of God*, Agege's disappearance provokes no less anxiety in them for fear of it disrupting the Oshun festival, held, significantly, during the harvest. The general public hopes for a quick resolution as much as Whitticar does but for culturally different reasons.

These repeated references to time function in two important ways. First, they crystallize and magnify the temporal tension inherent to the detective story. Each mention of calendars, timepieces, work hours, and deadlines refocuses the reader's attention on the time slipping away for the investigators to avert the disturbance of the Oshun festival. The second function is to underscore how the investigation, and along with it the narratological temporality of detection, operates as technology of colonial power. The police, courts, and Resident Officer are all agents of the repressive apparatus of the colonial state, and through them colonial power expresses itself directly and forcefully. Whitticar, for example, commands the Oba, with scant notice, to meet precisely at 11 a.m. (49) and compels a Nigerian doctor to abandon his waiting patients at a moment's notice to attend to the ill magistrate (81). But rather than dwell on blunt power, Ulasi emphasizes how the Resident Officer, the courts, and police are also agents of the epistemological colonization often associated with missionary work, schools, and other colonial institutions. Through the scheduling, sequencing, and structuring of policing and courtroom discovery, the juridical agents of the colonial regime enact and enforce Western temporal modes that undermine an epistemological order rooted in Yoruba cosmology.[5] For Whitticar's driver, who keeps his boss's schedule of work, lunch, tea-time, and European club visits better than the boss himself does, and for Duro Segun, who can only proclaim full daylight after confirming the time by his watch, the colonization of temporality is almost total. The public's impatience with the protracted police investigation indicates how they too have, at least tacitly, consented to colonial institutions and their temporal frameworks. Even the Oba, the character who should most faithfully represent the Yoruba cosmological order, reveals how deeply and subserviently he has internalized colonial juridical time when early in the novel he rushes, for fear of appearing to impede the prompt execution of colonial justice, to inform Whitticar of Agege's suspicious disappearance (16).

Another narrative strategy Ulasi deploys to illuminate the operations of colonial time is to incorporate forms of expositional delay that are unrelated to the investigation. Certainly, as Sternberg points out, the primary task of the mystery writer is to postpone, with great narrative pleasure and suspense, the revelation of that which has already taken place (180). Typically, the delayed payoff comes as the result of the time necessary for the work of investigation. The gathering of evidence, forensic analysis, false leads, and periodic explications of method to Watson-like reader stand-ins prolong the climactic reveal. Ulasi often defies this expectation by interrupting the investigation narrative with scenes that attend not to the investigation itself but dwell instead on the boredom and banality as well as the mores of British administrators and indigenous leaders. Ulasi employs this strategy less in *The Man from Sagamu* than in her first (1971) novel, *Many Thing Begin for Change*, which tests the limits of her readers' patience with descriptions of cocktail hours and other social events, but even with its tighter mystery plotting, *The Man from Sagamu* lingers on tea-time conversations between Whitticar and his wife, the magistrate's and Whitticar's assessments of the relative merits of Sagamu's assize court hostel, and the

---

5   In more than one novel, Ulasi depicts with great comic effect the discrepant definitions of causality, a battle over the conceptualization of time and space that might exasperate the colonial judges and magistrates but that the colonized can never win.

pageantry of the Oba's court. A full fifteen pages of the 124-page novel are also given over to the magistrate's illness (80–95). While the focus of these passages is on those characters directly or indirectly responsible for the execution of justice, they do not advance the investigation narrative. Instead, these instances of expositional delay further highlight the dominance of colonial temporality.

With this understanding of the disciplinary effects of colonial governmentality on lived time carefully established, Ulasi proceeds to undermine the generic codes with which she made this case. In the novel's final pages, Agege, like the detective of the locked-room whodunit, unravels the mystery of his disappearance for the audience assembled for the Oshun festival. In attendance for Agege's revelation are Sagamu's townspeople, Whitticar and his fellow colonial officers, the Nigerian magistrate in the colonial assize court, and the Oba and his confidants. Agege begins his oration by describing his own suspicious actions, his own motivations, and, crucially, his heretofore masked identity. In the very act of this narration, Agege usurps the detective's presumed prerogative to narrate the story of what will have happened, in this case denying Whitticar the authority over law and order vested in him by the colonial state. To emphasize this loss of authority, Ulasi all but erases Whitticar's presence in the novel's remaining pages. By usurping the colonial detective's position, Agege also reasserts the governing power of the Yoruba gods. Agege reveals to an astonished crowd that he, the vagrant in its midst for four decades, is actually an embodied avatar of the female god Oshun. It is a plot twist in which the accused enemy of both the colonial state and Yoruba community turns out to be the true sovereign authority of the region. While the typical detective symbolizes the omniscient surveillant eye of the state, Agege reveals that he does not merely represent that authority but is that authority. Agege, it turns out, is the law writer and law enforcer of the highest sovereign order.

After making this revelation to his assembled audience, Agege proceeds much like his detective counterparts would: by identifying the real violators of public trust. In a move that further displaces Whitticar's authority, Ulasi focuses Agege's judgement solely on the Oba and Nigerian assize court magistrate. Agege castigates them for consenting to a European episteme that serves to further colonize the people they ostensibly serve. Agege implies that, as the leaders best positioned to usher in independence and lead a politically sovereign Nigeria, the Oba's and judge's eagerness to buttress the colonial state and its governing epistemes threaten to arrest decolonization before it has even begun. No matter how lavishly leaders wrap themselves in symbolically saturated red, gold, and green garments, no nationalist teleology can take shape when political figures like the Oba and magistrate lack a critical stance toward colonial institutions, juridical frameworks, and policing methodologies. Under such circumstances, there could be no future fundamentally different from the present.

To avert that future, Agege proposes an alternative model of governance. In his address to the crowd, he enjoins the magistrate to remember that, although the magistrate 'had the power to sentence others' under colonial law, 'there was another power more than [the magistrate] had, that could make the magistrate incapacitated' (124). The admonition serves to remind the Nigerian magistrate to balance his obligations to the colonial state and those to Oshun but also to remind the magistrate of his responsibility to Nigeria's 'citizens' (124). He commands the magistrate to 'temper justice with mercy' and cautions the Oba to keep in mind that he is the ruler but also the 'father' of Sagamu's citizens (124). By speaking with divine authority, Agege re-establishes the primacy of Yoruba cosmology, not in place of colonial juridical power (or of the emergent nationalism referred to periodically throughout the novel), but as a tempering adjunct. Which is to say, he calls not for the abolition of the Nigerian state apparatus as it developed under British colonialism but instead for figures like the magistrate and Oba to preserve a Yoruba ethic within it.

Agege's revelations about his own movement through space and time elaborate on this idea of an interstitial cultural-political formation. During the weeks leading up to the Oshun festival, after turning himself invisible, Agege reappears in brief moments, either visually or audibly, four times. From the viewpoint of the colonial regime and the Oba's court, these actions are additional evidence of Agege's criminality. From the perspective of the public who encounter Agege only in the flashes of his appearances, Agege speeds up time, collapsing the temporal spaces of human chronology. Stitched together, the moments of Agege's appearances form a separate temporal narrative from that of the everyday life of the colony. The most obvious effect of this alternate temporal frame is to undermine the criminal investigation, based as it is on practices of colonial bureaucracy and Enlightenment temporal and evidentiary norms. But ineffective too are the time/space precepts of the Oba's powerful seer, whose tools of the trade – cowry shells, chalk markings, etc. – only reveal that Agege remains in town but not precisely where or in what state of visibility. By disrupting both colonial and 'traditional' temporal constructs, Agege underscores the limits of colonial power and of the chief's power as it has developed under British Indirect Rule. Moreover, by disrupting the hegemony of colonial time, Agege jars the people from what may or may not be their complacency to the colonial order.

The second, and no less significant effect of Agege's movement through time and space is that Agege recalibrates the human temporality of life in the colony to the temporal imperatives of the Yoruba cosmos. While Agege's divine temporality remains distinct from the secular human time increasingly dictated by colonialism, and while humans can never inhabit Agege's temporal sphere, the awe he inspires compels the public to acknowledge the eternal omnipotence of the Yoruba gods and cosmos. This is not to suggest that Agege demands

Nigerians to renounce secular time under colonialism for a return to some sort of precolonial ideal. In much the same way that Agege enjoins the Nigerian magistrate to temper his juridical authority in the colonial order with a Yoruba ethic, he calls on the Yoruba public to adopt instead an interstitial, hybridized temporality, a dynamic postcolonial temporality in the making. To live in modern time is to acknowledge the simultaneity of the cosmological time that he embodies and the secular time of clocks, watches, and colonial calendars. That is, it is to see modernity itself as being composed of both. In many ways, a postcolonial temporality such as this one is the one that the mass of Sagamu's citizens already live daily with their faithful observation of the calendar of Yoruba rituals conjoined with colonial government schedules, watches, and clocks. Agege validates the time of the people but also radicalizes it, insists on its primacy for the new nation's sovereignty.

Frantz Fanon famously warns of the dangers of reifying tradition in the name of national liberation. A postcolonial artist's turn to cultural forms from the past in order 'to illustrate the truths of the nation' risks, according to Fanon, the opposite result (2014: 225). To bring 'abandoned traditions to life again' (224), he declares, mummifies culture and delimits the formation of the national consciousness that is a necessary component of decolonization. The turn to tradition consequently arrests decolonization just as violently as bourgeois elites do when they perpetuate colonial models of governance and economic exploitation. As highlighted earlier, Ulasi has been criticized for a perceived lack of political commitment, though not necessarily in the terms Fanon lays out. A cursory reading of her colonial-era settings and the spotlight she places on divination and 'black magic' as markers of African authenticity might lead a reader to call to mind Fanon's warning. In *The Man from Sagamu*, after all, liberation comes from a renewed faith in the ancient gods. I hope I have made clear, however, that despite its outward lack of the normative markers of a resistance literature, the novel follows Fanon's injunction to the postcolonial artist to mine the past not for its own sake but 'with the intention of opening up the future, as an invitation to action' (232). For Ulasi, the Yoruba cosmos is not a relic of precolonial time. It retains its contemporary force. The same can be argued of the Igbo belief systems in Ulasi's first two novels, *Many Thing You No Understand* (1970) and its sequel *Many Thing Begin for Change* (1971), in which the central plots are set in motion by British attempts to undermine a ritual through which the antiquity of Igbo politico-cosmological time is reaffirmed and re-animated.

By making living Yoruba and Igbo cosmological temporal sovereignties central to her Africanization of the detective novel and to her reconstitution of postcolonial temporalities, Ulasi puts the crime mystery to the task of probing and shaping what Fanon describes as 'the fluctuating movement which [the people] are just giving shape to', that 'zone of occult instability' in which a new national culture and national consciousness are being formed through struggle for liberation (2014: 227). Moreover, within the context of Ulasi's other novels, the Yoruba-informed postcolonial temporal sovereignty of *The Man from Sagamu* is but one temporality among many within the incipient nation-state. Ulasi thus imagines a Nigeria comprised of a multiplicity of temporalities, the Nigerian nation-state as a chronotope of chronotopes, thereby further distinguishing the postcolony from metropole and demarcating its sovereign autonomy.

Conclusion

To read Ulasi's, Ike's, and Nwokolo's novels in reverse chronological order as I have just done is to trace a sequence of clues backward in time much like the detective does. The cynical destruction of government records and the blatant disregard for equitable mining allotments in *Dangerous Inheritance* point back to the weaponization of individuated economic relations and the resulting crises of value forms narrated in *Expo '77*, which in turn are layered atop the unresolved epistemological failures of decolonization that *The Man from Sagamu* outlines. Read this way, the culture of individual malfeasance of the 1970s and 1980s comes across as symptomatic of a much deeper problem that remains unresolvable and profoundly destabilizing. In fact, the failure to reconceptualize the hegemonic modernity of the colonial state stands as the ur-crime preceding and producing conditions for other forms of criminalization. Ulasi's vision thereby calls into question the heroic role ascribed to the detective in Nwokolo's and Ike's novels, and for that matter in the spy adventures that were popular while she wrote her later books. The Nigeria their protagonists rescue comes across in *The Man from Sagamu* as one worth saving but one that requires for its full realization more than the revelation of the mere mechanics of the criminalization of the state. The conceptual underpinnings of decolonization itself demand re-orientation. To do that work requires a careful interrogation of the logic of the postcolonial state. The detective novel is certainly not the typical narrative form for carrying out that critique, but for Ulasi it is an unusually productive one.

Early twenty-first century Anglophone African detective novelists will extend and expand the questions that Ulasi poses about historicity, temporal stasis, and the coloniality of time in the context of political and economic neoliberalism. It is to the neoliberalization of African social life and crime fiction writing that the remaining chapters of this book now turn. The crises of neoliberal governance, the privatization of risk, and the increasing valorization of market-based competitive social relations will animate detective fiction produced by Anglophone African writers from the 1990s into the second decade of the twenty-first century. For the continent's detective fiction writers, the future perfect will retain its value because the perfect future continues to elude its believers.

Part 2

Neoliberal Noir

Neoliberal Noir   4

During the final decade of the twentieth century Kenya underwent what one specialist calls 'the most rapid and total deregulation of an African economy ever seen' (Smith 2008: 33–34). The country had witnessed half of its International Monetary Fund and World Bank aid withheld from 1990–1992 for not implementing multiparty elections and again a few years later for not privatizing public corporations briskly enough for the funding agencies' managers. In response, finance minister Musalia Mudavadi took the steps of abolishing import licensing and price controls, floating the currency, ending restrictions on profit repatriation, and slashing public spending and civil servant roles and otherwise reshaping governmental priorities and processes to align with the IMF's and World Bank's neoliberal economic imperatives. On one hand, the public welcomed reforms like multi-party democracy and governmental transparency that checked the abuses of power endemic to President Daniel arap Moi's twenty-three-year rule. On the other, there was outrage at what was perceived as the international funding agencies' appropriation of Kenya's political sovereignty. Moreover, coming after a period when democracy had been associated with the equitable distribution of resources to the public, neoliberalism's valorization of individualized accumulation and income inequality left large segments of the population feeling that Kenya's social fabric had rotted (Smith 2008: 21, 31).

Variations on the Kenyan experience have played out across the African continent since the 1970s. With massive loans needed to mitigate the debilitating effects of the oil shocks and global recessions of that decade, African governments seeking aid from the World Bank, the IMF, and other global development banks were forced, like Kenya, to adopt a range of governance reforms that undermined the nationalist consensus that structured state-citizen relations during the first decades of independence. While tenuous in practice, that consensus was predicated on the developmentalist paradigms discussed in earlier chapters, through which governments would oversee jobs programs, price controls, and other forms of economic planning and lead the citizenry to the higher levels of prosperity enjoyed by the industrial nations of the Global North. The IMF's and World Bank's reforms impinged on the developmentalist program by demanding cuts to civil service rolls, the ending of price control regulations, the privatization of parastatals, and the contracting of services, including many of those associated with the police and military, from private suppliers. The imposed reforms also delimited domestic political autonomy by requiring individual nation-states to produce new constitutions that would secure private property rights and individual choice (but not public health or welfare), affirm the rule of law, and adopt homogenous global trade standards. In her ethnography of neoliberal governance in Ghana, Brenda Chalfin (2010) points out that countries under these mandates have, as a result, increasingly concentrated authority in agencies such as Customs that are responsible for facilitating frictionless cross-border movements of goods and capital while divesting most other agencies of their authority.

One of the central organizing conceits behind the neoliberal contraction and redeployment of state institutions is the idea that enterprising individuals are better able to govern themselves than governments can. Freed from governmental oversight and regulation, individuals can, and will, neoliberalism's proponents argue, make the most rational economic decisions for their individual situations. Responsibilized in this way, they are, moreover, presumed to be more likely to embrace entrepreneurial ventures in a competitive spirit that will drive local economic development, thereby obviating the need for state-owned businesses or development programs. In the history of post-independence Africa, few citizens of any country have enjoyed any other choice than to be entrepreneurial as few governments have had the resources to fund the robust welfare state safety nets that neoliberal governing rationalities seek to dismantle. This reality notwithstanding, the imperative of individuated self-governance has only expanded as governments have retreated from the state-driven modernization projects of earlier decades. Under these conditions, any residual faith in the sovereign state as the guarantor of the protections and rights of citizenship became increasingly difficult to sustain.[1] Even the social supports provided by kinship networks have become strained as individuals find it increasingly necessary to invest capital in their individuated economic selves. Additionally, the feminization of certain forms of labor and recalibration of gender relations, the decreasing visibility of experts for guidance in an increasingly complex social world, the spectral economies of global finance, and the proliferation of '419' and other financial scams have created a world of intensely competitive social relations in which few people can be trusted and every individual must assume near total responsibility for their own interests.[2] For these reasons, neoliberalism is often experienced at the level of the individual as a state of vulnerability, precarity, and paranoia.

---

1 The scholarship on this point is too extensive to list here. I found Birgit Meyer's (1998, 2007) and James Ferguson's (1999, 2006) thinking about the epistemological crises provoked by neoliberalization especially insightful as a starting point for further inquiry.
2 For an overview, see Comaroff and Comaroff (2000).

Given its historical engagement with the crises of liberalism and global capitalism, detective fiction offers an especially rich critical apparatus for investigating the morphing valences of sociability, criminality, and political legitimacy under these conditions of intensified social and epistemological recalibration. The genre's long-standing preoccupation with the mutually constituted sovereign bodies of the nation-state and the individual rights-bearing citizen enables a broad engagement with two interrelated problematics. The first concerns the capacity of the neoliberal state to regulate private interests through the rule of law and to contain both legitimate and criminal enterprise that exceeds the state's juridical boundaries and sovereign authority. The second involves the meanings of citizenship when individuals are increasingly redefined as autonomous economic self-governing agents who are subject to new privatized regimes of sovereign power. At issue for each of these problematics is the status of the postcolonial sovereign ideal itself.

It is perhaps not surprising, then, that of the more than two hundred English-language detective stories and novels published to date, the majority appear during the late twentieth- and early twenty-first-century decades when the wide range of dynamics associated with neoliberal capitalism reshape so much of African social life. The explosive growth of the crime mystery is partially a function of neoliberal publishing economics. After a period in the 1980s and early 1990s when the IMF's structural adjustment mandates decimated African publishing and book import economies, intensified profit pressures on publishers struggling to survive the increasingly competitive terrain of turn-of-the-century global capitalism began to generate unexpected opportunities for African writers to produce the kinds of mass-market genre fiction presumed to sell well domestically and internationally. But never slow to recognize an opportunity for socio-political critique even in the most commodified of cultural forms, a great many Anglophone African detective fiction writers also embraced the detective story for its capacity to dissect the profound crises of selfhood, sovereignty, and collective obligation wrought by political and economic neoliberalization.

In this chapter and the two to follow, I survey how Anglophone African novelists activate and further expand the detective genre's aesthetic and thematic capacities to grapple with the implications of neoliberal capitalist governmentalities for the ongoing project of decolonization. My aim is, moreover, to explore how these writers continue the project of their predecessors in putting the detective story to work in resistance to the social, economic, and political forces that delimit African self-sovereignties. Chapters 5 and 6 will consider specific manifestations of neoliberal capitalism in the postcolony as they are animated in select Anglophone African mysteries. Chapter 5 also includes a discussion of Anglophone African detective fiction in relation to neoliberal capitalism's pressures on the publishing industry. But first, I outline the broad themes and modes of critique evident in Anglophone Africa's 'neoliberal noir'.[3] My use of the term neoliberal noir is not to suggest that the fiction is itself neoliberal in its expression or values. Rather, it is to evoke the neoliberal phantasmagoria in which the authors locate the violence and disorder of late twentieth- and early twenty-first-century life and to highlight the generically specific ways that they make sense of it. In this chapter, I analyze four criminal investigation novels that I see as paradigmatic in articulating the broad consequences of neoliberalization, especially as it is experienced by the individuals and communities for whom privatization, deregulation, and individuated self-governance lead not to wealth or security but to exacerbated economic and social precarity. Tony Marinho's *The Epidemic* (1992), Unity Dow's *The Screaming of the Innocent* (2002), writing duo Wahome Mutahi and Wahome Karengo's thriller *The Miracle Merchant* (2003), and Diale Tlholwe's *Ancient Rites* (2008) emerge, respectively, from the diverse political and cultural geographies of Nigeria, Botswana, Kenya, and South Africa to tell similar stories about neoliberalizing Africa. In their multi-layered reimaginations of the detective story's historical liberal registers, the four writers suggest productive mystery genre protocols for challenging neoliberal capitalism's cultural logics.

New Realities, New Plots

Before delving into the four novels, it is helpful to know something about the broader evolution of Anglophone African detective fiction of which they are a part. As Ghana's achievement of self-rule in 1957 ushered in new investigation plots and inventories of villains and heroes from those seen in the colonial era and as the failings of African governments in the 1970s and 1980s to fulfill the promises of self-rule produced yet others, the neoliberal turn likewise generates its own unique storylines and characters. To be sure, mysteries featuring egregious abuses of power by seemingly untouchable politicians continue to find favor well after the first moves toward liberalization.[4] So, too, the secret agent adventure and police procedural reappear periodically. But the crises of governance that follow liberalization usher in new kinds of mysteries investigating both new and intensified disorder in the postcolony. Writers begin experimenting with the genre's conventional treatment of law and order to assess the perceived escalation of domestic economic crimes and violence, on the one hand, and the incapacities of the postcolonial state to deliver the order,

---

3 As indicated in the Introduction, this term comes from Misha Kokotovic (2006).
4 These include, among others, Amaechi Nzekwe's *A Killer on the Loose*, Chuma Nwokolo's *Dangerous Inheritance*, Femi Osofisan's *Pirates*, and Akosua Gyamfaa-Fofie's *Murder at Sunset* each referenced in earlier chapters, and Adimchinma Ibe's *Treachery in the Yard* (2010), and Leye Adenle's Amaka mysteries (2016, 2018, and 2022).

security, and economic well-being promised by the nationalist meta-narratives of decolonization, on the other.

Predictably, in turning their focus to emergent forms of political and economic disorder, many of the mysteries written beginning in the late 1980s pivot on murder, fraud, and graft by rapacious business elites rather than politicians. The crimes of the wealthy to preserve power gain significant currency and feature prominently in the works of South Africa's Gomolemo Mokae (1995), Diale Tlholwe (2011), Lauren Beukes (2010), and Omoseye Bolaji (2000); Botswana's Lauri Kubuitsile (2008); Sudan/Egypt's Parker Bilal (2012); Nigeria's Henri Eyo (2004); and Kenya's James Irungu (1987), to name just a few. And, in the face of increasing political and juridical incapacity, Uganda's Ulysses Chuka Kibuuka (1991), South Africa's Deon Meyer (2000), and Kenya's Mukoma Wa Ngugi (2010, 2013) fashion detective thrillers about transnational criminal syndicates able to operate across state borders at will. For the first time, African detective novelists also begin to experiment in significant ways with that staple of the interwar British mystery, private interpersonal grievance as a motive for murder. Kwame Anthony Appiah re-invents this plot device in his three Sir Patrick Scott mysteries (1991, 1994, 1995), set within the not-so-genteel orbit of Cambridge University, as do Angela Makholwa (2007) and H.J. Golakai (2011), who dramatize particularly effectively South African class anxieties as they are bound up with gender and race. Kwei Quartey's six Darko Dawson mysteries similarly chart interpersonal conflicts against a backdrop of economic deregulation, the circulation of global capital within and across Ghanaian borders, and the growth of evangelical churches and their prosperity gospels.[5]

The diverse body of writing is linked by a constellation of overlapping economic anxieties characteristic of the neoliberal era. In different ways, the novels illuminate the insecurities produced by an increasingly competitive marketplace for wealth and power where the transferal of sovereign authority from the state to the entrepreneurial subject exacerbates existing precarities and generates new forms of internecine violence. Repeatedly, their investigation plots unfold in environments of state incapacity and under the shadow of bankrupt developmentalist paradigms and visions of state-led collective liberation. Published by Nairobi-based Phoenix Books in the wake of Kenya's break-neck neoliberalization, Mutahi and Karengo's *The Miracle Merchant* captures the general sentiment of Anglophone African neoliberal noir by

---

5   In addition to this multiplication of plots and forms of villainy comes the appearance of various previously unseen subgenres, such as the historical crime mystery, of which South Africa's Malla Nunn's three Detective Emmanuel Cooper novels stand out, and new subgenres, such as the 'truth commission thriller', so named by Shameem Black (2011).

conveying this emergent reality as loss. From their villain's fraudulent evangelical healing ceremony set in Nairobi's Uhuru Park, which opens the novel, to his assassination in the Kenyan Port Authority's Exhibition Grounds that ends it, *The Miracle Merchant* traces the arc of a dying nationalism as neoliberalism's market rationalities dismantle the ethos of collective struggle that is signified historically in the Swahili word '*uhuru*' and that was so vital to the country's anticolonial nationalist movements. That arc, and the forms of violence and vulnerability it produces, could be said to structure nearly the entire body of Anglophone African detective fiction that follows the neoliberal turn. It clearly haunts each of the four novels I consider in the following pages.

A Dying Nationalism

One of the first Anglophone African detective novels to focalize the crises, insecurities, and violence of neoliberal governance is Tony Marinho's 1992 biothriller, *The Epidemic*. Of Marinho's two mystery novels, *The Epidemic* is the more compelling and not just because the author brings his professional training as a doctor to his portrayal of public health catastrophe.[6] Marinho published the novel in Ibadan as part of Heinemann's Frontline series, an imprint for the Nigerian market that mixed literary and popular genre titles and included works by Chinua Achebe, Tess Akaeke Onwueme, Niyi Osundare, Gabriel Okara, and many other prominent Nigerian writers. Set in Toro, a fictitious West African country dependent on oil and tourism revenue, *The Epidemic* unfolds in a barely concealed post-oil boom Nigeria where a mysterious health crisis is taking lives by the thousands. Working to solve the mystery are doctors, epidemiologists, and research scientists from the country's hospitals and universities.

Toro's extensive medical facilities, mobile health clinics, active university research centers, vast highway networks, and well-educated professional class index real-life Nigeria's massive petroleum-funded nation-building projects of the 1970s. Despite these superficial signs of national prosperity, outdated medical equipment, dilapidated transportation, unreliable phone lines, decaying infrastructure, petrol shortages, and venal kleptocrats situate *The Epidemic*'s narrative firmly in the hangover of the petro-naira oil boom. If, as Andrew Apter argues about the oil boom years, the 'tangible signs of progress and abundance … ratified the new prosperity with visible evidence, producing a national dramaturgy of appearances and representations that beckoned toward modernity and brought it into being' (2005: 41), *The Epidemic* points to the hollowness of the spectacle. The hospitals and research labs at best signal a utopian future that never materialized, and in their tarnished state give lie to

---

6   The other is *Deadly Cargo*, a novel in the spy thriller mold that I reference in Chapter 2.

illusion of prosperity and functionality that the fictitious country's leaders so desperately seek to sustain.

Seven years prior to *The Epidemic*'s publication, under IMF and World Bank pressure, Nigerian president Ibrahim Badamosi Babangida, initiated a broad liberalization of the Nigerian economy. In a bid to lure foreign investment and consolidate his personal power after having claimed the presidency in a military coup, Babangida floated the currency, deregulated banking, and welcomed other familiar IMF structural adjustment conditions.[7] Marinho's choice of the medical mystery/biothriller is particularly suited to exploring questions of sovereignty and the health of the body politic that can result from such a move. As Ruth Mayer notes about the genre, the 'particularly protean character of the virus, its capacity to invade a foreign "body" on the sly and use the host's metabolism to self-replicate, allows for its spread into many fields of cultural expression and exchange' (2007: 1). Marinho makes starkly evident in his first pages how the neoliberal imperatives of the IMF and World Bank read like viruses commandeering a body's metabolism, turning the government's own self-interest into a mechanism for propagating neoliberal rationalities.

The novel opens at a presidential cabinet meeting in which the head of state and his ministers confront the horrifying scene of a seemingly unstoppable disease that rapidly bloats the bodies of its victims in the process of killing them. Before the nominally civic-minded health minister can demand emergency funding, and before the unapologetically self-interested president can instruct his cabinet to avoid any action that might lead to his loss in the next elections, the exterior minister quietly points out that publicly acknowledging the epidemic could decimate the country's nascent tourism industry, just as official government reports about AIDS rates had in East Africa. He further predicts that the IMF and World Bank will call the country's loans if revenues dip too precipitously, which they certainly will when reduced tourist inflows compound already depressed oil profits (2).[8] He need not state explicitly that, were the loans to be called, there really would be no money to treat the epidemic's victims or to contain the health threat. As self-serving as the ministers are, their fear that word of the biomedical terror would destroy their tourism industry and, in turn, would trigger debt obligations, speaks to the very real ways that governments internalize and thereby propogate the IMF's and World Bank's neoliberal rationalities. In this case, the internalization of balance-of-payments priorities prevents the state from taking an active role in controlling public health.

The protagonists of Unity Dow's and Diale Tlholwe's crime mysteries and the cases they investigate are not impacted in such obvious ways by the

---

7   See Apter (2000: 269).
8   Unless indicated, all parenthetical citations for Marinho's writing in this chapter refer to *The Epidemic*.

neoliberalization mandates of the IMF or World Bank, but they are similarly haunted by the conflict between older statist-developmentalist ideals and neoliberal realities. In *The Screaming of the Innocent*, which was published in Australia by the feminist press Spinifex, Dow introduces her principal protagonist, Amantle Bokaa, as an eager participant in Botswana's national service program, Tirelo Sechaba. The program's intention, the novel's third-person narration explains, 'was to give young people an opportunity to serve the nation before they embarked on their long-term career or work path' (42). Moreover, the government was asking everyone, local communities included, 'to make sacrifices in order to ensure the success of the scheme' (42). Depicted as a flailing initiative rife with exploitation and abuse – in a play on its initials, host wives refer to female Tirelo Sechaba Participants only half-jokingly as 'Temporary Sexual Partners' for their husbands (25) – Tirelo Sechaba nevertheless represents the enduring promise of state-led development, and Amantle remains genuinely dedicated to its nationalist mission.[9] Furthermore, Amantle's discovery of a box of blood-encrusted clothing on her first day of duty sets in motion an investigation into the murder of twelve-year-old girl Neo Kakang, an inquiry that results less in conventional generic discovery or punishment than in Botswana's marginalized and dispossessed communities asserting their claim to citizenship rights and procedural protections within a nationalist developmentalist framework. This is a theme that runs across all of Dow's novels. As one critic notes, Dow's female characters repeatedly 'assert themselves … by knowing how to access the rules of law' (Darlington 2013: 80).[10] Given Dow's primary professional career as a lawyer, legal scholar, and High Court judge, this focus on the jural mechanisms of a sovereign nation-state is not surprising.

But, as in *The Epidemic*, these nationalist decolonial ideals are almost impossible to sustain against the rising neoliberal tide. In a 2005 interview Dow laments: 'We are a people in transition, a people in cultures that are weak in terms of our relationship to global power' (qtd in Kalua 2009: 48). Dow represents this unequal relation of power through her depiction of a Botswanan state that has been captured by a coalition of enthusiastic entrepreneurial subjects and traditional patriarchs seeking to secure their competitive advantage against their

---

9 It is worth noting that Dow's given name, Unity, reflects the idealism of African nationalism. She explains,
   'I was born in 1959. Those were the days of African nationalism, African self-realisation; and it really came from that. I think I am right that the [apartheid-era] South African coins used to have the motto "Eendrag maak mag" (Unity gives strength) on them, and my father's attitude was: if it can give them strength, it can give us strength. It was a hijacking of that idea' (Daymond and Lenta 2004: 50).
10 Annie Gagiano (2004) develops a similar line of argumentation about the centrality of legal knowledge to the feminism of Dow's fiction.

rivals and against the women and others whom they view as undeserving. The novel's criminal mastermind, Mr. Disanka, for example, is by all appearances an emblematic entrepreneurial subject, meritorious in capitalist terms for building his family cattle post into a multipronged vertically integrated enterprise with a meat processing facility, a retail butcher shop, and a variety of other investments and ventures. He is, moreover, a man described as having an acute awareness of appropriate consumer choices and of the most self-servingly advantageous forms of private philanthropy. For these reasons, he is viewed as a 'good man' (1), a sobriquet that gets repeated in different variations (good husband, good lover, etc.) over a dozen times by his admirers, even as they envy his prosperity, and by local and national government officials, who need his favor to retain power. He is, moreover, untouchable by the police and judiciary because it is his class interests that they serve. And his neoliberal interests stand in stark opposition to Amantle's nationalist ideals.

The tension between neoliberal and collectivist-nationalist ideals in Tlholwe's *Ancient Rites* inflects both the central plot conflict and the protagonist's self-conception. Readers learn that Thabang Maje, Tlholwe's detective in *Ancient Rites* and its follow-up, *Counting the Coffins* (2011), both published by South Africa's Kwela Books, works for a private sector investigation and security firm that serves post-apartheid South Africa's entrepreneurial classes. In *Ancient Rites*, a school administrator with ambitions for lucrative private sector work hires Maje to ascertain the whereabouts of a missing teacher whose disappearance might tarnish his public image. Despite Maje's service to South Africa's corporate capitalists, his background and beliefs reflect the ideals of collective action and state-sponsored nation-building. A secondary school student during the mass student uprisings of 1976, Maje had initially pursued a teaching career in the apartheid-era Bantu Education system, not as a Boer apologist but with the heady ideals of radical change. Along with many other idealistic Africans, Maje 'had prophesied a new type of education, like countless others in all revolutions that the world has ever seen' (26).[11] Even though Tlholwe's two novels find Maje working in the private sector, those ideals persistently motivate his actions.

Given his professional milieu, Maje's collectivist, nationalist commitments are continually strained by the imperatives of the 'new South Africa' (23). Tlholwe depicts the neoliberalization of post-apartheid South Africa as being equally, if not more pervasive than Dow does in her evocation of early twenty-first-century Botswana. Regarding the impossibility of his generation's idealistic teachers implementing their radical vision, Maje declares, 'we had failed to foresee our own demise, our inevitable irrelevance in the new order' (26). 'Management' individuates and pathologizes Maje's ensuing disillusionment

---

11 Unless indicated, all parenthetical citations for Tlholwe's writing in this chapter refer to *Ancient Rites*.

as depression and casts his refusal to medicate in the consumer-capitalist logic of his 'right to choose' (27). In both of Tlholwe's mysteries, nearly everywhere Maje looks, a profit-driven market logic has infiltrated institutions including those whose primary mandate is not, in Maje's eyes, revenue generating. In *Ancient Rites* Maje sarcastically dismisses the economic language that dominates social discourse by describing the murder of a mistress 'as a misguided cost-cutting measure' (54) and laments that the police are subject to 'arrest targets' (98) and other quantifactual measures of achievement. The individuals who surround Maje are, as well, partisans of this late-capitalist logic. His own fiancée comes across as a paragon of the entrepreneurial subject. She is a property developer 'whose whole world is urban and upwardly driven' and who views society as a competitive battle between the 'hunters and the hunted' (110). Anyone who sees the social order differently is, according to her, 'out of the mainstream' (32). Moreover, Tlholwe depicts a new South Africa in which untrammelled self-interest has been elevated to a virtue. Among the most devoted adherents to this neoliberal ideal is Regional Education Director J.M.B. Tiro, the man who hires Maje to investigate the disappearance of the teacher. Tiro sees in the new South Africa only opportunity for personal advancement, first 'to be the next Provincial Minister of Education. Then, with luck … a national position. That will lead to a fat directorship in some private company looking for a high-profile black face' (119). In the meantime, Tiro operates as a keen advocate of the 'progressive management' overseeing the neoliberal restructuring of the education system, the same restructuring that led Maje to early retirement and to his job as a private investigator and security consultant.

Where Tiro, Maje's fiancée, and Maje himself inhabit the class, educational, and status positions to capitalize on the opportunities available in the neoliberal order that is the new South Africa, the Marikong villagers Maje encounters on his assignment in South Africa's North West province do not. Excluded from the new South Africa and from the opportunities afforded to the new Black elite, they occupy 'a fast-changing world that seems to be leaving them behind' (41). Maje sees in the villagers' eyes the 'look of a people who sensed that when humanity finally gathered around the last fire, they may be absent, their tongues long stilled and their last prayers unheard' (39). While 'there is nothing here for them anymore' (42), the few who venture to the cities discover that 'they were not expected' (121), that they have become so extraneous as to be excluded even from the category of unwelcome competition. There is as a result little more left for them to do in the new South Africa than to watch their 'community sliding towards dissolution' (98), all the while nursing resentment and competing for scarce resources and scarcer opportunities.

Fig. 4. *The Miracle Merchant* by Wahome Mutahi and Wahome Karengo (2003). Cover by John N. Nyagah. Published by Phoenix Publishers, Nairobi.

Pentecostal and Occult Economies

Neoliberalism's ethos of individuated economic self-governance and its radically uneven distribution of resources have propelled the closely related proliferation of charismatic Pentecostal Christianity and occult economics discourse across large swaths of the African continent, just as it has as globally. In three of the four novels under consideration in this chapter, one or both dynamics feature prominently. To solve their criminal mysteries Mutahi and Karengo's, Tlhowlwe's, and Dow's protagonists must tease out how Pentecostalism and/or accusations of witchcraft fill the spaces vacated by the liberalizing postcolonial state, organize neoliberal modes of sociability, and, perhaps most significantly, proffer non-state-based systems of law, order, and punishment for already precarious populations forced to bear the disproportionate risks of privatization and self-governance.

Mutahi and Karengo bring together neoliberalism's entrepreneurial market ethos and evangelical Christianity in the criminal mastermind Apostle Paul Meshack Mpevu. Apostle Paul is a self-styled religious leader who preaches the Pentecostal gospel of economic salvation to worshippers across East Africa and whose African Church of Modern Apostles (ACMA) fronts a diverse conglomeration of businesses ranging from fresh flower plantations and children's clothing factories to heroin and military-grade arms markets. Less a criminal thug than a chief executive officer, Apostle Paul runs ACMA like a modern multinational corporation, with unit directors, cross-marketing strategies, offshore tax havens, board meetings, and a contempt for governmental regulation. For his follower-customers who purchase his self-help videos as eagerly as a favored militia buys his assault rifles, Apostle Paul offers the neoliberal-inflected rhetoric that salvation in its spiritual and economic forms is a function of economic self-governance. The most prized workers in his conglomerate are recognized within ACMA as the 'Chosen Few', and among the members of ACMA's community of believers, financial wealth signifies nothing less than God's approval of one's personal choices (17). Apostle Paul makes no actual personal claims to Christian belief; rather, the church is simply one of the most lucrative niches available in the local market, and more so because its customer base is as vast as the global population.

As in Latin America, the United States, and other regions of the world, one of the most pronounced social responses to liberalization in much of sub-Saharan Africa has been the rapid spread of Pentecostal charismatic Christianity such as that represented by ACMA. Reasons for this expansion into the spaces vacated by the state are complicated and vary from location to location, but scholars have identified a number of 'elective affinities' (B. Meyer 2007) between evangelical Christianity and neoliberal capitalism that may account for their frequent cohabitation.[12] With their for-profit structure and free-market ethos, Pentecostal-charismatic churches have aggressively capitalized on economic crises to expand market share.[13] Individual adherents are often drawn by the prosperity gospels proffered in sermons, religious tracts, and videos. As Birgit Meyer (2007) emphasizes in her study of Ghanaian Pentecostal communities, the middle-class business owners and office workers

---

12 Birgit Meyer rethinks Max Weber's arguments about Protestantism and the birth of capitalism to account for the primacy of consumption, pleasure, and sensation in evangelical piety. See also Sasha Newell (2007).
13 For global contexts, see Bethany E. Moreton (2007), Matan Shapiro (2019), and Robert W. Hefner (2010).

who make up a large proportion of congregants are also attracted to evangelical Christianity for its spiritual frameworks for managing the dilemmas posed by neoliberal capitalism. In the wake of the collapse of nationalist metanarratives of decolonization, membership in a global Christianity thus offers 'a community of a new type, proper to the forms of diffuse, individualized, non-isomorphic forms of connectedness in our globalized world' (Marshall 2009: 208). Given the destabilizing effects of neoliberalization on most Kenyans, Mutahi and Karengo are careful not to patronize Apostle Paul's adherents as dupes of a charismatic charlatan. But nor, as we shall see later in the chapter, are they hesitant to indict Apostle Paul for using Christianity to usurp sovereign powers from a hobbled postcolonial state.

Alongside and in many cases inseparable from the growth of Pentecostal Christianity has been an intensification of accusations of witchcraft and other malevolent spiritual practices. Meyer (1998, 2007) notes the unusually prominent presence of witchcraft accusations in African Pentecostalisms, for instance. She argues that such accusations often function to legitimate the cutting of financial obligations to poorer kin demanding support. Defined as vampiric witches, relatives demanding money or jobs can be more easily dismissed, thereby better enabling the individual capital accumulation necessary for success in a liberalized economy (Meyer 1998: 235–236). But to the poor and disenfranchised, it is the wealthy and powerful who practice the dark arts of occult accumulation. As it has since at least the early years of the transatlantic slave trade, witchcraft has proved to be capacious in its explanatory power to make sense of the asocial logic of market economies.[14] Where wage work is scarce and long-standing forms of production are disappearing, any form of accumulation or economic security can appear to come unnaturally. In an age when outsized accumulation and consumption are severed from any visible means of production, as is so often the case in late capitalism, such forms of wealth generation can look especially devilish.

Mutahi and Karengo highlight one manifestation of neoliberal occult economics in an underdeveloped subplot in *The Miracle Merchant*. The laborers in Apostle Paul's factories and on his plantations, it is revealed, are literal zombies, formerly autonomous humans whose brains have been reprogrammed with proprietary technology developed by neuroscientists in Paul's employ. Occult economics here highlights how 'otherwise inexplicable accumulation' in the absence of visible markers of production, as in Apostle Paul's case, has come,

---

14 During the years of when human bodies filled European and American slave ships, entrepreneurial West African merchants would justify selling community members to slave ship captains by accusing them of witchcraft. So too, the potential victims of such accusations perceived the same merchants' unprecedented new wealth and power as evidence of occult mastery. See Rosalind Shaw (2002).

in many parts of the world and not just Africa, to be crystallized in the figure of the living dead, the zombie (Comaroff and Comaroff 1999: 290). Zombie discourse is especially prominent where wage work is increasingly scarce and the 'chosen few' consume ever more conspicuously and with ever less restraint. Mutahi and Karengo seem to forget about these zombies as they close their detective in on his criminal target, but by highlighting the connection between the charismatic Christian preacher and zombie labor they draw attention to the inseparability of Pentecostalism and occult belief systems in neoliberal contexts.

Where Mutahi and Karengo relegate the problem of occult economics to a minor subplot, Dow and Tlholwe make central to their plots the occult's intimate entanglements with neoliberal life for already precarious populations forced to bear the disproportionate risks of privatization and self-governance.[15] Tlholwe's detective Maje learns that Mamorena, the missing schoolteacher, and her family are the subject of persistent accusations of witchcraft and 'rumors of missing body parts' (77). The villagers suspect Mamorena's family of enriching themselves through occult means at the villagers' expense. A matriarch of the family tells Maje: 'We have always been hard-working, prudent and frugal. Wherever our people settled, they thrived' (72). Mamorena, the missing schoolteacher, had thrived not just locally but had seemingly secured a rare foothold in the neoliberal new South Africa. To the local population left behind and outside of the pathways to power in the new individuated and competitive dispensation, which is nearly everyone in the impoverished province, Mamorena is viewed as the 'over-educated witch' (75), mysteriously able to harness the seemingly occult forces of a liberalizing economy and state. The matriarch tells Maje that she believes that the villagers killed Mamorena as punishment for her perceived occult crimes against the community.

Writing in the wake of two prominent cases in which the disappearance of young girls assumed to be the victims of ritual murder incited mass demonstrations against the Botswanan government, Dow similarly highlights the salience of occult accumulation to contemporary understandings of inequality and power.[16] 'Throughout the village', Dow writes about Mr. Disanka, the wealthy entrepreneur and unofficial suspect in the disappearance of Neo Kakang, 'people were circulating rumors about him – but then, people circulated rumors about any successful man. It was common for people to suspect that a man attained his political position, business success, academic kudos or professional promotion – any type of success, for that matter – by devilish means' (4–5). Whether or not Mr. Disanka committed the specific ritual

---

15 In this respect, the novels repeat, with a new level of intensity, the Victorian gothic detective genre that registered analogous kinds of precarity.
16 For references to the two disappearance cases, see Comaroff and Comaroff (1999: 299 note 55).

murders that the people's court of gossip and rumor allege he did, Disanka is, in the community's eyes, guilty of the antisocial crime of becoming wealthy and powerful while his neighbors languish, all the while committing the equally grave crime of profiting off them every time they are compelled to spend their meager earnings in one of his businesses. In the avaricious exchange, Disanka gains potency as their life force withers. In contrast to Mamorena, who lacks the protections of money and patriarchal status, Disanka remains unassailable. But in both examples, a conjoined logic of occult culpability and vigilante justice is shown to fill the vacuum left by the state in its neoliberal contraction.

The profound tragedy of occult discourse, as Dow presents it, is that Disanka and his accomplices come to see occult murder and organ harvesting as simply additional methods of securing advantage in a competitive economic arena. So tempted are they by the power and riches promised by the discourses of occult economics and so insecure in their ability to compete in an unregulated free market that they do in fact abduct and ritually kill prepubescent girls for their organs. From these they produce a variety of 'medicines' to be deployed to boost their own power and to diminish that of their rivals.[17] Disanka's brutality is all the more horrific for his inability to comprehend that his economic and professional achievements are the result of his privileged position in a patriarchal capitalist economic system rather than of his occult practices.

It is necessary to note that Dow leaves little to the imagination in the scenes depicting Neo Kakang's evisceration. Crafting crime tales that revolve around any indigenous spiritual belief system, let alone the form of organ harvesting that Dow depicts, risks reaffirming even for African readers the most pernicious stereotypes of African savagery and superstition. That *The Screaming of the Innocent*, like all but the first of Dow's novels was published by an Australian press with only one other African novelist on its lists and distributed almost exclusively in the Global North makes Dow's representational decision more fraught still.[18] For precisely these reasons, Ghanaian mystery novelist Kwei

17 Disanka's partners are similarly motivated. Headman Bokae's existence is defined by the desire to regain an ancestral chieftaincy that a previous generation had lost due to the adept maneuverings of another branch of the family. Defined by his outsized entitlement, a deep hostility to the concept of individual rights, and a complete lack of aptitude for the new economic order, Bokae assumes his right to power and wealth without any of the effort put in by Disanka. After all, 'being a chief meant having a good job for which no training was required' (10). But even for village headmen such as Bokae, 'the job market was becoming more and more competitive' (10) and Bokae finds that his already vulnerable social position is increasingly precarious. The third partner, teacher Sebaki, bridges the other two. Like Disanka, Sebaki is professionally ambitious, seeking to rise to the administrative ranks in the education system, but like Bokae, he is lazy and undeserving. On the basis of his own merit, his career would go nowhere.
18 The question of the role of publishers of African fiction is always a complicated one. Whether a press such as South Africa's Kwela, which published both of Tlholwe's novels,

Quartey (2019) writes that Dow crosses a line he cannot. 'Every author', he says, 'has a "don't-go-there" limit, and that is one of mine'. In depicting Neo's killing so graphically, Dow also risks producing what crime fiction scholar Glen Close describes as 'necropornography' (2018: ch. 2), a depiction of female corpses that lends itself to a particularly intractable misogynistic voyeurism that potentially objectifies the girl whose subjectivity Dow otherwise wants to affirm. These are serious and valid concerns. But, as we will see later in the chapter, Dow, ever the lawyer, builds a carefully constructed case that Neo Kakang's mutilation is no more or no less than the brutality of neoliberal capitalist pragmatism taken to its unspeakable extreme. Which is to say, radical dehumanization is the logical result when the cravenly ambitious come to view ritual killing as simply one more potential instrument for professional self-optimization in an individuated competitive socio-economic world.

Neoliberal Death-worlds

The story of the victim in the murder mystery typically begins with the loss of subjecthood and ends with its recovery. In the classic mystery, the victim might lose his or her identity in death, but, as Sean McCann contends, the freedom and autonomy of the individual liberal subject and his or her status as a subject under the law ultimately gets reaffirmed and celebrated (2000: 8). This is in large part because restitution comes in the form of legal recognition of the victim, even in death, as a rights-bearing subject under the law. So long as the detective symbolizes the Law, he or she need not formally turn the perpetrator over to the police for this recognition. Glen Close agrees that detective story ends with the achievement of subjecthood, but not that of the victim. Close contends that that subjectivity belongs instead to the detective. With regard to the female cadaver, Close writes: 'Death obliterates us. It suspends signification and subjectivity, and cancels identity and differentiation' (2018: 13). But, in turn, the lifeless female body, in its abjection, secures the male detective as a subject according to Close. Standing over the body, visually dissecting the corpse, the hard-boiled investigator marks himself as the 'autonomous, armored, invulnerable phallic subject' (10), an act that, through its repetition in novel after novel and film after film, solidifies the misogynistic subject/object relation.

There is no shortage of Anglophone African crime mysteries that revel in the sort of necropornographic abjection that Close describes. Mbokotwane Manqupu's 'Love Comes Deadly', Amaechi Nzekwe's *A Killer on the Loose*, and

---

would have been as comfortable with the mutilation scene, for example, is impossible to know. After all, the Botswanan publisher Pentagon released Lauri Kubuitsile's mystery *Murder for Profit* (2008) with similarly graphic depictions of pubescent mutilation six years after Dow's novel came out.

David G. Maillu's two Benni Kamba novels come immediately to mind. Nor is there a paucity of detective stories that endeavor to re-establish the legal subjectivity of the victim. Sam's *Who Killed Inspector Kwasi Minta?* and Ekwensi's *Yaba Round-about Murder* work in this vein. But for the four novels under consideration here, neither McCann's or Close's conception of the victim as a generator of subjectivity adequately explains the states of exception, exclusion, and expendability in which vast swaths of the populace exist under the new economic sovereigns of the neoliberal era. While Dow and Tlholwe fashion narratives around individuated victims, their novels, along with Marinho's and Mutahi and Karengo's, focus their detective stories more expansively on the death-worlds that structure the neoliberalized postcolony. Like the femicides of Roberto Bolaño's *2066*, the victims in their novels occupy those social spaces of neoliberal society – its death-worlds – wherein individual lives are expendable by virtue of their availability to being 'harvested', whether for the purposes of increasing the perpetrator's individual vitality or of supplicating the IMF. In a world where economic subjectivity comes to replace political subjectivity, an individual who is not advantageously positioned as an entrepreneurial agent does not, in their telling, exist. The novels' victims are thus, for the most part, biologically alive but politically dead, subject to the biopolitical regimes of neoliberal global capitalism. They are the *homo sacer* of Giorgio Agamben's description (1998).[19] Across the four novels, investigation serves in crucial ways to illuminate and map these death-worlds.

In Mutahi and Karengo's *The Miracle Merchant*, for example, Apostle Paul's greatest danger stems from the way he harnesses neoliberal market and spiritual rationalities to appropriate sovereign right from the state in ways that dispossess his adherents of political subjectivity. The clearest example of his expropriation of sovereign power is his support of a Ugandan militia to create a deregulated transnational border zone to facilitate the free flow of his goods between Kenya, Uganda, and Tanzania (38). Achille Mbembe views this species of privatization of violence in the service of the market as a new, distinctly neoliberal form of the colonial state of war. For Mbembe, the 'erosion of the state's capacity to build the economic underpinnings of political and economic authority' after the imposition of neoliberal restructuring leads inexorably to the re-emergence of a colonial-era relation of domination in which 'the controls and guarantees of juridical order can be suspended – the zone where the violence of the state of exception is deemed to operate in the service of "civilization"' (2003: 24, 22). Neoliberal governance extenuates the individuated sovereign right assumed by the colonizer, Mbembe posits, when violent coercion is made a 'private commodity' (32) available to militias like Apostle Paul's, and subject to market

---

19 See Giorgio Agamben (1998).

forces. That Apostle Paul's followers view him as blessed and, as Jean and John Comaroff have described the perception of successful entrepreneurs elsewhere in Africa, preternaturally able to harness the 'vast, almost instantaneous riches to those who master [neoliberal capitalism's] spectral technologies', the same technologies that simultaneously 'threaten the very existence of those' like them, 'who do not' only further authorizes his sovereign right (2000: 298).

Like his Kenyan counterparts, Tony Marinho understands that under neoliberal governing rationalities, the state is just one competitor in the global market dealing life and death to subalterns like Toro's citizens. In his telling, the global pharmaceutical industry also jockeys for domination in this marketplace. No matter how well Toro's doctors on the ground heroically identify the cause of the epidemic in their underfunded and outdated labs, they simply lack the resources to develop a serum to treat the general population. Nor does the country have the capacity to produce pharmaceuticals even if the research teams could develop them. At the end of the novel, it is instead a British university research scientist who develops and patents the serum to treat the infected. His better-equipped lab and access to profit-generating production facilities ensure that he can produce medicines while the state-employed scientists in West Africa cannot (92–93). Thus, while the president's and cabinet ministers' ethical violations are unspeakable, Marinho illuminates how, as Jean Comaroff puts it elsewhere, the 'independent hold of biotechnology and the pharmaceutical industrial complex over significant dimensions of the life process makes them consequential forces in the operations of sovereignty' (2007: 213) and, therefore, advantaged players in the competition to deal directly in the power over life. Compelled to work within this global economic order in order to preserve the basic biological viability of the general population, Toro's own doctors and scientists become the unwitting agents of this modern biopolitics.

The inhabitants of *The Epidemic*'s and *The Miracle Merchant*'s death-worlds are defined primarily by the markers of class and, in Marinho's case, location, with the most vulnerable situated in rural agricultural zones. Tlholwe and Dow share this focus on the rural poor but make additionally explicit the gendered dynamics at work in the production of neoliberal states of exception. Tlholwe does this by crafting a diversionary plot element that hints that Mamorena's disappearance might somehow be related to the nearby serial murders of young female sex workers who ply their trade to long distance truckers carrying goods and materials between South Africa and points north of the border. Sex work in this context of global capitalist trade is presumably not a matter of choice, certainly not in the manner that Maje's school bosses cast his refusal to medicate as a personal choice, nor of entrepreneurial spirit, in the way that Maje's fiancé understands it. Prostitution is instead one of the few financial avenues open to the region's women in neoliberal South Africa, a circumscription of opportunity produced by the post-apartheid government's embrace of neoliberal capitalism in the first place. The women are, moreover, an expendable resource to fuel the drivers – in this case literal – of global commerce, and they exist outside the already delimited protections of the law in a state of legal exclusion. The connection between Mamorena and the murdered sex workers turns out to be a red herring, but by asking the reader to consider the possibility that Mamorena, with all her relative privilege and mobility, might have something in common with the women, who lack both, Tlholwe draws attention to the gendered facets of her precarity in neoliberal South Africa and to gendered states of exclusion broadly.

Dow identifies a similar intersection of class and gender at work in the operations of the postcolony's death-worlds. Within the first few paragraphs of the novel, Dow reworks a common trope in narratives about ritual murder: that to its perpetrators it is an act 'of harvesting fertility' (7) of prepubescent or virginal girls.[20] As the novel opens, readers witness Mr. Disanka voyeuristically assess Neo Kakang's 'impala legs', her lean torso with 'no bulbous protrusions yet', and 'tight little butt' (5). He assures himself of her presumed virginity. Dow is careful to stress the class relations of such targeting. Because Neo is female and comes from a poor family, she is exploitable and targeted in a way that Disanka's similarly aged daughter, sitting next to him in the protected space of his expensive truck as he watches Neo, is not. In Dow's depiction of Disanka's scouting mission, she hints, however, that the trope of harvesting fertility and the typical class dynamics at play might not fully capture the full range of economic rationalities that motivate ritual killings by men like Disanka. As Disanka surveils Neo skipping rope with her friends, he sees a girl focused entirely on skill and achievement. Watching her tuck her skirt 'into the legs of her panties', Disanka admires the fact that 'she did so not out of modesty but to make sure that she successfully completed the task at hand' (5). Disanka singles her out as much for this productive vitality, her ability to dedicate herself so entirely to achievement, as for her latent fertility. It is that vitality that Disanka wants to vampirically suck from her to ensure that he can 'expand his business as well as to buy a new car within the next year', install 'a hot-water geyser at the mistress's house', and 'remain involved in the community projects by chairing the various development committees' (4). To the 'good man', the paragon of neoliberal virtue for whom the state exists and serves, Neo exists not as a subject under the law, not for herself as a self-owning sovereign subject, nor does she exist for others in the sense of 'ubuntu' as Mamorena describes the regional Southern African concept of collectivity in *Ancient Rites*. Rather, Neo exists as an object for others in capitalist and patriarchal terms, her life force 'harvestable' for other's consumption and deployment for personal gain. Neo's fate is horrific,

---

20 See Comaroff and Comaroff (1999) and Adam Ashforth (2005).

but as the endpoint of gendered 'labor' extraction in a neoliberal economy, it differs from that of *Ancient Rite*'s sex workers and many of the other women in the novels only in the scale of the bodily violation.

Privatization and the Private Detective

The focus on death-worlds, as opposed to individuated victims, raises ethical questions concerning the act of detection when the rules of the game have been neoliberalized and the jural mechanisms of the state primarily serve agents of neoliberal capitalism such as the Mr. Disankas and Apostle Pauls, the tourism ministers, and the global pharmaceutical corporations vilified in these novels. The first question is, can any form of detection in these contexts ensure basic legal recognition for putatively rights-bearing citizens let alone restitution or the holding accountable of criminals, moral or legal? Stylistically, these four novels bear little resemblance to the American hard-boiled tradition of Hammett, but like him and his acolytes, the African novelists under consideration in this chapter suggest that the matter of detection in an age of market liberalization, privatization, and self-governance, especially in the African postcolony, is fraught. In a context where individuals are so thoroughly stripped of their bodily sovereignty and where state sovereignty is so concentrated in institutions that facilitate capital flows, the detective's common arsenal of powers are rarely sufficient to the task of containing the metaphysical disorder produced by neoliberal governance. At best, little can be resolved, and the fundamental corruption of the neoliberal world remains.

The Epidemic underscores the detective's constrained powers to ameliorate societal problems produced under neoliberalized governments by depicting a socio-political landscape in which detection can only ever accomplish partial results. Proceeding slowly, inefficiently, and without knowledge of one another's findings, the two medical research teams that have taken it upon themselves to solve the medical mystery confirm independently that the epidemic is nothing more than a strain of easily managed rinderpest, which had spread from cattle to humans. Inadvertent double-blind review here is about the only positive outcome of the government's fettered response and post-oil boom infrastructural decay. The doctor-detectives could, in theory, subsequently trace the chain of responsibility for the unmitigated dispersion of the epidemic all the way to the highest levels of the government. They do not because, as happens to one of their colleagues, they would get stripped of their jobs and punished by ministers who remain terrified of their IMF and World Bank overseers (114). But even were they to conduct these additional investigative labors, they would uncover neither crime nor culprit because, properly speaking, no crime, legally or constitutionally defined, is ever committed. To underscore the point, the novel withholds the cathartic relief that might follow from the Minister of

Health's rinderpest-related death during his attempted escape from the country (59). Whereas in other crime novels the minister's death might bring satisfactory narrative closure, if only through schadenfreude, it comes across here just as hollowly as the discovery of the biomedical mystery. He dies, the mystery is solved, but the inextricable web of global and local structural conditions that enabled his ethical violations and that fueled the epidemic remains firmly in place. Detection in this case can, and does, make visible how for the common man and woman of the country, subject to assault by state leaders, international banks, and global pharmaceutical corporations, the state of exception has become unexceptional. The detective cannot, however, provide victims any form of restitution, jural recognition, or justice.

The figure of the *private* detective in an era of economic privatization poses its own problems in relation to the question of which forms of justice a detective can achieve while working within neoliberal death-worlds. Mutahi and Karengo in their novel and Tlholwe in *Ancient Rites* make starkly apparent the private detective's agential complicity with the very regimes of neoliberal governance that produce the death-worlds they are ostensibly battling. In Mutahi and Karengo's hands, the disorder produced by Apostle Paul's violent iteration of neoliberal global capitalist production exceeds any single state's jural reach; but private justice, normatively figured in the extrajudicial work of the private investigator, risks turning their detective protagonist into one more representative of a new sovereign disorder in which autonomous economic agents assume authority once invested in the state.[21] Therefore, narrative resolution through Dhlakama's capture and punishment of Apostle Paul would risk reproducing the same neoliberal formations the plot critiques. Not surprising, given the late Wahome Mutahi's reputation as Kenya's premier satirist, he and his co-author emphasize this threat by turning Dhlakama into a satirical caricature of the very dangers he poses.[22] Without apparent irony, for instance, Dhlakama takes his nickname from the well-known Mozambican anti-communist guerrilla leader of the 1980s, Afonso Marceta Macacho Dhlakama, who received support from both the white Rhodesian and apartheid South African governments. Ever faithful to his namesake, the former police officer serves the privatized desires of entrepreneurs like himself (49), complains about the hindrances posed by the regulatory requirements of the government (115), and, whenever possible, makes

---

21 See Pahl (2018) for a similar discussion of African detective fiction in relation to crime that exceeds the state's jurisdiction and capacities.
22 From the mid-1970s until his death at age forty-nine in 2003, Wahome Mutahi's weekly newspaper column, 'Whispers', exposed with withering humor the hypocrisy and corruption of Kenya's elite. Satire figures less prominently in *The Miracle Merchant* than in 'Whispers' but deserves more attention than I can give it here. For essays on Mutahi's life and writing, see Hervé Maupeu and Patrick Mutahi (2005).

opportunistic use of state resources to serve his and his clients' private needs, as he does, for example, when he cajoles an assistant commissioner of police into assigning him a police team to execute a sting on Apostle Paul's operations (120). Mutahi and Karengo trust their readers to recognize the satirical critique in this characterization, but they also recognize that satire does not fully mitigate the ideological risks posed by letting such a detective replace the police or other state law enforcement agents. Therefore, they take the additional steps of refusing him psychological transformation often seen in the hard-boiled detective and the satisfaction of capture and kill.

Regarding psychological growth, the novel's anticipated climax arrives without the protagonist gaining the new ethical insight that hard-boiled genre conventions condition readers to expect. Antonio Gramsci and others view the radical, oftentimes antisocial, individualism of the hard-boiled detective that emerged in the 1930s as a counterweight to the increasing limitations placed on individual liberty by various political and economic forces of the period, but it was an individualism tempered by ethical obligation.[23] Slavoj Žižek posits that, as the result of the realization that their actions can injure others, hard-boiled detectives like Dhlakama typically come to view their investigation as an ethical responsibility: 'The guilt he thus contracts', Žižek contends, 'involuntarily propels him to "honor his debt"' (1991: 63). In other words, the characteristic antisocial individualism that could otherwise threaten the cohesion of society is transformed into an ethical force for reaffirming social ties. Mutahi and Karengo resist ascribing a similar feeling of debt to Dhlakama. The imperious, possessive tone he adopts with the assistant police commissioner reflects a managerial approach, not unlike Apostle Paul's, that Dhlakama applies to the case from beginning to end. Of course, by making the apparent good guy a paragon of neoliberal rationalities the authors risk affirming those values, but this characterization better permits Mutahi and Karengo to suggest that under neoliberal hegemony privatized justice, regardless of motivation, produces the same necropolitical threat as Apostle Paul's privatization of sovereign rights.

As if to emphasize this point, Mutahi and Karengo deflect the narrative closure that would come from Dhlakama's successful capture of Apostle Paul. Just as the private detective's police team storms an open-air stage to apprehend the crime boss, Paul's ex-militia commander assassinates Apostle Paul and slips away from his hiding spot undetected. For Dhlakama and the reader alike, the manner of Apostle Paul's assassination provides a hollow resolution. Certainly, Apostle Paul's death closes the case, and the assassin's escape promises the possibility of another Dhlakama mystery, but the ending resists cathartic closure. Fredric Jameson cautions against reading too much into open-ended

---

23 See Antonio Gramsci (1985), C.L.R. James (1993: 127), and Fay and Nieland (2009: 6).

detective stories like this because, he argues, they often reconfirm 'the value of closure ... by [their] intent to thwart and frustrate it' (1993: 35). In this case, however, Mutahi and Karengo's critique of neoliberal governance hinges precisely on the conspicuous absence of a satisfactory solution to the thriller. Had Dhlakama captured and punished Apostle Paul with the assistance of the police but without formal recourse to the law, his privatized detective work would only have exacerbated the state of war initially promulgated by Apostle Paul. Dhlakama would, in effect, operate as a second war machine, securing forcibly the result desired by his client but not the justice or safety of the public as a civic body. Dhlakama's success would signal no less than the collapse of the dream of nationalist liberation into the violent disorder of a completely free market. By denying Dhlakama his expected success, Mutahi and Karengo refuse to ratify Apostle Paul's or Dhlakama's individuated sovereign authority or the necropolitical order it represents.

In *Ancient Rites*, Tlholwe treats the problem of private detection in the public sphere in similar ways. Like his Kenyan counterparts, Tlholwe makes his detective the explicit agent of neoliberal capitalist enterprise. Recall that Tiro, the man who hires Maje for the case, sees in the new South Africa only opportunity for individual advancement through the ranks of public service to riches in the private sector. Tiro, Maje eventually learns, fathered the missing woman's daughter, and cannot afford as a Black man, even in the post-apartheid racial order, the reputational stain of an illegitimate child. While Tiro comes across as too feckless to have had Mamorena murdered, let alone to do it himself, it is in his interest to know for certain that she is 'dead and safely buried. And that nothing negative will find its way back to him' (119). As a private detective, Maje thus serves not as an agent for the public good nor to carry out the revolutionary ideals that initially propelled him into education. Instead, as would have been his fate had he remained in the classroom, he functions as another type of tool for the achievement of successful entrepreneurial subjecthood. In this case Tiro's, but also his own as a private sector professional.

As Mutahi and Karengo do with Dhlakama, Tlholwe denies Maje the power to pursue his investigation to its expected conclusion. Its endpoint comes relatively quickly, and with a similar effect as in the Kenyan novel. Maje has only advanced into his investigation to the point of speaking to the police about their inquiry into Mamorena's disappearance and to meet the local family that had cooked and cleaned for her, neither of which unveils any significant clues, when Mamorena herself simply reveals herself to him. From that moment onwards everything that Maje learns about why Mamorena went into hiding, about the murders of the local sex workers, and about the region's precipitating economic crises, he learns not because of his investigatory labors but because Mamorena chooses to admit him into the moral community of which she is a part. What she reveals is that a secret spiritual community has coalesced around her, hence the ancient rites of the novel's title, whose function is, like the evangelical church but without the individuated market logic that Pentecostalism so often promulgates, to supplement the collectivist ethos of an increasingly bankrupt postcolonial nationalism. In the faces of the adherents, Maje sees 'a beautiful and heady mixture of people from every African nation' (137), a physical manifestation of 'ubuntu' (121), reclaimed and revitalized from its hollowed out appropriation by the dominant market ideologies of post-transition South Africa.[24] Mamorena chooses to admit Maje not because he is a private detective and security consultant nor because he can provide the physical protection that the state, in its blistering race to liberalization, cannot. Despite his professional service to South Africa's neoliberal elite, Mamorena trusts him and takes him into her and her community's confidence because she believes that his deeper motivation is ethical and rooted in their shared past. 'You came here because of our past, and that's good', she tells him, adding, 'the people who say that they don't care about the past are just a short breath away from saying that they don't care about the future, and therefore cannot be trusted with it' (120). By taking him into her confidence, she transforms his generically traditional role of discoverer and revealer of truths into caretaker of truths. She makes him a guardian of communal knowledge. Effectively, Mamorena places a demand on Maje to honor a debt as an individual to a community, to the very ethos of community. Mamorena thus undermines the detective's ability to serve the neoliberal rationalities that have rendered expendable huge swaths of South Africa's population.

As the examples of Dhlakama and Maje suggest, compelling critiques can be made of both neoliberal governance and the ideological workings of the detective genre by undermining the detective's normative powers of identification and containment. Significant questions persist, however. If the private detective remains too much of a risk, too complicit with emergent structures of domination, too powerful of an agent for the forms of neoliberal governance that dictate life in the postcolony to be trusted to carry out his or her normative labors, if in fact he or she cannot be trusted to fulfill his or her generic duties, does the crime

---

24 'Ubuntu' served as the rallying catchphrase of the South Africa that came to birth in 1994, a term broadly understood to mean that 'a person depends on others to be a person', a collectivist ideal that values 'interdependence, justice, solidarity of humankind, respect, empathy and care' (Matolino and Kwindingwi 2013: 200). To this conception, South Africa's first post-apartheid president, Nelson Mandela, appended the affirmation 'one people, one law', a state-centered notion of governance that set the terms for an emergent social contract of the newly reconfigured nonracial democratic nation-state. Not surprising, 'ubuntu' was quickly 'appropriated by pro-market interest groups – from nationalists who use the concept to argue for a "rebranding" of the country to business leaders and government policy-makers keen to make South Africa a more business-friendly place' (MacDonald 2004: 139).

mystery have a future in which it accomplishes anything more than to merely point out its own limitations with regard to neoliberal reason? Similarly, given the crime mystery's propensity for ideologically conservative articulations, can it be made into a reliably productive literary genre for imagining justice, for righting historical wrongs, for imagining decolonized futures, for modeling the sovereignty of both the state and the individual citizen? Where does that leave marginalized communities, the expendable, the homini sacri? If they remain unrecoverable to legal subjectivity in fiction, what are their chances in real life? In short, without viable detectives fulfilling their generically conditioned duties, to what extent can the crime mystery avoid becoming merely another genre of neoliberal reason? Mutahi and Karengo and Tlholwe are equivocal on these questions. Dow and Marinho, on the other hand, are not. Through attentive transfiguration of the investigatory process, they affirm the detective genre's ongoing potential for achieving more than self-critique. They do not embrace the private detective or police investigator as normatively constituted, but nor do they abandon the figure of the detective altogether. Instead, they turn the work of investigation over to civil society and activist coalitions. Detection in their hands becomes a collective endeavor in which diversely constituted and differentially scaled communities band together to uncover wrongs and to demand legal recognition by the state.

As indicated earlier, *The Epidemic* dispenses with the heroic individual detective in favor of a dispersed collection of medical professionals committed to the ethical obligations of medical practice and to the greater public good. Detection, consequently, reads as a tool of civil society to mitigate, if perhaps not fully counteract, the most debilitating effects of political and economic liberalization. Unity Dow, too, represents socially productive detection as a collective endeavor. Almost instinctually, Amantle Bokaa, the young woman who discovers the box of long-lost evidence during her national service assignment, pulls together a coalition of villagers and city dwellers, legal professionals and illiterate farmers, activist youth and weary elders to ensure that Neo Kakang receives justice under the law. The coalition members are acutely aware that collective action can only carry them so far. They recognize, for example, that in the best of circumstances that they could not 'pretend much can happen after a five-year cold trail' (166). They also understand that the killers were powerful enough to scare the police off from an investigation the first time around and that it is unlikely they will ever be identified, let alone prosecuted (167). What the assembled group can do is work collectively to piece together disparate bits of information about the girl's disappearance to reconstruct a narrative of what might have happened. With echoes of the 1988 and 1997 civil unrest against governmental inaction in similar suspected occult violence cases, collective rage follows the ensuing collective investigation. Dow's villagers take over local government buildings and force a meeting, on their terms, with government officials and the Minister of Safety and Security. And despite almost certain failure, the collective formally demands that the case be officially reopened with the goal of getting 'the authorities to admit their mistakes … explain why it happened' and to punish the officers involved (166–167).

A celebrated feminist legal professional, Dow is the least willing of the four novelists under consideration in this chapter to relinquish the political subjectivity of her victims. Her protagonists' most vociferous demand is that the case be formally reopened. Their goal is to ensure Neo's recognition by the state as a rights-bearing subject deserving of police inquiry, even if she is no longer alive to enjoy the protections of the rule of law. By fighting for her jural recognition, the surviving community members effectively assert their own rights as citizens to be recognized as such. In the collective action of demanding that the state fulfills its obligations to its citizens, they remind the police, the courts, high-ranking government officials, and, just as importantly, themselves that the state exists as an expression of the will and consent of the people. Which is all to say, Dow never fully relinquishes the individual political subject as a bearer of political rights, not even when its objectified form is literally dismembered and dematerialized and when individual police officers and politicians remain unwilling to deploy state power to enforce the law or to ensure the protections and rights of legal personhood for anyone other than neoliberal sovereigns. What the villagers and their allies understand most acutely is that the state's recognition of individual rights under the rule of law can only be secured by collective action, by an assertion of popular sovereignty against the neoliberal sovereigns that have come to dominate the postcolony.

Conclusion

None of the four novels ultimately accede to the reader's potential desire to see justice served or punishment meted. Each ends pessimistically: the political conditions that fueled the rinderpest epidemic remain firmly in place in Marinho's novel; R.E.D. Tiro murders Mamorena near the end of *Ancient Rites*; Apostle Paul's assassin escapes uncaptured and unidentified in *The Miracle Merchant*; and, in *The Screaming of the Innocent*, the coalition investigating Neo Kakang's murder unwittingly hands the only remaining evidence to the girl's killers who will surely destroy it. That the novelists tease their audiences with the fantasy of securing judgement against seemingly omnipotent forces only to withhold it and leave their protagonists in a state of exacerbated disorder should not, however, be read as defeatist or as a capitulation to the new market regimes. Rather, it is through the delicate dance of offering and transfiguring familiar aesthetic pleasures that the four texts bid their readers to weigh the meanings of social justice, the political formations required for securing it, and their own complicity in its compromised condition five decades after independence. By holding up for scrutiny the neoliberalized governing apparatuses and practices of economic self-governance that capture individuals like Dhlakama, Apostle Paul, Disanka, Tiro, and Toro's governmental ministers, the novelists guide their audiences through these questions and provoke them to envision alternative formations of self and society. None of the five writers willingly relinquish the expectation of a post-independence and postcolonial state with its effective institutions, high standard of living, and inclusionary public sphere. Each, in their own way, reaffirms the ideals of collectivist state-driven decolonization.

Through their complex engagement of the relationship between literary form and political formation, their texts also interrogate the political effects of genres themselves. As genre fiction and film proliferate across the continent, especially as Nollywood-style films reach ever wider audiences, the likelihood that crime and other popular genres will reify neoliberal formations grows. By holding the aesthetic forms of the crime genre up for interrogation, *The Miracle Merchant*, *The Epidemic*, *The Screaming of the Innocent*, and *Ancient Rites* help foster a critical framework for reading the ideological operations of genre fiction. Thus, in their appraisal of both literary form and political formation, the diversely located authors of these detective novels offer crucial protocols for reading the genres of neoliberalism to precisely the populations most likely to consume popular genre texts.

5 Seriality, Stasis, and the Neoliberal State

While the neoliberalization of the African state has generated new conditions of political exclusion and new forms of violation for those individuals and communities unable to harness capitalism's privileged mechanisms of economic advancement, the neoliberalization of the publishing industry during the same period has, paradoxically, given African writers of detective fiction a new instrument to represent and critique some of the specific neoliberal rationalities responsible for these emergent forms of subjugation. The new tool is the franchised novel series. While not new per se, novel series publication only becomes widely available to African writers in the first years of the 2000s. Once accessible, writers from West, East, and Southern Africa began to experiment with the narrative possibilities of seriality to build profitable brands, but also to explore the types of critical engagements made possible by a long-form series.

I have emphasized elsewhere in this book that the crime mystery is as much a genre of time as it is of investigation and discovery. Within an individual story, a detective fiction writer's ability to make effective use of suspense, delayed exposition, and a future perfect narrative grammar, as well as to play on the genre's implicit promise of future justice, is as important in sustaining a reader's attention as the fabrication of a seemingly unsolvable mystery. As the Nigerian writers of the 1970s and 1980s whom I examined in Chapter 3 additionally make clear, the strategic manipulation of narrative time also expands the genre's potential for social critique, especially for what the mystery genre can be made to reveal about the arrested teleology of decolonization. With seriality's expanded repertoire of temporal devices – namely, multi-novel plot lines and repetition – the series affords writers additional and unique opportunities to historicize the neoliberalization of everyday social life. The series format turns out to be equally productive for dissecting neoliberalism's own temporalities for their material and epistemic impact on the ongoing decolonial project.

As critical theorists emphasize, those impacts are significant. David Harvey (1991), for instance, contends that the delinking of nation and capital in favor of flexible production and flexible accumulation on a global scale has put the notion of national development, and with it its temporal registers, at risk of becoming irrelevant. Anthropologist James Ferguson (2006) nuances Harvey's claim by arguing that, as global capitalist forces have undermined African governments' authority over collective development, the temporal emphasis of modernity has given way to a spatial focus. With the erosion of the nation-state as a vehicle for collective progress, people no longer see themselves as catching up to modern societies, but instead, Ferguson argues, understand themselves as being stuck below them (189–190). Development does not, then, hinge on societal transformation over time, but on individualized movement upward (174–175). Neither he nor literary theorist Simon Gikandi (2001), who has also written on postcolonial African temporalities, find that very many of the African communities or individual culture producers they study have abandoned the teleological developmentalist notions of modernity so important to the mid-twentieth-century discourses of decolonization. What Ferguson does identify is an ever-engulfing confrontation between teleological thinking and a spatial conception of hierarchical development. Ferguson elaborates:

> Insofar as such ranks have lost any necessary relation to developmental time, they become not stages to be passed through but non-serialized statuses that are separated from each other by exclusionary walls, not developmental stairways. Modernity in this sense comes to appear as a standard of living, as *a status*, not a *telos*. The global hierarchy is thereby de-developmentalized and appears as static, without the promise of serialization. (189)

It is worth noting that Africa is not unique in this regard. Much the same assessment could be made of the twenty-first-century West as well.

To focus too closely on the spatial aspects of de-developmentalization, however, is to overlook other equally significant disciplinary effects of late capitalism's dominant temporal modalities in the Global South. In his provocative work on time and sovereignty under neoliberalism, Robert Hassan (2017) argues that the emergent global hegemony of what he calls 'network time' is defined by ever increasing speed and fueled by flexibility, efficiency, and the digital technologies of the network. Hassan writes: 'What is revolutionary (and post-modern) about the production and experience of time is that the clock-time rhythm of modernity and the clock's *basso continuo* role in modern life have been undermined, displaced and increasingly replaced by network-generated temporal flux, temporal contingency and temporal acceleration' (35). Hassan regards this as a form of 'universal temporal domination' (37) that has undermined local 'sovereign authority over lived time' (39). Even those spaces lacking the resources to maximize or basic infrastructure to connect to the networked late capitalist economy are subject to its hegemony. In her exploration of the biopolitical effects of the space-time compression associated with late capitalism, Sarah Sharma argues that the much-celebrated acceleration of late capitalist life is predicated on the slowing down of time for the legions of hotel cleaners, taxi drivers, security guards, and other similar workers in the Global North and South who make possible the conditions for the corporate classes to maintain a state of perpetual acceleration. But, Sharma counters, those for whom late capitalism means temporal stasis remain no less subject to the disciplinary regime of speed. She explains:

> It is not speed per se but the explanatory power of speed that I argue has the undue effect of preparing more and more sites for the institutions of modern power to intervene in bodies in increasingly invasive and inequitable ways … Shared across the temporal differential is not so much the general speed of life but rather the expectation that one must recalibrate. (2014: 18)

Sharma elaborates elsewhere that:

> Recalibration accounts for the multiple ways individuals and social groups synchronize their body clocks, their sense of the future or the present, to an exterior relation, be it another person, a chronometer, an institution, or ideology. That you will synch up is a demand of economic encounters and most of the productive and institutional arrangements in which we live. A deliberative recalibration is the expectation of all responsible self-governing citizens within late capitalism. (2011: 442)

In short, citizens of the postcolony find themselves subject to a new form of domination emanating from geographical spaces and economic-technological systems that look strikingly like the old colonial order.

If neoliberal temporal sovereignty constitutes a new mode of domination that dispossesses African communities of their own conceptions of time, it is not criminal in the way that the detective fiction writers of the 1950s defined colonial domination as criminal. Neoliberal temporality does not in itself violate bodies, take lives, or steal resources in any of the ways that detective fiction normatively defines criminality. Nor does it create the conditions for new forms of violation or dispossession in the way that other elements of neoliberal governance do. What the new hegemonic temporal order does do is exacerbate the insecurities, vulnerabilities, and anxieties inherent to postcolonial life in the twenty-first century. De-developmentalization, stasis, and recalibration signal the further erosion of the state's sovereign authority to oversee the mechanisms of justice, fair play, and social equilibrium. Constrained by temporal regimes not of their own making, African nation-states simply cannot lead their populations to the future anticipated by any discourse of decolonization. In place of the promised future comes entrapment in a perpetual precarious present where recalibration is expected but impossible to achieve. If the fictional detective's traditional task is to manage popular fears about emergent social relations such as these, it is thus not surprising that into this neoliberal phantasmagoria again steps the African detective, but this time pitted against multiple foes across multiple novels, demonstrating in both form and content how neoliberal time gets experienced in the postcolony as de-developmentalization, stasis, and recalibration, which is to say as an obstacle to the collective justice promised by decolonization.

Of the recently serialized Anglophone African detective fiction novelists, Parker Bilal's hard-boiled detective thrillers and Kwei Quartey's police procedurals stand out for how they illuminate ways that detective genre serialization can be made to register the shifting parameters of neoliberal time in the Global South. In content, Quartey's and Bilal's series investigate the violence that inheres to market rationalities. Like the African detective novels examined in the previous chapter, the crimes at the center of Bilal's Makana thrillers and Quartey's Darko Dawson procedurals are prompted by the crises of a hegemonic market logic in which the novels themselves have been produced and circulate. The novels are set in Egypt and Ghana, respectively, countries where corporate capitalists, entrepreneurial gangsters, foreign fortune-seekers, and politicians jockey for control over the spoils of the loosely regulated economy. These are emphatically settings where any vestiges of Nasser- or Nkrumah-era nationalism have been overwhelmed by the virtue of heedless and cynical self-interest and the unshakable logic of the market. On the whole, the two series read like mini histories of the recent neoliberal past: Quartey traces Ghana's evolution into a late capitalist market economy through the criminality it engenders; Bilal reconstructs an Egyptian narrative of state financialization as it intersects with Islamist politics and U.S. imperial intervention and destabilization of the region. The two series offer their readers variations on the same narrative formula: while the crimes themselves typically turn out to hinge on private interpersonal jealousies and resentments, Quartey and Bilal situate those conflicts within the broader context of the dangers posed by the unequal distribution of capitalism's spoils. In their novels these dangers include, but are by no means limited to, the social and environmental costs of unregulated markets, the assertion of sovereign right by market makers, and the perception of the poor as disposable and unworthy of the state's protection.

In mapping these material manifestations of neoliberal reason, the two series reveal a great deal about the resulting reconceptualization of time, both in terms of the difficulties of resisting the hegemony of speed and efficiency and of the violence inflicted on those unable to achieve its velocities. But insofar as the two series share a common focus on the insecurities wrought by neoliberal capitalism, they diverge in their approach to the implications of its temporalities. They diverge, too, in their employment of seriality as a means of critical engagement. While Quartey's series seeks to sustain an older nationalist teleology, its series-spanning umbrella narrative, conversely, encodes the values of speed and efficiency as a pathway to that future. The series consequently generates significant measure of consent for neoliberal temporalities in a manner that obscures their threat to postcolonial temporal sovereignty. By contrast, for Bilal, the series format offers the opportunity to explore seriality as a narrative technology for illuminating how the stasis and expansion of time characteristic of neoliberal capitalism in the Global South has all but overwhelmed the nationalist temporalities so frequently invoked in the series' individual instalments. Which is to say, Bilal puts seriality to work to explore a radically different experience of the end of history than is envisioned by global capitalism's champions. And it is a dystopic vision that registers as critique. A comparison of the two series thereby illuminates both the limits and possibilities of seriality for critically engaging the problematics of neoliberal sovereignties.

Quartey's and Bilal's Neoliberal Social Worlds

First published by U.S.-based press Random House and later by its imprint Soho Crime, Kwei Quartey's Darko Dawson police procedurals take the whole of the Ghanaian nation-state for their setting, stitching together urban and rural, port city and capital, ancient governing seats and modern centers of power through the hard-won achievements of police inspector Darko Dawson.[1] Quartey's is the Ghana that Brenda Chalfin describes 'as a neoliberal pacesetter (and supposed success story)' (2010: 6) on the African continent, having begun the implementation of austerity measures, deregulation, and the privatization of state industries and services earlier than other countries. By the time of the publication of Quartey's first novel in the series, *Wife of the Gods* (2010), market reform in Ghana had already led to a significant realignment of the state's remaining resources and sovereign power away from those governmental agencies responsible for social welfare. The costs of such priorities are reflected in Quartey's narratives. Minimally funded HIV-prevention programs, unfettered electronics-waste importing and dumping, loosely patrolled offshore oil drilling, unregulated gold mining, and rapacious commerce in the name of Christianity provide the context for the flourishing of the abuses and crimes that Dawson investigates. The victims of his stories are typically those individuals most at risk of predation in the market economy. They include women sold into marriage by poor families, brutalized miners in Ghana's illegal and ecologically disastrous gold mines, homeless youth eking out a living by melting down dumped electronics for salvageable copper, and even middle class but nevertheless economically precarious wage workers. Moreover, the diffusion of Pentecostal Christianity into the spaces vacated by the neoliberal state is touched on as

---

1 Quartey has yet to receive extensive critical attention. Two articles to make more than a passing reference to his novels are: Patricia Fox (2019) and Kate Horsley (2013).

a plot line in *Death by His Grace* (2017) and, obliquely, in the character of Darko Dawson's mother-in-law who regularly implores Dawson to attend her charismatic church.

Individually, the novels read as morally salutary social problem novels with Dawson as an identifiable everyman looking to get by and to do his small part in mitigating the new vulnerabilities suffered by the larger part of Ghana's population. As a series, the novels trace an arc of social transformation. Near the beginning of the fourth novel in the series, *Gold of Our Fathers* (2016), Dawson laments 'Oh Ghana … Why can we never get it right the first time?' (11). To Dawson's attentive readers, the lament reads as a reminder that the series has, all along, been crafting a longer serial narrative of the Ghanaian state, symbolized by its ace police investigator, finally making progress on 'getting it right'. As a law enforcement officer, Dawson understands 'getting it right' in terms of ensuring the legal rights and protections of the country's citizens. Through his experiences as a working man struggling to traverse clogged roads, as a community member fostering a homeless youth, and as a biological parent of a child with chronic health problems, Dawson also understands this notion in terms of the myriad ways that the African nation-state after independence was supposed to oversee infrastructure, healthcare, education, and the other markers of modernization and collective development.

In significant respects, Dawson's motivations align with this statist conception. In *Gold of Our Fathers*, for instance, Dawson endeavors to uncover the identity of a murderer but also hopes that his investigation will motivate the government to draft and enforce stronger labor and environmental regulations of the country's informal gold mines. In *Children of the Streets* (2011), Dawson's identification and arrest of a serial killer who targets unhoused youth prompts him to outbursts of frustration with Ghana's education system and social work services for failing to keep the children in school and in secure home environments, whether with their biological or foster families. He adopts one of those children but maintains no illusions that individual efforts such as his can replace governmental programs. In these examples and others, Dawson demonstrates a deep faith in a progressivist vision of the postcolonial state as the driver and, indeed, moral authority for achieving collective justice, security, and betterment over time. With his first-hand knowledge of the Ghana Police Service's (GPS) many shortcomings, Dawson sets himself the task of transforming the entire institution of the police to better serve Ghana's citizens. In what develops as a series-spanning narrative, Dawson slowly remakes the institutional culture of the GPS from the inside in ways designed to maximize its institutional capacity as a vehicle for national development.

Published in England by Bloomsbury, Parker Bilal's six Makana mysteries are more cynical and violent than Quartey's morally salutary and optimistic tales.[2] They bear hallmarks of the police procedural used so effectively by Quartey, but Bilal's works are hard-boiled thrillers almost as much as they are detective mysteries. 'Parker Bilal' is the pen name for the British-Sudanese literary novelist Jamal Mahjoub, who explains that his own motivation for turning to crime fiction was in no small part financial, but whose longstanding literary preoccupations are decidedly historical (Crace 2013).[3] Caroline A. Mohsen sees in Mahjoub's literary fiction a 'clear historiographic project ... in which Mahjoub seeks to find the early reasons for the failure of the present-day [Sudanese] nation' (2000: 541).[4] His literary novels focus extensively on memory, cultural amnesia, migrancy, exile, and landscape. These thematic foci also pervade his Egypt-set Makana mysteries. After a visit to his parents who were living in exile in Cairo, Mahjoub found himself trying to make sense of the conditions that led to Egypt's 2011 revolution and precipitated its apparent failure (Crace). The result was his series of private detective stories set in late twentieth- and early twenty-first-century Cairo – and the creation of the writing persona Parker Bilal. Where the historical meditations on Sudanese nationalism in Mahjoub's literary fiction look back as far into the past as the Mahdi's anticolonial resistance in the 1880s, Bilal's meditations assess the much more recent past of the region as it has been impacted by two American wars, the rise of Islamist radicalism, and the proliferation of neoliberal economic rationalities that link them.

Bilal's protagonist, Makana, inhabits Cairo as an outsider, a former Sudanese police officer forced to flee his homeland in the 1990s after running afoul of the regime for investigating its leaders for criminal activities. Throughout the series, Makana remains haunted by exilic loss and the guilt of having abandoned his wife and daughter to a likely death in Khartoum. Working in Cairo as a private investigator instead of as an official of the state as he did in Sudan, Makana offers the promise of privatized justice for those ill-served by a corrupt, self-serving, and inefficient Egyptian government. In these respects, Bilal offers his reader a radically autonomous and atomized protagonist with no claim to any of the social supports of family, community, or state and whose precarity remains mitigated only by his wits, his always provisional entrepreneurial alliances, and, on very rare occasions, his pistol. He would appear to represent the radically

---

2   To distinguish the critical engagements of the author's detective novels from his literary novels, I hereby refer to Mahjoub as Bilal when discussing the Makana mysteries.
3   In the same interview, Mahjoub reveals that his first attempt at a thriller, written before the Nordic Noir boom, was set in Copenhagen. He jokes that were it not for better timing he could have 'cashed in' (Crace).
4   For a representative sampling of the scholarship on Mahjoub's writing, see Yasemin Mohammad (2017), Jacqueline Jondot (2015), and Jopi Nyman (2011).

free individual economic agent fantasized by Friedrich von Hayek, Milton Friedman, and other theorists of the free market. Moreover, the Cairene social world he inhabits remains wary of the state and not just because its inhabitants work outside the law or are disproportionately vulnerable to state sanctioned violence. Yet, Makana's ethical drive for collective justice and the series' larger historical frames suggest not celebration of radical autonomy or privatization but their critique.

Like Quartey's series, Bilal's stitches together a multi-novel narrative arc. But it is not one that depicts Egypt finally 'getting it right'. Instead, each instalment incrementally widens a historical contextual frame for the interpersonal violations Makana is tasked with solving. The series begins with stories of localized, seemingly private crimes. Makana investigates a case of extortion against a conglomerate owner in *The Golden Scales* (2012) and violence against children in *Dogstar Rising* (2013). Subsequent novels widen the frame by illuminating the local fallout from U.S. imperial adventures in the region in the years following the first and second American invasions of Iraq. Peppered through the six novels are references to the two American invasions, the anti-American fervour of dispossessed young Arabs, 9/11, and the extrajudicial renditions carried out by the CIA. In the series' second instalment, for example, Makana encounters one Egyptian, burning with jihadi fervour, who tells Makana of his flight training, clearly in preparation for the 11 September 2001 attacks, and in *The Burning Gates* (2015), a promising lead directs Makana to an American private contractor officially working for the U.S. military in Iraq but offering surreptitiously his 'security' services beyond Iraqi borders.

In equal measure, Makana uncovers intrigues prompted by local manifestations of regional and global conflicts over unregulated financialization and trade. *Dogstar Rising*'s central conflict, for instance, turns on the quasi-criminal machinations of an Islamic bank seeking to drive financial returns for its legitimate enterprises. In *The Ghost Runner* (2014), the mystery hinges on the unregulated cross-border flow of consumer goods and military matériel. With each new title in the series, Bilal fleshes out an increasingly detailed portrait and chronology of the complex interconnections of local, regional, and global power players, including corporate capitalists, financial institutions, government officials, organized crime syndicates, and Islamist political groups. Consequently, the series reads as a mini historical narrative of the jockeying for the outsized power and profits that have become newly available with Egypt's neoliberalization. If the military destabilization wrought by the United States and militant Islamist groups provides a dramatic backdrop for the series, these economic transformations prove to be much more significant in the narrative foreground in terms of generating the risk, precarity, and exploitation that fuel the crimes Makana gets tasked with investigating.

Makana's commissions are typically of the low-budget variety that a socially marginal exile like him could expect, but they put him in regular contact with a cast of powerful figures in neoliberal Egypt. As his investigations of small-scale crimes reveal the broader social destabilizations wrought by unregulated capitalist markets, one or more of the men repeatedly show up as a key market maker, profiteer, or enforcer of Egypt's economy, and whose activities indirectly precipitate the crimes that Makana investigates. Included in this cast are Daud Bolat (*The Golden Scales, Dark Water*), a freelance thug whose acute understanding of the logic and profit centers of Egyptian corporate capitalism give him an outsized advantage in wringing revenue from its ruling elite; Lieutenant Sharqi (*The Ghost Runner, The Burning Gates, Dark Water*), a high ranking counter-terrorism officer in the Egyptian state security forces who oversees an unofficial free trade zone on the Egypt border and monitors the official flow of people and goods at Cairo's international airport; and the Zafrani brothers (*Dogstar Rising, The Burning Gates*), powerful crime bosses who might be better described as conglomerate co-CEOs of Egypt's informal economies and who like to invoke rhetoric about the inefficiencies of the state and the social benefits of their entrepreneurial approach. As one example of the Zafranis' market-based ethos, Zayed Zafrani makes a case for the greater effectiveness of private development at a construction site that 'back in the heady days of 1960s Nasserist socialism … had been open farmland allocated to young technocrats' (2015: 112). He explains, not entirely cynically, that 'for decades now the government has failed to help the weakest in society … In the meantime, we do what we can' (113–114). In the series' symbolic landscape, Bolat represents the blurred line distinguishing extortion from legitimate production in a loosely regulated economy, Sharqi signifies the shift in postcolonial governance from the management of public security to the management of cross-border commercial flows, and the Zafrani brothers reflect the anti-statist rationality of entrepreneurial self-governance. Also included in most of the instalments are two police officers, Inspector Okasha and Makana's former Sudanese rival, Mek Nimr, archetypes in the global hard-boiled canon whose heedless careerism regularly undermines the workings of state-enforced justice.

Seriality and Its Uses

Crime mystery writers have access to two types of seriality. The first is the serialized story in which a single mystery develops over several instalments, each punctuated by a cliff-hanger ending and the last delivering an anticipated resolution. These typically appear in magazines and other serial publications. The second is the detective story or novel series such as is employed by Quartey and Bilal. These are usually authored by a single writer and feature a single detective protagonist over the course of successive texts. Each individual story or novel in the series narrates a discrete self-contained mystery. With his three Auguste Dupin mysteries, Edgar Allan Poe inaugurated the latter form of detective fiction seriality simultaneously with his solidification of the genre itself.[5]

Seriality is in no way new to African crime fiction writers. The earliest identified Anglophone African detective stories are serials of the first type and appear in magazines, newspapers, and on the radio. As detailed in previous chapters, Arthur Maimane's for *Drum* magazine in the 1950s, *African Film* and *Boom* serial photonovels in the 1960s, and Ghana's serialized newspaper fiction and comics in the 1960s and 1970s simultaneously Africanized the crime mystery and earned their protagonists the same kind of name recognition with African audiences as Christie's Miss Marple and Hammett's Sam Spade enjoyed with theirs. Like their global counterparts, Anglophone African detective fiction writers have embraced seriality to explore the repertoire of their creations' ingenuity and heroism and, of course, to seek the profits that come with a successful series. For the writers and their publishers, an individual instalment in a mystery series is the paradigmatic commodity, designed for quick obsolescence while fueling the reader-consumer's addiction-like desire for its successor. Matthias Krings highlights South Africa's Drum Publication's success in generating steady readership from issue to issue of *African Film*, for instance, when he describes the anticipation with which Anglophone African consumers waited to turn over their savings for each new instalment in Lance Spearman's ongoing battle against his criminal foes (2015: 71–78). With cliffhanger ending after cliff-hanger ending, the Ghanaian newspaper serials from the 1960s and 1970s, which I discussed in Chapter 2, simultaneously helped sustain consumer loyalty to the papers themselves. Fledgling magazines also turned to serial crime stories as a way of establishing readerships. During its brief 1971–1974 run, *Pleasure: Ghana's Sunshine Magazine*, for example, ran at least two overlapping serialized detective stories, Cofi Quaye's six-part 'The Copper Wire Conspiracy' and Ali Yemoh's (1973) multi-instalment graphic narrative featuring the mystery adventures of Oko and Ebo.

Despite these experiments in story serialization, the second type of serialization remained underrepresented in Anglophone African writing into the 1990s. Writers and readers in Anglophone Africa had at their disposal imported mass market series featuring Doyle's Sherlock Holmes, Christie's Hercule Poirot and Miss Marple, and Fleming's James Bond. Flora Nwapa is reported to have been an avid reader of Agatha Christie mysteries (Ogunyemi

---

5   One might include a third type of series, genre-based series such as Macmillan's Pacesetters, which publish a specific literary genre though not necessarily multiple titles by the same author. This type is not my interest here. See Chapter 2 for a discussion of Pacesetters and other similar publishing series.

1996: 195), Cyprian Ekwensi was a regular consumer of such detective novels (Lindfors 1982: 37), and Bloke Modisane poured over every Leslie Charteris detective novel he could get hold of (Modisane 1963: 166–67). African writers themselves, however, were not producing novel series. The few exceptions include James McClure's eight Kramer and Zondi mysteries, David G. Maillu's two Benni Kamba 009 secret agent adventures, Hope Dube's and Victor Thorpe's respective two-title series for Pacesetters, and Sola Oloyede's two novels in his Brotherhood of the Silk Handcuff series. Otherwise, the 1970s and 1980s were marked by stand-alone titles.

Beginning in the late 1990s these patterns change when single-author series publication emerges as a viable option for Anglophone African authors. In addition to Quartey and Bilal, Mukoma Wa Ngugi, Lauri Kubuitsile, H.J. Golakai, Michael Stanley, Margie Orford, Jassy MacKenzie, Malla Nunn, Omoseye Bolaji, Deon Meyer, Diale Tlholwe, Leye Adenle, Adimchinma Ibe, and the Rhodesia-born Scottish writer of 'Botswanan' mysteries, Alexander McCall Smith, all launched detective franchises, often for large multinational publishing conglomerates or for independent African presses such as South Africa's Kwela Books capable of striking international distribution contracts. On screen, Ghana's Shirley Frimpong-Manso's subscription-based streaming video service, Sparrow Station, also experimented with the series format in its 2010s investigative drama *Peep*. And when Nigerian novelist Helon Habila (2013) announced the creation of Cordite Books, an imprint of the Nigerian publisher Paréssia, he declared his intent to give West African readers African alternatives to franchise stalwarts 'Robert Ludlum, and Hadley Chase, and the Scandinavians'.

In Anglophone African writing, the shift to the single author series occurs in tandem with two broader, interrelated changes in the economic landscape in the late twentieth and early twenty-first centuries. The first is the transformation of the global publishing industry under the rationalities of neoliberal global capitalism. The initial stage of this transformation was disastrous for African writers of popular fiction. The IMF's and World Bank's structural adjustment programs in the 1980s decimated African publishing industries and the book trade. Currency devaluation, a cornerstone of IMF efforts to promote exports and balance payments, made the importation of paper and ink prohibitively expensive for African presses and simultaneously put imported books entirely out of reach.[6] But while World Bank and IMF marketization requirements cut off the dominant publishing avenues writers had come to rely on in the 1970s and 1980s, the increasing global consolidation of the publishing industry, itself a symptom of and survival tactic against the era's profit and efficiency

---

6 See Walter Bgoya and Mary Jay (2013).

pressures, would in the decades to follow provide African crime fiction writers unanticipated new publishing opportunities. The explosive worldwide success of Scandinavian crime fiction in the 2000s, referenced by Habila, underscored for international publishing conglomerates that well-branded crime stories, even when translated from minor languages and/or rooted deeply in unfamiliar local social milieux, could generate efficient, steady, and substantial profit. Karl Berglund notes that the scramble to sign potential blockbuster authors has, counter-intuitively, benefitted unknown writers from the global periphery whose potential profitability remains unexploited (2017: 81). But more important still, according to Berglund, is the foreignness and exoticism that generically familiar crime narratives from the contextually unfamiliar periphery represent. On this point, Berglund cites Eva Erdmann's argument that setting, rather than plot, has become a primary reason for readers turn to crime fiction because, Erdman posits, the 'inventories of criminal motives and case histories have been exhausted' (qtd in Berglund 2017: 84). Consequently, what stands out for readers in the global book market is contextual particularity, no matter how stereotypically exotic it might be in its ethnographic treatment of place.[7] One could argue that setting began supplanting plot as early as the 1930s in both whodunits and hard-boiled detective novels, but Erdmann's historicization is relevant where Anglophone African writers are concerned insofar as it signals an intensification of the dynamic and its expansion to previously peripheral global spheres.[8]

Like their Scandinavian counterparts, African franchises provide familiarity to their smaller domestic audiences in, say, South Africa or Ghana while functioning as exotica for readers located elsewhere. The snow-packed covers on Scandicrime titles find their counterpart in the international editions of African crime novels whose covers feature images of the South African veld, Nile landscapes, or other nature scenes that tap romanticized Western clichés about the continent.[9] Attentive to global scale, marketing departments highlight the familiar codes of foreignness of their products, pitching individual series as new but recognizable commodities for non-native consumers content with proven formulas but bored with a particular type of exotica. Lest readers miss the point, Mukoma Wa Ngugi's publisher Melville House, an imprint distributed by Random House, features this blurb on the front cover of his second Black Star Agency mystery, *Black Star Nairobi*: '[Ngugi's detective] may

---

7   Lauren Goodlad (2021) similarly highlights the centrality of place in serial crime genre texts but with a focus on what spatio-temporal geographies produce ontologically.
8   I am thinking of Dorothy Sayers' ethnographic treatment of the Lincolnshire Fens in her 1934 novel *The Nine Tailors* and of Hammett's Personville in *Red Harvest* (1929).
9   See, for example, Simon and Schuster's cover for Malla Nunn's *A Beautiful Place to Die* (2009) and Bloomsbury's covers for all of Parker Bilal's novels.

not as yet have taken over from Kurt Wallander in our affections, but … it's only a matter of time' and this one on the back cover: 'If you're weary of the glut of Scandinavian crime fiction, take a trip to Kenya's teeming capital city'. This seemingly contradictory messaging is anything but. Foreignness itself has become part of the familiarity of the global crime novel. Again, this dynamic is not necessarily new. Chester Himes' so-called Harlem novels benefitted from similar messaging by their French publisher in the 1950s and '60s, for example.[10] But it must be viewed as an important driver of Anglophone African popular genre writing in the late twentieth and early twenty-first century.

Given these economic dynamics, seriality's cultural affordances are multifaceted. From one perspective, seriality can generate consent for hegemonic value systems much like the detective genre itself does. As a commodity designed for continual consumption, for example, the series has long played a critical role in forming capitalist subjectivities. Film scholar Ruth Mayer highlights this problematic when she contends that twentieth-century literary and filmic seriality remain inseparable from industrial modes of production and consumer-capitalist consumption. By organizing 'time into units, modules, or segments' and through 'sequentiality, brevity, and modularity', the series and serial, Mayer writes, 'correspond to the structures of industrial modernity' (2017: 22–23). Thus, serials are not only capable of representing 'the abstract process of industrialization, social organization, and spatiotemporal structuring' but also, she argues, 'need to be seen as integral elements of these processes' (24). Mayer's emphasis on industrialization reflects her focus on early cinema. Her point that seriality has come to construct modern temporality and that modern time has come to be experienced as seriality is, however, equally relevant to late capitalist modes of production and accumulation. Network time, flux, speed, efficiency, space-time compression, and the other markers of neoliberal temporality get reflected in and encoded by contemporary modes of seriality, especially where they intersect with the multiple channels of content delivery, distribution, social media, and branding that attend commercial publishing within twenty-first century global capitalism.[11]

---

10 See Higginson's (2011) introduction for a discussion of Chester Himes and his French publishers.
11 I am thinking here also of websites and social media interaction, including, for instance, crime series author Mike Nicol's CrimebeatSA blog, which during the 2000s and early 2010s when was it most active, generated steady streams of new content and reader comments about nearly every newly published Anglophone South African crime novel and public event featuring crime fiction writers. Included too are the literary festival circuit appearances, teaser chapters for forthcoming instalments that appear at the end of some of Kwei Quartey's novels, traditional television adaptations of print novels as in the case of Deon Meyer and Alexander McCall Smith, and web series adaptations of traditional cinema releases as pioneered by Shirley Frimpong-Manso.

Yet, in much the same way that the detective genre itself is elastic in its political-ideological expressions, seriality's effects are not limited to the interpolation of writers and readers as capitalist subjects. Wielded tactically, seriality can also be employed to critique and rethink what it means to be a (neo)liberal subject under the hegemony of global capitalism. Where Quartey's and Bilal's series are concerned, two counter-hegemonic uses stand out. The first is the considerable power Benedict Anderson (1991) ascribes to seriality in fostering imagined communities. The chronotopic thickening produced by long-form series, whether in print news, the serial novel, or serial screen media, reshapes the collective experience of time and produces, per Anderson, new imagined collective pasts and anticipated futures (ch. 2). No matter its means of production, seriality remains central to the construction of modern political formations, including but not exclusively the postcolonial nation-state. Quartey and Bilal clearly put this use of seriality to work with their series-long narrative arcs. The Swaziland-born mixed-race South African novelist Malla Nunn does as well. Her four-novel crime mystery series (2009, 2010, 2012, 2014) traces the implementation of the first of the Afrikaner-led Nationalist Party apartheid laws from the late 1940s to the early 1950s in ways that simultaneously serialize white supremacist state-making and the formation of a collective Black and mixed-race racialized anticolonial consciousness.

The second opportunity afforded by seriality is its power to encode bildung's opposite, narrative stasis. For writers probing the problematics of neoliberal temporal hegemony in the postcolony, narrative stasis generates several challenges that chronotopic thickening does not. But it affords compelling opportunities for critique as well. Regarding the challenges, to franchise a detective series is to make a near fetish of repetition – of plots, tropes, themes, settings, and characters – repetitions that not only secure each series its brand identity, efficiencies, and profits, but that can also potentially structure the series as perpetually presentist and ahistorical, thereby complicating any attempts at chronotopic thickening of nation-time or at reigniting stalled liberationist teleologies such as those seen in the Nigerian novels discussed in Chapter 3.[12] But stasis can also be deployed as a narrative strategy in and of itself. One of the most fascinating ways to mobilize narrative stasis as critique is to make repetition itself historicize the stasis associated with neoliberal de-developmentalization. This can be achieved by drawing attention to the ideological and material conditions that lock characters and plots in a perpetual present. To accomplish

---

12 In the same vein, while crime series continue to gain their identities from their distinctly national settings and the citizenships of their producers, their production as global novels by global presses for global markets risks disaggregating them from specific material histories.

that requires putting seriality's two temporal propensities – bildung and looping repetition – in productive tension with each other.

In different ways, Kwei Quartey and Parker Bilal employ seriality's two temporal propensities to make sense of the de-developmentalist effects of neoliberalization. Of the two, Bilal more effectively generates the productive tension necessary to historicize and critique neoliberal economic and temporal hegemonies. Quartey's series, by contrast, gives a contradictory account. As outlined above, Quartey's five-novel series locates the violent disorder of twenty-first century Ghanaian life firmly within the context of neoliberalization and stitches together a series-spanning metanarrative of state-led collective development. However, its uses of seriality contravene this statist framework by encoding the neoliberal temporal recalibrations described by Hassan and Sharma as the pathway out of neoliberal violence. Despite never resolving this contradiction, the Darko Dawson series remains useful to students of African genre fiction for illuminating the significant challenges involved in turning neoliberal seriality in resistance to neoliberal capitalist rationalities. To understand the ends to which Anglophone African novelists might put seriality in their dissection of the crises of twenty-first-century African society, it is thus helpful to assess the contradictions of Quartey's series before turning to Bilal's nuanced critical engagements.

Efficiency, the Meritorious Self, and the State

For Darko Dawson, efficiency, and its resulting velocity, is crucial for the Ghanaian state's achievement of its long-anticipated promise. Indeed, a regular feature of the series is Dawson's routine articulation of his dismay with the inefficiency resulting from the poor state of the GPS's record keeping and forensics resources. His frustration functions in part as a broader commentary on the adverse impact of governmental austerity and the general budgetary constraints of countries in the Global South. Readers learn in the first novel of the series, for instance, that GPS can afford only twelve forensic pathologists for the entire country (2009: 59) and in the fourth novel that the DNA lab lacks the financial resources to meet demand (2016: 13). But Dawson's exclamations about these shortcomings also serve to highlight inefficiencies and waste in the use of those resources that the GPS does have at hand, particularly in the form of human intelligence and labor power. Dawson's efforts are often made grossly inefficient when crime scene reports can get issued in 'a week … or next year' (2009: 71), while case files lie in 'chaos on the floor' (70), digitization progresses at a 'snail's pace' (2017: 107), and lackadaisical, lazy, and inept policing leads to missed evidence, shoddy records, and wrongful arrests (2009, 2011, 2016), but also while institutional procedure and Ghanaian law sometimes stymie expedient discovery. These obstacles to Dawson's efficient labor serve, at least in part, the narrative demands of generating of suspense, which requires delays in the detective's race against time. However, Dawson's practical efforts to correct these inefficiencies and thereby improve the performance of the GPS turn into a secondary plot line for the series. In *Gold of Our Fathers*, for instance, readers find Dawson organizing years' worth of case files that have been so chaotically arranged as to be useless (2016: 31, 33); in the same novel he also instills better discipline in the logging of station activity, making the logbooks more immediately effective for identifying patterns, suspects, and witnesses (29); and he regularly chides his lazy colleagues and gets the most negligent suspended (for brutality in *Wife of the Gods* and for drinking on the job in *Gold of Our Fathers*). In short, Dawson devotes himself to making GPS more efficient and faster in achieving its desired outcomes.

As Darko Dawson adjusts himself to an expectation of synchronization to a hegemonic accelerated network time, despite the absence of the robust and reliable infrastructure to support such acceleration, he seeks to discipline those around and below him to it as well. In this way he becomes a vehicle for a temporality of neoliberal capitalism that rests uneasily with the developmentalist nationalism otherwise advocated by the novels. Dawson's greatest effort in maximizing the GPS's institutional potential comes in the form of modeling a meritocratic, achievement-oriented ethos that produces the velocities and efficiencies he sees as necessary. Throughout the series, Dawson offers himself as much as possible as a model of personal responsibility, self-sacrificial hard work, and continual self-improvement. He freely reminds his colleagues that he will not waste GPS's limited human resources by discussing sports or politics on the clock (2016: 13). In a climate where police officers routinely extort bribes from victims for preferential service, he is considered 'a saboteur' for following protocol strictly and equitably (2017: 123). Moreover, he makes transparent the increasing self-control and self-discipline that he brings to his work. In the early novels of the series, Dawson's inability to contain his anger at those who abuse their power or the public trust leads him to commit his own acts of police brutality that break the laws he is charged with upholding. By the fourth instalment in the series, Dawson's dogged efforts to channel his rage into disciplined, professional investigatory labor pay off in the form of a reputation for superior results and a promotion from Detective Inspector to Chief Inspector (2016: 16). With his institutional authority, he rewards others for enacting similar values, as he does from the first to the second instalments when he orchestrates a desired transfer for Constable Gyamfi, a junior officer with 'great integrity and promise' (2011: 7).

The most dramatic impact of Dawson's modeling of self-improvement and goal-oriented achievement comes in the transformation over the course of several novels of his boss's nephew, Philip Chikata. Quartey introduces Deputy Sergeant Chikata in the first instalment as an unqualified and entitled nepotism hire, more inclined to prop 'his gigantic feet on his desk as he listened to the call-in morning show on Happy FM' (2009: 26) than to solve homicides, or indeed to act with any sense of urgency. When first partnered with the 'spoiled ... lazy' young man in the second novel of the series (2011: 30), Dawson is commanded to give the unmotivated Chikata more responsibility than he is prepared for. Dawson hopes that Chikata's missteps will reveal his unworthiness to their chief, Chikata's uncle. Chikata initially falters, wasting already limited time and resources, but by giving the younger officer a challenging goal and competing with him to complete it, Dawson unintentionally unlocks Chikata's potential, triggering Chikata's pride in hard work and hard-won achievement. So successful is Dawson in developing Chikata's individual initiative that by the third novel in the series Chikata has not only become one of Dawson's most trusted colleagues but has been given cases and a team of his own to train and mentor. By the fourth entry, so valuable are the two men to the GPS individually that Dawson, newly promoted, and Chikata, in training for its most elite tactical unit, must scheme to work a case together. The fifth novel sees Dawson's role as mentor formalized, working regularly in the police academy to similarly professionalize new recruits, turning them, like Chikata, into additional vehicles for neoliberal rationalities and the calibration to the hegemonic temporalities of late capitalism.

All these demands for efficiency, meritorious achievement, and recalibration are presented in terms of their benefit to Ghana's most at-risk citizens and as interventions into the forms of patronage and nepotism that have foreclosed economic security for those outside existing networks of power. In this way, Quartey's seriality relies less on the future perfect narratological grammar that Robert Champigny (1977) argues is so important to the detective genre than it does on the future conditional of what *could* be.[13] For Dawson, and perhaps for Quartey himself, efficient disciplined labor by individuated achievement-oriented citizens could easily lead to the long-promised realization of a modernist postcolonial state. The responsibilized actions of individuals, not structural transformation, offer the clearest pathway to that future. By repeatedly emphasizing that the institutions and bureaucracies of the state need to accommodate such figures as are willing to recalibrate themselves and their underlings to a culture of speed, Quartey's series thus normalizes as common-sense neoliberalism's foundational rationalities. As I suggested earlier, these neoliberal methods rest uneasily with the novels' portrayal of the economic and physical vulnerability suffered by large swaths of Ghana's citizenry who must live with material manifestations of twenty-first-century global capitalism. Haunting the novels' depiction of environmentally disastrous electronic waste dumping from the Global North, inaccessible hotels built for multinational

---

13 See Chapter 3 for my discussion of Champigny's argument.

oil executives, and the uncheckable power of Pentecostal churches is the cost of global capitalism on Ghana's most precarious populations. Quartey never resolves this tension, shying away from opportunities to link this precarity to the neoliberal behavioral and economic precepts that it otherwise affirms. Furthermore, while the cultures of speed and meritorious achievement may indeed improve the measurable markers of state efficacy, they risk turning citizens and the state alike into participants in a sovereign governing and temporal order whose terms and conditions continue to be dictated elsewhere.

Serializing Neoliberal Stasis, Resisting Neoliberal Time

Insofar as Quartey's seriality risks encoding consent for neoliberal capitalism and its temporal registers, the twenty-first-century detective series is not an inherently consent-producing mechanism for them. On this point, Quartey's British-Sudanese counterpart Parker Bilal stands as a useful counterpoint. Where Quartey uses the opportunities provided by the series format to narrate the virtues of a culture of speed, Bilal plays on the detective series' static impulses to illuminate and assess the physical and epistemic violence that result from the stasis of neoliberal time in the Global South. Bilal establishes the thematic centrality of temporality in *The Golden Scales*, the first instalment in the series. In the novel's repeated juxtaposition of Cairo's shiny new skyscrapers, manicured gated communities, and luxurious golf resorts with the city's visibly sedimented ruins, dating back millennia, Tina Steiner sees an attempt to illuminate the multiple time frames within which Egyptians experience and comprehend progress, social change, and futurity itself. Steiner argues that the novel's depiction of Cairo's ruins reveals the ways that Egyptian history has been defined by successive revolutions, each doomed to failure and replacement: the physical traces of the ancient monarchy giving way to the public monuments and agricultural projects of Nasserist socialism giving way to the privatized enclaves of neoliberal global finance capitalism (2018: 111). In the moment of anti-statist neoliberalism in which Bilal locates his detective, *The Golden Scales*, Steiner writes, imagines 'an alternative future nurtured by a deep yearning for equality, for the rule of law and for a sense of social justice' but repeatedly sets this future against the signs of its impossibility (114).

Over the series, Bilal's interest in time centers less on the longue durée of Egyptian history and its succession of unrealized teleologies than on the experience of time in the neoliberal present. He develops this focus in and through the interplay of the twinned poles of seriality's narrative progression and stasis. The first glimpse of this polarity comes in the series' second novel, *Dogstar Rising*. Makana's journalist friend, Sami Barakat, laments that in Egypt the future that was eagerly anticipated in the early days of nationalist independence remains farther away than ever. He asserts, 'We're going backwards in time. This country used to be the vanguard of the Arab world. Books, movies, we made the best. Dissidents from less fortunate places flocked here in search of freedom. Not anymore' (2013: 59). As a recurring figure in Bilal's mystery series, the journalist retains older postcolonial nationalist commitments to progressivist-developmentalist teleologies, and his pronouncements in each instalment tend to give a larger social-structural context to Makana's investigations. But in the same novel, Bilal illuminates another experience of time, one that has come to define the lives of more and more residents of the Global South. Hired to identify the source of a threatening message sent to a tour agency catering to European and American holiday-seekers, Makana finds himself overpowered by a sense of temporal stasis. The sensation begins when Makana is left waiting in the lobby of the agency with a three-day-old newspaper and thoughts of how 'work had been slow' (4). Impatient, he glances 'at his watch to see if the minute hand was still doing its job' (5), skims belated news, and is reminded of Egypt's leaders' perpetually unfulfilled 'promises of change to come' (5). Posing as a business efficiency consultant, Makana is told that, while the tour business is predicated on speed, low margins, and high volumes (21), 'there's hardly enough work to keep one of us occupied' (131). To maintain the appearance of productive labor, and so to keep their jobs, the agency's employees fill the expansive hours with pretend work (134). For the agency's employees, time is experienced not so much as reversing, as it is in Makana's friend Sami Barakat's description, as it is slowing to a standstill.[14]

On the surface, the absence of work and the lost sensation of temporal progression that comes with it is a function of the contraction of the tourist industry in the wake of growing Islamist militancy in the region. In the novel, however, Islamist militancy is revealed to be just a single symptom of the supplanting of state-directed developmentalist paradigms by the ethos and mechanisms of an unregulated free market. Like Pentecostal churches in Africa and elsewhere across the Global South, the Islamist organizations depicted by Bilal fill the spaces evacuated by the neoliberalized state with promises of both spiritual and economic security, and they increasingly function as profit-seeking entities. When Makana peels back the layers of intrigue behind the series of threats to the tour agency, he finds not fundamentalist ideologues angry at a business that caters to scantily clad infidels but instead a finance bank, outwardly

---

14 The tour agency workers Bilal depicts are not alone in experiencing neoliberal time as stasis. From his fieldwork on unemployed university graduates in Ethiopia, ethnographer Daniel Mains notes, for example, that the boredom of joblessness and the deferral of adulthood make individual days, weeks, months, and years seem unending. For communities such as these comes the perception that time has radically expanded rather than contracted and accelerated (2007: 660). They are, Mains contends, cognizant of the expectations of the velocities described by Hassan and Sharma but self-conscious of their external relation to them.

abiding by Islamic lending principles, that has quietly purchased a stake in the same agency in order to hide off-balance sheet revenue and surreptitiously fund sectarian violence as a way of generating the kind of fear and insecurity that will increase deposits by the bank's target middle class consumers. Religious fundamentalism appears in this instance as little more than a marketing strategy. For the tour agency workers and the Egyptian middle-class that they represent, the result is yet more temporal stasis. Where the tour agency sells the image of a timeless Egypt of pharaohs and pyramids to its European and American customers, it itself has become a vehicle for the timelessness emblematic of the broader stasis produced under neoliberal capitalism.

In the context of the full series, the neoliberal stasis emblematized by the tour agency reads as a key to understanding one of Bilal's larger critical engagements. Bilal employs seriality to emphasize how temporal stasis has come to define Egyptian social life and, more importantly, uses it to historicize that stasis as a function of the region's neoliberalization. To emphasize how progressive postcolonial time has slowed to a halt, Bilal turns to the crime mystery series' propensity for repetition. The detective series is relatively unique among literary genres in that the same protagonist returns in novel after novel to solve variations on the same catalogue of crimes. While there is nothing inherently ahistorical to narrative repetition, scholars have highlighted its privileging of a perpetual restoration of a past condition over transformation or bildung. Umberto Eco contends of detective fiction serials, for instance, that:

> Instead of having characters put up with new adventures (that would imply their inexorable march toward death), they are made continually to relive their past ... Characters have a little future but an enormous past, and in any case, nothing of their past will ever have to change the mythological present in which they have been presented to the reader from the beginning. (1985: 168–69)

Franco Moretti argues similarly that

> detective fiction's characters are inert indeed; they do not grow. In this way, detective fiction is radically anti-novelistic: the aim of the narration is no longer the character's development into autonomy, or a change from the initial situation, or the presentation of plot as conflict and an evolutionary spiral, image of a developing world that is difficult to draw to a close. On the contrary: detective fiction's object is to *return to the beginning* ... So too it is with the reader who, attracted *precisely* by the obsessively repetitive scheme, is 'unable' to stop until the cycle has closed and he has returned to the starting point. (1983: 137, emphasis original)

Eco and Moretti base their arguments primarily on the golden age British whodunit, so their comments tend to overlook the modernist portraiture of alienation and psychological damage that begin to inflect the genre with the advent of hard-boiled detective narratives in the 1930s.[15] But their attention to broader patterns of character presentation and narrative progression is not altogether misplaced. The mise-en-scène might change, historical time might be shown to pass over the course of a series, but characters and plots rarely develop: new case, old methods, same starting point, a mode of repetitive looping unique to the mystery series. It is this looping repetition that highlights an ahistorical propensity in the genre even when seriality itself has been critical to temporalizing the collective historical experience of the imagined community.

Bilal activates this form of repetition to place Makana in a static present. In each successive novel Makana takes a case, identifies one or more suspects, follows various leads, and, in the end, successfully identifies his criminal antagonist. But unlike Quartey's novels, in which Darko Dawson's investigatory efforts from novel to novel get Ghana incrementally closer to an idealized future, Makana's individual cases do no more than solve individual isolated crimes. In effect, he begins each new instalment investigating the same sorts of crimes as the previous instalments with no progress toward a transformation of society through which such crimes would disappear. Bilal accentuates this stasis by highlighting his detective's inability over the series to contain Sharqi's, Bolat's, and the Zafrani brothers' marginally lawful to outright criminal dealings as they reshape Egyptian society around their entrepreneurial ambitions. Because Sharqi, Bolat, and the Zafrani brothers pose a larger threat than any of the primary criminals in any of the novels, the reader expects Makana to eventually check their individual power. Over the course of series, Bilal consequently provokes an expectation of progress and of the social or political development promised by it. Again, however, Bilal reproduces the sensation of time stopped. Instead of defeating his antagonists and thereby freeing Egyptian society from their destabilizing behavior, Makana only ever blunts a fractional edge of their power. If anything, they grow in stature and authority over the arc of the series. Retaining a cast of powerful antagonists is, of course, a productive narrative strategy for sustaining the series over time as it means Makana's work never ends. But repeating these characters is equally useful, in this case, for representing

---

15 A quick perusal of American and English television and film offerings indicate how well Sherlock Holmes, Hercule Poirot, and Miss Marple stories lend themselves to seemingly infinite recycling, with the characters and plots remaining true to formula over decades and in the hands of successive generations of novelists and screenwriters. So, too, the hard-boiled detective's psychic damage and alienation have secured themselves as generic tropes to be repeated from instalment to instalment.

the arrested telos of Egyptian decolonization as lamented by Makana's friend, Sami Barakat.

To serialize stasis is nevertheless to historicize it. For all its ahistorical repetitive propensities, the series always retains its potential for historicizing social relations over time. As I indicated earlier, the Makana mystery series reads as a mini history of late twentieth- and early twenty-first-century Egypt, and Makana's confrontations with Daud Bolat, Lieutenant Sharqi, and the Zafrani brothers over the course of the series are central to understanding Bilal's historiographical project. They, their actions, and the economic rationalities they represent provide the historical context to understand the temporal stasis that Bilal sees as defining modern Egyptian life. Makana's recurring confrontation with the state security agent Lieutenant Sharqi is a good example. Makana's first major clash with Sharqi comes in the third novel of the series, *The Ghost Runner* (2014), when an investigation into the apparent honor killing of a teenage girl unexpectedly uncovers a battle among competing government and military figures, as well as organized crime bosses, over control of the quasi-free trade zone at the Egyptian border. Makana eventually discovers that the girl's killing is one of several acts of violence that have occurred in the lawless space following the withdrawal of the formal apparatus of the state in the interests of untrammelled trade. With the weight of state power behind him and no direct connection to any of the murders, Sharqi prevails to take over the smuggling network and makes no effort to hide his new role from the stateless Makana. When Sharqi returns in the fourth instalment, *The Burning Gates*, Makana finds that Sharqi's ability to deploy state power to facilitate private trade – in this case, the art and antiquities flowing out of Iraq in the aftermath of the U.S. invasion – has become even more concentrated. And when in the sixth novel, *Dark Water*, Makana encounters the recently promoted Major Sharqi at the airport, controlling not the private movement of arms and household goods but instead the official flow of people through Cairo International Airport's immigration desks, Makana sees a man whose authority over the forms of transborder commerce previously controlled entirely by the state is almost complete. In this neoliberal milieu, Sharqi and his ilk enjoy individual elevation in status, much in the way that Ferguson identifies the new spatial understandings of modernity, with stasis the reality for everyone else.

While Sharqi is not precisely a paragon of neoliberal virtue, his incremental accumulation of the sovereign power previously held by the state frames historically neoliberal capitalism's transformation of postcolonial political, economic, and social relations. The ancillary crimes that result from his assertion of sovereign authority read as direct effects of this historical transformation. So, too, does the series' temporal non-progression. If each novel widens incrementally the series' historical contextual frame, each ultimately returns Makana to the same starting point wherein social relations remain dictated by avarice and heedless self-interest and no better for Makana's efforts in the previous instalments. If progressive time has come to a standstill, it is because the neoliberal economic and governing rationalities represented by figures such as Sharqi have subverted the traditional vehicle of the nation-state for sustaining it. The potential progress promised by seriality, so central to Quartey's narrative of ever-increasing institutional efficiency, is unavailable. Bilal preserves the sense of temporal inertia Eco and Moretti highlight, but he transforms it from the mythical to the historical. Put differently, Bilal refashions seriality's propensity for narrative non-progression, threading it through seriality's equal propensity for narrative bildung to illuminate and evaluate the historical conditions structuring neoliberal time in the postcolony. If Bilal's use of looping and eternal returns registers the valences of neoliberal temporalities, they thus simultaneously serve to serialize the Egyptian nation-state, to sustain its ongoing evolution. But rather than serialize development and incremental progress, as Quartey's Darko Dawson novels do, Bilal's Makana mysteries serialize stasis as a primary historical condition of the Egyptian postcolony in the twenty-first century. Stasis, the novels suggest in their performative seriality, has become the changing-same over time.

Re-animating the Future

In Sir Arthur Conan Doyle's stories or Agatha Christie's novels, the repetition of storylines has the effect of asserting the timelessness of liberal capitalist values. Even if temporal progress – that article of liberal capitalist faith – remains stunted in the classic whodunit, as Moretti and Eco contend, the so-called golden age writers' vision of liberal capitalism offers the promise of a viable and glorious future. In Parker Bilal's Makana mysteries, liberalism, in its late capitalist 'neo' iteration, comes across as not so much timeless as inescapable. It offers not equality and liberty but exploitation and violence, material and epistemic in similar measure. The novels end not by restoring an idealized neoliberal social order but instead by checking only its worst excesses. In this regard, Bilal's seriality signifies the 'end of history', to take neoconservative Francis Fukuyama's (1992) catchphrase very much against the grain of his meaning. For all the genre's obsession with who did what and where in the past and its mapping of the temporal logics of modernity, the future exists for the Sudanese refugee detective as little more than a bleak extension of the present.

Despite the series' bleak perspective on neoliberal social relations, it retains a glimmer of hope in older ideals of Nasserist state-led Egyptian nationalism to survive the emergent neoliberal order. Bilal signals these ideals with another series-spanning repetition, the reappearances of Makana's journalist friends, Sami and Rania Barakat. In much the same way that the Barakats supply Makana with historical context for his investigations, Makana's discoveries provide essential evidence for their stories – their news articles and his discoveries thereby merging into a serialization of Egypt's neoliberalization. Bilal's Makana mysteries depict the journalists as the keepers of a secular modern national temporality. Within the series' fictional world, Sami and Rania Barakat sustain the work of narrating the nation through their journalism, lamenting, as we have seen, the seeming reversal of nationalist teleologies, but still practicing journalism as an ethical project of fostering collectivity. For them, investigative journalism remains a potent force for sustaining national time in the face of neoliberal market rationalities. Their presence in Bilal's novels echoes earlier Anglophone African journalist detectives. Like the Barakats, Cyprian Ekwensi's Amusa Sango, Hilary Ng'weno's Scoop Nelson, Mohamed Tukur Garba's Tahir Hussein, and Chuma Nwokolo's Biodun Beckley similarly come from the investigative journalist ranks to uncover the forces allayed against African sovereignty.

Neither does Bilal abandon the promise of the modernist bureaucratic state as the vehicle for decolonization. Like their Nordic noir counterparts, Bilal's novels' critique of the state affirms rather than rejects its idealized form.[16] There is little to celebrate about the Egyptian state as Bilal presents it. And Sami Barakat's lament for the days when Egypt stood at the vanguard of the Arab world might suffice as little more than nostalgia. But Bilal's choice of a rising star of the Khartoum police in neighboring Sudan, who would still be the exemplary agent of the state were it not for forces beyond his control, is suggestive of a deeper assertion of the ideals of the post-independence developmentalist paradigms. Makana takes up the work of private investigation in Cairo because it is work that he knows, of course. He also comes across as driven by an ethos, more suited to the earlier era recalled by Sami Barakat, to carry out the work of ensuring public justice despite the absence of welfare-statist governmental authority, which is to say of ensuring the functioning of the state even where the state's sovereignty has been eroded.

---

16   Various scholars have identified what they view as a strong strain of neoliberal anti-statism in Scandinavian crime writing, highlighting for instance recurring examples in the novels of the bureaucratic inefficiencies of the police and corruption in the ranks of law enforcement, anti-statist staples of American hard-boiled crime writing but presumably previously rare attitudes in Scandinavia's robust welfare states. At the same time, however, Bruce Robbins (2015) makes the counter-argument that Nordic noir should not be viewed as a narrative of the 'decay of the Swedish welfare state', but instead as a reassertion of its necessity in an era of neoliberal capitalism. Robbins acknowledges the critiques made of the welfare state in the Scandicrime novels but identifies an equally recurrent counter-narrative in the fiction which warns against the dangers of circumventing the law or otherwise celebrating the dismantling of the centralized bureaucratic administrative state. The central motif Robbins identifies is that public justice 'can only be properly dealt with, therefore, from outside the family: by the cold, inexpressive, unlikely representative of the state'.

The detective series format in the iteration associated with Bilal's books might be born out of neoliberal restructuring of global publishing. The format might lend itself to an ahistorical presentism. The series-spanning narrative arc might, moreover, privilege a narrative of the decay of the developmentalist state under the emergent hegemony of neoliberal economic and governing rationalities. Yet, like so many of his fellow Anglophone African detective fiction writers, Parker Bilal puts the genre's narrative logic and its ideological engagements to work to re-animate and sustain the project of decolonization.

Managed Risk and the Deadly Allure of Transparency

6

Rosina Umelo's *Finger of Suspicion* (1984) and Angela Makholwa's *Red Ink* (2007) emerge, respectively, from the diverse political and cultural geographies of late oil-boom, military dictatorship Nigeria and post-apartheid South Africa, which is to say just prior to the extensive IMF-directed liberalization of Nigeria's economy and a decade after South Africa's new post-apartheid constitution enshrined free-market rationalities as the path to racial equality. In contrast to the crime mysteries discussed in previous chapters, which spotlight some of neoliberal capitalism's most abject victims, Umelo's and Makholwa's novels focus on the lives of neoliberal capitalism's presumed beneficiaries, the upwardly mobile business owners and corporate managers who make up a small but important segment of African society. Their protagonists are in many ways exemplars of neoliberal virtue. They embrace unreflexively both the core liberal values of individual freedom and unfettered entrepreneurialism and the neoliberal-inflected ideals of data-driven decision-making, self-branding, and continual improvement. They are, in short, keen adherents of the neoliberal conceit that economically self-governing individuals drive societal progress. Crucially, they demonstrate their virtuous self-governance publicly through a devoted practice of personal transparency. By making visible their own investments in the self, they publicize their worthiness in communities ruled by the demands of flexibility, measurable outcomes, and meritorious reward. They demonstrate Cynthia Katz's contention that to make one's value publicly transparent through techniques of self-branding is to make oneself 'sensible to those with money and resources – to be codified as (worthy) partners' (2005: 625). By their own markers of achievement – regular promotions, an expanding client base, and increasingly lucrative contracts – the characters reap the rewards for broadcasting their neoliberal prowess.

Umelo and Makholwa test their protagonists' faith in the ideals of self-governance and transparency by plunging them into nightmare worlds where their carefully calibrated acts of self-disclosure threaten to undermine every form of security that they take for granted. Chief among the threats is the calculated charge of wrong-doing leveled by rivals seeking to gain their own personal economic advantages. For individuals whose livelihood and whose self-conception are so fundamentally predicated on unblemished reputations for being 'worthy partners' such accusations are devastating. Moreover, in a world where only those who can successfully play by the market's rules are afforded societal protections, to be declared a criminal is to be declared undeserving. To be falsely named, whether maliciously or through mistaken identity, and to find one's community suddenly allied against one is thus to face a special kind of terror. Umelo and Makholwa compound these terrors by subjecting their characters to allegations that are based on information that the protagonists themselves freely divulge in their efforts to make their value publicly visible. With echoes of Walter Benjamin's adage that 'in times of terror, when everyone is something of a conspirator, everybody will be in the position of having to play detective' (Benjamin 2006: 21), the novels' protagonists respond by propelling themselves into an investigatory frenzy to prove their innocence and re-establish their public reputations as deserving entrepreneurial subjects. For them, detection comes to function as another practice of transparency, one with the added value of assuaging the terrors of competitive economic and social relations.

Umelo and Makholwa are less interested in employing the prove-one's-innocence plot to restore their protagonists to a state of neoliberal grace, however, than they are in mobilizing it to probe the contradictions inherent to their protagonists' neoliberal conception of the sovereign self. Previously blinded by their own achievements, the protagonists are forced to recognize the contradictory nature of transparency, that it can be wielded by economic and social competitors to very different ends than those intended, and that it can only be productive when combined with strategic obfuscation. And rather than assuage the terrors of neoliberal social relations, detection is shown to magnify the persistent menace of uncontainable private desire. Left damaged if not corrupted, their protagonists emerge both paranoid and cynical, cognizant that perpetual self-vigilance is both necessary and hopelessly impossible to achieve.

By elucidating the narrative tension between celebration and phantasmagoria and between self-disclosure and mystification as symptomatic of the tensions in neoliberal reason, the arguments that follow suggest a framework for reading even those Anglophone African detective novels that are not explicitly critical of emergent neoliberal formations as diagnostic of their perils. As in the previous chapters, my comparative framework endeavors to reveal commonalities in the mobilization of the detective genre at two distinctly different moments in the African history of neoliberalization, while also allowing for attentive focus on the geopolitical unevenness and distinct local iterations of that process.

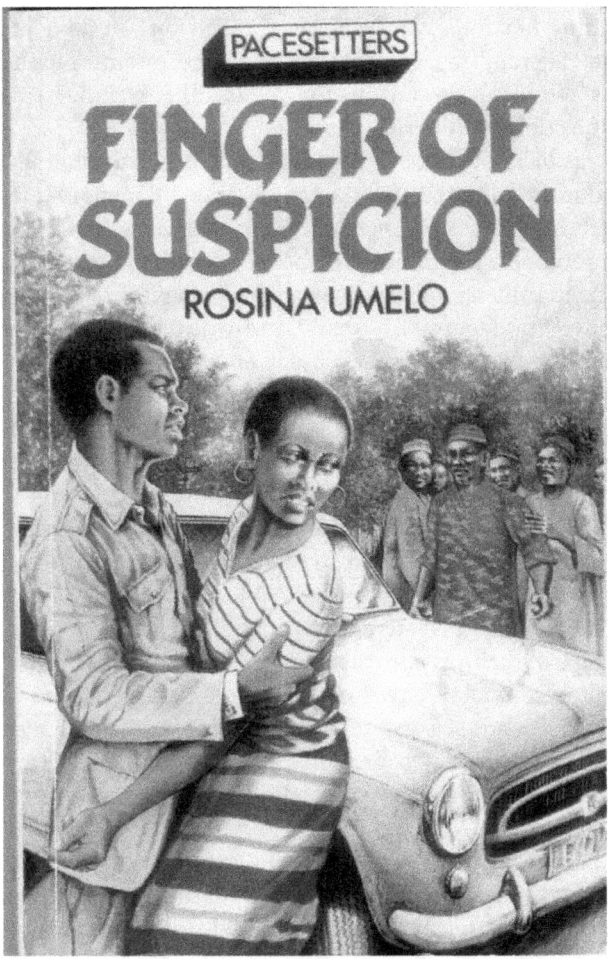

Fig. 5   *Finger of Suspicion* by Rosina Umelo (1985). Reproduced with permission of Springer Nature Limited through PLSclear.

Merit and the Visible Self

Rosina Umelo was born Rosina Martin near Liverpool, England and met the working-class Nigerian immigrant John Umelo in London in the late 1950s. They would eventually marry and move to Enugu, near John's family in southeast Nigeria. Through the years of Nigeria's civil war, its oil boom and bust, its successive military regimes, and its years of neoliberal austerity, Umelo worked as a schoolteacher, novelist, and editor. She authored eighteen books, many of them for adolescent readers and several for Macmillan's Pacesetters series, including her 1984 work *Finger of Suspicion*.[1] In its content, themes, projected audience, and engagement with broader economic rationalities, *Finger of Suspicion* stands in sharp contrast to Umelo's other writings, especially those focused on the adolescent perils of maturation.

Finger of Suspicion came out just prior to the broad liberalization of the Nigerian economy initiated in 1985 by President Babangida, the outline of which I sketch in Chapter 4. *Finger of Suspicion* reveals, however, a neoliberal ethos already enjoying a significant measure of popular consent. Like the large class of educated professionals who were able to capitalize on the country's oil wealth, the novel's protagonists, husband-and-wife pair Agu and Ebere, display a seemingly unshakeable faith in meritocracy, entrepreneurialism, and the market rationalities of self-improvement and self-governance.[2] Undergirding Agu and Ebere's faith in meritorious reward is a confidence in the value of self-disclosure and transparent data. In the novel's opening chapters, for instance, Agu's first project as a newly promoted deputy human resources manager is to implement a process for collecting data on the company's employees' outside educational achievements, an aggressive transformation of the old-boy nepotistic corporate culture that compels workers to make visible how they are investing in their individual identities as private assets (69). Ebere and her business partner extend this logic in their private catering enterprise. With a flexible production and service work model, Ebere hires workers on an as-needed basis with no attention to social status or educational achievement outside the workplace. All that matters is measurable performance: she pays higher than average wages to those who meet her rigorous expectations and refuses to re-contract those who do not (56).

Angela Makholwa's novel *Red Ink* offers its readers a protagonist similarly emboldened by the logic of neoliberal market rationalities. Intensely entrepreneurial and attentively self-governed, Johannesburg resident Lucy Khambule's first thoughts in the novel's opening are whether to launch her own public relations firm only months after joining a friend's company as a prospective equity partner, a move that she believes would secure her freedom and permit her to fully capitalize on her talents, chief among them the ability to maximize the economic benefits of branded self-disclosure. Makholwa, herself a public relations manager by profession, is recognized as South Africa's first Black woman detective novelist, and as she explains in a 2008 interview, she is 'particularly interested in the current mindset of young professional urban South

---

1 For details of Umelo's life, see S. Elizabeth Bird and Rosina Umelo (2018).
2 For an overview of the rise of Nigeria's oil-boom-fueled professional class, see Apter (2000: 274–75).

Africans ... to show that there is life beyond apartheid' (Matzke 2012a: 229).³ Indeed, the novel offers few references to the daily sufferings of life prior to 1994. In her ambitions, consumer tastes, and faith in taking individual responsibility for economic security, Makholwa's protagonist reflects the aspirational culture of the Black middle class that expanded rapidly with the ending of apartheid-era restrictions on property ownership, debt finance, and mobility.⁴ Only in her late teens at the time of the transition to democracy, Lucy reflects more specifically the generation that came of age under South Africa's break-neck economic liberalization. After decades at the forefront of collective struggle, South African youth again led the way to fashion new modes of selfhood that elevated, in Sarah Nuttall's words, 'the first-person singular within the work of liberation' (2004: 432). Utopian in spirit and neoliberal in form, South Africa's post-apartheid youth culture, Nuttall adds, tended to replace the resistance movement's vision of participatory democracy with consumer citizenship and to supplant an ethos of collective obligation with one that privileges individuated identity as 'a manipulable, artful process' (438). Like many of her peers, Lucy generally believes that liberty extends from unrestrained individualized expression and that economic reward is best secured through transparent meritorious enterprise.

The models of individual merit to which the protagonists of the two novels subscribe follow a fundamental neoliberal market rationality: as long as initiative and outcomes are made legible, every individual is equally deserving – or undeserving – as an entrepreneurial subject.⁵ But while the protagonists abide by these neoliberal ideals, the texts make equally apparent that these models of merit dispense with the safety nets provided by traditional kinship, the state, and, in its own way, the corporate enterprise. Agu, Ebere, and Lucy are consequently marked as subjects of neoliberalization, no less by their entrepreneurial and meritocratic fervour than by the risks, vulnerabilities, and microeconomic dilemmas that structure their daily existence.⁶ In this regard, they resemble closely the many protagonists and victims of the fiction that we encountered in my earlier chapters. None of the three fears falling into destitution, but their constant preoccupation with the debilitating costs of automobile breakdowns, housing, and family obligations reveals creeping anxieties about the privatized risk that they are compelled to manage in the absence of social safety nets. By

---

3   See also Makholwa (2012). Critical studies of Makholwa's writing focus primarily on her later novel *Black Widow Society*. See in particular Binder (2021) and de Kock (2016).
4   The neoliberal frameworks through which the transition was implemented are well documented. For analyses with special pertinence to the current discussion, see Jean Comaroff and John L. Comaroff (2006), Deborah James (2012), Detlev Krige (2012): 69–92; and Andrew Ross Sorkin (2013).
5   For more on the gendered entrepreneurial subject, see Carmela Garritano (2020).
6   For a discussion of the microeconomic mode, see Jane Elliott (2018).

magnifying the reader's perception that the protagonists' economic security rests on a tissue-thin foundation, these forms of precariousness heighten the novels' narrative tension. So too they permit a broader assessment of emergent social formations that the characters' own contributions to neoliberalization exacerbate, and that transparency itself is supposed to manage.

What the protagonists will discover is that transparency is not itself transparent. While the disclosure of self-investments might aid the entrepreneurial individual in attracting clients and partners, the imperative for economic self-care under capitalist social relations produces a conflict between the benefits of transparency and of mystification: that is, between broadcasting reliable information for informed risk assessment and choice on the one hand and calculating obfuscation for individual competitive advantage on the other. At risk is the veracity of information itself in what are supposed to be increasingly information-driven economies. Thus, calculating and evaluating individually generated data, with all possible permutations of self-interest, becomes one more paranoia-inducing task for the already risk-laden individual.

Competition, Mystification, and the Imperative of Detection

Umelo's *Finger of Suspicion* opens with the disappearance of Agu and Ebere's house girl, Caro, whom the couple had taken in from Agu's home village and sent to vocational school in Lagos in exchange for household labor. Agu and Ebere initially experience the eighteen-year-old's disappearance as more a nuisance than as a cause for legitimate concern. They assume that Caro, like many young women in her situation, has run off with a secret paramour to enjoy the imagined glamour of city life. Other people see the matter differently. Agu and Ebere discover that mounting ill-will toward their entrepreneurial and corporate successes, antagonism toward Agu's data-driven transformations at work, and incredulous suspicion of the efficacy of meritorious reward get condensed in the figure of the young woman's missing body. Unable to discredit Agu and Ebere without sounding merely envious, the couple's rivals, neighbors, and family members impugn their reputations by implying that they are responsible for the young woman's disappearance. The most serious charge is that the couple engaged in an act of occult violence, exchanging Caro's life for unearned wealth and power. This accusation taps the increasingly common 'satanic riches' discourse that has proliferated widely across the continent since the first moves toward market liberalization, in which the wealthy are understood to be those who have mastered the seemingly occult forces of late capitalism's spectral and speculative economy. As discussed in Chapter 4, far from representing an expression of 'traditional' belief, the charge of satanic riches represents what many scholars view as a distinctly modern response to extreme inequality.

While these reputation-wrecking efforts only reconfirm the market-based rationalities so unsavoury to the couple's antagonists – directed as they are at the couple's private selves and motivated by anger at falling behind more skilled competitors – the attacks on Agu and Ebere are also attacks on the entire neoliberal apparatus of economic self-governance. For as much as Agu and Ebere are targeted as individuals, the ethos they represent emerges as the more dangerous threat to their opponents. Thus, falling back on the same technologies of the self that have served them so well, Agu and Ebere defend their investments – in themselves, in their entrepreneurial ventures, and in neoliberalism's meritocratic ideals – in the most effective way they know: they double-down on the work of making their worthiness as transparent as possible. In this case, transparency demands that they make Caro's absent body publicly visible.

In Agu and Ebere's search for their missing house girl, Walter Benjamin's contention that the terrors of bourgeois capitalism compel everyone 'to play detective' is enacted and updated for a neoliberalizing Nigeria. Each instance in which Agu and Ebere are confronted with a false accusation or malicious workplace gossip is followed by a renewed commitment to investigating Caro's disappearance and perfecting their methods of evidence gathering and puzzle-solving, which, like the detectives of Benjamin's fascination, focus on the material traces of the woman's private life. These efforts do not, in themselves, uncover their object, but they do produce enough evidence to reassure the couple that their initial hypothesis that the young woman ran off with a lover was correct. They thereby affirm their faith in the power of self-transparency and in the necessity of playing detective as an imperative of vigilant self-governance. And, like the classic British mysteries of the late-nineteenth century and interwar years – referenced explicitly when Agu recalls Sherlock Holmes' actions in *The Hound of the Baskervilles* (77) – the couple's successes would appear also to reconfirm the broader virtues of bourgeois civil society; in their view, their own rational self-interest provides the bulwark to secure society against the abuses of the irrational desires of others.

But all the while, we as readers suspect that this faith in making one's worthiness visible to others is naïve and leaves the couple vulnerable to the darker forces of individuated competitive social relations, in which self-interest can be advanced by dissimulation, illusion, and mystification just as effectively as by disclosure. This suspicion arises contextually and textually alike. From a contextual perspective, at the time of the novel's 1984 publication, escalating competition for jobs in a contracting oil sector incentivized the falsification of educational certificates and the other visible markers of self-improvement upon which Agu bases his faith in achievement data. As professional credentials increased in importance for Nigerian job seekers in the 1970s, Andrew Apter (2000) points out that the first signs of the 'politics of illusion' that would come to pervade Nigerian political and economic culture in the era of neoliberalization were visible in the widespread exam cheating and diploma counterfeiting scandals of the late 1970s, the same ones that Chukwuemeka Ike mines for his detective novel, *Expo '77*, which I discussed in an earlier chapter. About the broader art of the '419' confidence scam that was taking shape with the neoliberalization of Nigerian society, Apter adds, 'the "seeing is believing" of the oil boom has given away to the visual deceptions of the oil bust, a social world not of objects and things but of smoke and mirrors, a business culture of worthless currency, false facades, and empty value forms' (2000: 279). To the novel's Nigerian readers in the mid-1980s, Agu's faith in credentials and other outward markers of worth would quite likely come across as dangerously misplaced.

Just how misplaced becomes clear textually when Agu finally makes the girl's living body publicly visible but without producing the results he and Ebere anticipate. Upon encountering Caro along a back road into his family's village, Agu wrings a confession from the villagers. They grudgingly reveal that they, abetted by Agu's immediate family, had constructed an elaborate ruse about Caro's disappearance to cover up a sexual scandal and thereby protect the village's reputation. They chose Agu because, for all his efforts to create conditions in which others can make themselves visible, he took little interest in uncovering Caro's motives for leaving the village. They continued to deceive him because of his propensity to beat 'the drum' of his personal business (142). In other words, to protect the future market value of the village as a competitor in the modern marketplace, they take advantage of both Agu's naïve faith that everyone will voluntarily make their value visible and of his single-minded, blinkered self-promotion. The villagers are successful because they resort not to a valorized practice of transparency, but to mystification. In a final cynical play on filial duty, they coerce Agu and Ebere into silence, leaving them unable to make transparent their own innocence and thus, their, trustworthiness as partners in the economic marketplace.

Left to make sense of his and Ebere's treatment by the villagers, Agu finds himself increasingly cynical about the beliefs he once held dear. When faced with an ambitious colleague who seeks to capitalize on Agu's inability to clear his own name, Agu himself turns to the dark arts of mystification to combat this rival and gives in to what he still views as the corruption of dissimulation and intimidation. With evidence of the colleague's involvement in a shady real estate deal – uncovered in Agu's investigatory frenzy to protect his own reputation – Agu secretly terrorizes the co-worker into a state of such profound paranoia that the man flees the company. Successful in his deception, Agu secures his upward corporate trajectory but is left corrupted. Hence, the work of disclosure, of demanding and managing transparency, serves to mitigate Agu's individual risk and to heighten his value as a site for 'foreign investment', but it also embeds him ever deeper in the morally murky social relations of a neoliberalizing world.

In narrating Agu and Ebere's confrontations with the dark underbelly of their economic value system, Umelo's novel articulates for its readers a fundamental tension of transparency as a technology of neoliberal self-governance. To make transparent one's worthiness is to confirm the promises of liberalization, but competitive social relations simultaneously incentivize self-interested mystification. Value forms, such as educational credentials, HR progress reports and other markers of meritorious achievement, are not so much emptied and made illusory as they are made unstable and unreliable so that to exist as a self-governing individual is to not simply manage economic precarity but to live in a state of permanent insecurity about the value forms by which rational self-interests are to be calculated. The novel's final lesson appears to be that to survive as a neoliberal subject is to be permanently vigilant against the self-interested deceptions, mystifications, and dissimulations of one's competitors, who are everywhere and everyone.

Managing a Public Relations of the Self

If *Finger of Suspicion*'s ultimate lesson is that neoliberalized, self-governing individuals must guard themselves against their competitors' cynical self-mystifications, Angela Makholwa's *Red Ink* makes the case that self-transparency in any form is only valuable as a strategic technology of the self and only economically productive when that which is concealed is as carefully managed as that which is made visible. Mystification is not a perversion of neoliberal ideals, but simply another tool for self-optimization. As a condition of neoliberal selfhood, Lucy must learn this lesson, applying to her private self the same risk-management branding strategies that she sells to her corporate clients. She only comes to appreciate the value of mystification after the twinned high-stakes projects that would secure her entrepreneurial ambitions plunge her into a free-market grotesquery of interlaced, competing avaricious self-interests. Lucy discovers that her friends, colleagues, and clients will eagerly exploit her skills and vulnerabilities to serve their own ends, leaving her permanently paranoid about the motivations of even those closest to her. Thus, not only does she discover, as Agu does, that she is too trusting of others' public articulations of self, she also learns at great personal and professional peril that she makes many of her own qualities, desires, and motivations too visible and, therefore, vulnerable to the machinations of others. Lucy's recognition, not unlike Agu and Ebere's, comes when detection, as a formal ordering of neoliberal society, is confronted by neoliberalism's internal contradictions. She too is consequently overwhelmed by a cynical vision of an atomized society ruled by 'bloodsuckers' (60).

Set in 2002, *Red Ink* places Lucy in a transitory moment when the public staging of the individuated self was about to be liberated officially from the collectivist claims of the anti-apartheid struggle. Less than a year later, South Africa's Truth and Reconciliation Commission (TRC) declared its work complete, and the country sufficiently unencumbered by its apartheid past to embrace a democratic free-market future. As commission architect Desmond Tutu explains, the primary goal of the TRC was to 'rehabilitate the human and civil dignity of victims' by allowing them to tell their stories of brutalization (1999: 26). Through a model of forgiveness, the commission also offered amnesty for those who voluntarily confessed to committing acts of brutality in the service of perpetuating white rule. While the TRC endeavored to defuse the resentments and demands for retribution resulting from nearly fifty years of racial tyranny, these two modes of truth-telling – perhaps unintentionally but no less potently – functioned pedagogically to help produce the self-governing subjects appropriate for the neoliberalized state enshrined by South Africa's post-apartheid constitution. For victims, the imperative to offer personal testimony reformulated the collectively experienced and resisted violence of the apartheid era as discrete individuated occurrences of suffering. For perpetrators, individual confession had the effect of recasting structural state-sponsored violence in the idiom of personal accountability. Thus, in post-TRC South Africa, the grammar of personal responsibility had come to structure the language of market-oriented self-governance. And critically, in an era of compulsory self-branding and fetishized self-transparency, these forms of individuation needed to be publicly staged.

The TRC generated its own body of investigatory crime fiction, 'truth commission thrillers' in Shameem Black's (2011) formulation, wherein detection plots function as literary analogues to the formal Truth and Reconciliation Commission proceedings. The novels are far from laudatory of the court's rhetoric or precepts. Some, including Gillian Slovo's *Red Dust* (2000) and Jann Turner's *Southern Cross* (2002), are set in TRC chambers and use the court's own suspenseful narrative codes to highlight how, through the sanctioned discourse of the perpetrator's confession, the proceedings can re-wound those whom they are intended to heal. In others, such as Malla Nunn's historical murder mystery *A Beautiful Place to Die* (2009), the police procedural is adapted to investigate the gendered collateral violence unaccounted for within the TRC framework. Yet others, including Diale Tlholwe's *Counting the Coffins* (2011), Liberia-born H.J. Golakai's *The Lazarus Effect* (2011), Deon Meyer's *Dead at Daybreak* (2000), and Margie Orford's five Dr. Clare Hart mysteries (2008, 2009, 2009, 2011, 2013), challenge the very notions that sublimated violence from the past can be safely contained or that ritualized reconciliation can deflect the desire for retribution. But as these novelists 'challenge the ideal of national disclosure before the law', they welcome the genre's normative requirement of full, unambiguous revelation (Black 2011: 48). Motives are revealed, the most unspeakable psychic trauma is expressed, and, in conspicuous contrast to the TRC's non-punitive approach, culprits are subject to the possibility of punishment. Moreover, as Black argues, disclosure and resolution 'allows for a form of knowability denied to the TRC', such that the crime mystery generates fictive truths to mediate the chasm between popular and official narratives of collective justice (55).

One of those truths is that in South Africa disclosure and transparency have long been dangerous to the country's Black, mixed-race, and Asian communities. When not carefully calibrated, self-disclosure provides a pathway not to freedom or collective justice, as promised by the TRC, but to bodily and psychological violence instead. Set in the early 1950s during the first years of the Nationalist Party's escalation of racial segregationist law-making, Nunn's *A Beautiful Place to Die*, for example, narrativizes the tensions between disclosure and concealment that would define life, and ensure a modicum of survival, under apartheid law. Her protagonist, Detective Emmanuel Cooper, serves the apartheid state in its national police force where his professional responsibility is to make visible that which is hidden, thereby ensuring the lawful and orderly functioning of the racially segregated nation-state. The specific case he works sees him investigate the murder of a stalwart of Afrikaner society, a family patriarch, farmer, and descendant of the voortrekkers of Afrikaner mythmaking. The victim's family and community expect the investigation to reveal that Black communist radicals perpetrated the killing. Cooper's work uncovers instead the murder victim's extramarital romance with a mixed-race woman. Nunn propels Cooper's investigation by fueling the reader's desire to see him make visible Afrikaner moral and racial hypocrisy. But to accomplish that in the wake of the 1949 Prohibition of Mixed Marriages Act, Cooper must fiercely guard the secret of his own mixed-race ancestry, a genealogy that is not visible on his body but which is documented in his and his parents' birth records. Under the new anti-miscegenation laws, Cooper is unlawful by virtue of the circumstances of his birth and criminal for defying South Africa's newly codified racial geographies. As his case increasingly threatens to destroy the myths of Afrikaner morality and racial purity, Cooper's antagonists, suspicious of his conspicuously concealed history, threaten to produce the documents that would deny him of his legally recognized whiteness. Such a revelation would strip him not only of his job, freedom of movement, residential privileges, and liberal selfhood, but, significantly, also of his power to make visible Afrikaner hypocrisy, venality, and criminality. But if successful concealment is the condition for successful disclosure, it is also the precondition for reaffirming apartheid racial classifications. To fight white supremacy, Cooper must cling to the privileges and power of whiteness as fiercely as he can. Nunn's great accomplishment is her elucidation of how contradictions of disclosure are foundational to South African social and political life.

As a brand manager who suffers not from the political violence of South Africa's apartheid past but from the travails of its entrepreneurial present, *Red Ink*'s protagonist Lucy is offered as a test case for the new modes of selfhood expected from the country's self-governing citizens. From the outset, Lucy is confronted with the contradictions inherent to neoliberal modes of transparency and the necessity of a more carefully managed disclosure of the self, though she neither appreciates their magnitude nor comprehends their longer South African history. The plan she formulates in the novel's opening chapters to pursue her own entrepreneurial venture is prompted by the discovery of her partner's efforts to under-compensate her for her disproportionately high contributions to the firm's profits. By chalking up her partner Patricia's self-dealing contract to her own failure to study up on legal questions, Lucy frames her plight within a familiar neoliberal rhetoric of personal responsibility. In this way, she is quicker than Agu and Ebere to learn that detective-like due diligence is a foundational quality of an entrepreneurial ethos. However, in her rush to claim her autonomy, she fails to notice that Patricia herself is being played by a boyfriend to capitalize on Lucy's baldly visible eagerness to gain an equity stake in Patricia's venture. By limiting her frame of reference to a single other person, Lucy fails to see how competitors such as Patricia are themselves entwined in larger webs of competing, parasitic self-interests. She also fails to understand that the apparent virtues of transparency are contravened by the forms of vulnerability entailed in her own public declarations. She cannot see what Nunn's Detective Cooper knows to be true about the value of mystification.

Myopic but driven to capitalize on her liberty and merit, Lucy plans a two-pronged escape. The first, as indicated, is to establish herself as an independent entrepreneur with her own public relations firm. The second, more dubious component, involves accepting an invitation from convicted serial sex crimes killer, Napoleon Dingiswayo, to tell his life story. By taking on what is effectively a PR campaign on the behalf of South Africa's most notorious sexual predator, Lucy tells herself that she will be fulfilling a childhood dream to author a book. She also admits more revealingly to taking on the project to make a public name for herself, to increase, in other words, the value of her personal brand (40). But in taking on this project, Lucy reveals the extent to which she has failed to internalize the full complement of lessons about neoliberal selfhood that her dealings with Patricia should have taught her. With the limited understanding gained from that experience, Lucy does recognize that she must employ the tools of detection to make visible Napoleon's private desires; she sees in Napoleon's motives only a simple egotistical longing for public acknowledgement of his expertise as a killer. She takes comfort in the belief that the state, here in the form of a maximum-security prison, will secure her against the risks posed by entering a commercial transaction with a convicted criminal. What she fails again to see, as she did with Patricia, is that other figures stand behind Napoleon, hidden and working in tandem to get the convicted killer's life story publicized and commoditized. One is KK Mabote, an apartheid-era political opportunist turned post-apartheid business tycoon. The other is Sifiso, Napoleon's brother, an apartheid-era petty criminal and thug-for-hire turned post-apartheid corporate manager. With much to gain and much to lose financially from the project, Sifiso and KK deploy their diverse resources to mobilize Lucy's skills as a PR wunderkind, and, as she painfully learns, to exploit for personal advantage every private detail she shares with Napoleon. In the game of wits, they have the initial advantage insofar as Lucy fails to apply more than a modicum of neoliberal common sense.

In the figures of Sifiso and KK, Makholwa highlights two central figures in South Africa's pervasive post-apartheid crime discourse who signal the country's discrepant perspectives on law and disorder in the wake of economic liberalization. The first, represented by Sifiso, is the pathologically violent Black township criminal, the *tsotsi*. The end of apartheid intensified white South Africa's phantasmagoria of this figure. During apartheid, the country's white population enjoyed the disproportionate protection of the state's security apparatus but after the end of white rule and the redistribution of policing resources, it could no longer count on the state to secure private property and physical well-being. For white South Africans, the figure of the *tsotsi* served both to depoliticize enduring grievances about racial injustice and to discredit the ANC government for its failure to contain social disorder.[7] The second figure, represented in different ways by both Sifiso and KK, is the self-dealing African businessperson who has betrayed the promises of liberation. For many of South Africa's Black citizens, who have seen few of the economic or social benefits of liberation and whose relationship to the repressive apparatus of the state remains fraught, crime emerged as an index of the perceived failures of the state and of the new racial and economic order. While the African National Congress party remained popular during the first decades of full democracy, the Black political opportunist who sells out the collectivist project of the anti-apartheid struggle for outsized personal gain became a central villain in popular discourse. Indeed, he (nearly always *he*) emerges as one of the most prominent criminal antagonists of the country's post-apartheid crime-fiction boom.[8] Makholwa herself returns to the figure of Black political opportunist in her follow-up novel,

---

7 For more on post-apartheid social panics and the figure of the Black outlaw, see Rita Barnard (2008) and de Kock (2016).
8 Three novels that stand out for featuring this figure include Thabo Nkosinathi Masemola's *Mixed Signals*, Gomolemo Mokae's *The Secret in My Bosom*, and Diale Tlholwe's *Counting the Coffins*.

Black Widow Society (2014), a noir in which a group of economically elite Black women seek murderous revenge against wayward and abusive husbands.⁹

Makholwa's interest does not appear to lie in dissecting these figurations of the Black criminal in post-apartheid discourse. In fact, she leaves them largely unproblematized. Instead, she employs them to assess the contradictions inherent in the neoliberalized work of disclosure. As in Umelo's *Finger of Suspicion*, Lucy is pressed into compulsory detective sleuthing as the price of her individual liberty. Much of the narrative details her efforts to identify and peel away the layers of subterfuge employed by Napoleon, Sifiso, and KK to manipulate her labor and capitalize on her already tenuous security. In much the same way that Agu and Ebere's investigative work does, Lucy's private efforts to make transparent that which is masked eventually pay off insofar as she escapes the men's clutches. In this way, vigilant self-governance is suggested to stand at the core of the liberal social order. But again, paranoia and cynicism intercede in the classical vision of detection as a method of affirming those liberal virtues. *Red Ink* reveals instead the underlying contradictions of neoliberal transparency. For all the ways that self-transparency elevates Lucy's investible worth-value in the eyes of her clients and for as much as she secures the larger neoliberal social order by illuminating the hidden avariciousness of others, unregulated self-disclosure simultaneously amplifies Lucy's precariousness as a private self-governing individual.

Nowhere is the failure to manage the risk entailed by reckless self-disclosure clearer than when Lucy reveals to Napoleon her anger at Patricia's self-dealing, her anxieties about a romantic involvement, and her excitement about landing a lucrative campaign to rebrand the city of Johannesburg not as a center of crime and decay but as a global capital for the creative class. Napoleon passes these revelations along to Sifiso and KK, who, in turn, use the information against Lucy for their own ends. As Lucy persists in thwarting their efforts to control her labor, they begin to kill off her enemies and friends, seeking alternately to frame her for their crimes and to terrify her into submission. Taking no chances, they also plot to ruin her entrepreneurial future. On the eve of her Johannesburg campaign debut, they telephone the city hall liaison with lurid fabrications of past prostitution and drug convictions, charges that are at carefully calibrated cross purposes with the goal to brand the city's clean-up (161). Even though the accusations are false, they capitalize on unnecessarily divulged information about the content and economic importance of the PR project. And, as is the

---

9 De Kock writes that the 'Black Widow Society is shown to operate in a world where political connections, struggle credentials, daughters, sons, nieces, nephews of exiled politicians washed up and renewed [*sic*] to emerge as BEE entrepreneurs or "tenderpreneurs" (Makholwa 11). That is where conventional politics has brought matters' (2016: 114).

case for Agu and Ebere in *Finger of Suspicion*, the accusations simultaneously undermine Lucy's entrepreneurial initiative and cast her as an undeserving criminal outsider to the meritocratic order. The liaison's own detective-like due diligence deflects that attack, but no amount of sleuthing can obviate Lucy's insecurity so long as she persists in making fully public the private details that lay bare her self-investments. In the larger parable of the novel, this reckless publicizing of her anxieties and strategic plans reads as the complete failure to protect her personal brand in the competitive marketplace of a post-apartheid South Africa in which everyone is out to take advantage of everyone else.

So again, as in Umelo's novel, *Red Ink* illuminates a series of contradictions in neoliberal reason: to make one's value publicly transparent is to subject oneself to the avariciously self-interested machinations of economic competitors; transparency provides a central technology of self-care and simultaneously the ammunition for one's destruction; and the technology that is touted as essential for privatized security is, at once, the same technology which amplifies one's precarity. In *Red Ink*'s final pages, after Lucy has prevailed over Sifiso in a bloody confrontation, she attempts to reconcile these contradictions. Ever the responsibilized private economic agent, she fulfills her contract with Napoleon, but does so with a clear demarcation of her professional and private selves, revealing nothing to the pathological killer that might compromise her economic or bodily security. If a chastened, and now permanently paranoid, Lucy proceeds into a future beyond the narrative with a clearer understanding that, if transparency remains a critical tool for self-governance, it exists as such only insofar as that which is made visible is as attentively calibrated as that which is obscured. Lucy's hard-earned knowledge that she must make visible the hidden motives of her competitors and simultaneously more carefully manage her own immerses her more fully than Agu or Ebere in the enveloping, perilous waters of neoliberal reason, but the reader is left with the same doubts about the viability of her efforts to reconcile neoliberalism's contradictory imperatives.

Conclusion

As tempting as it is to read formal critiques of neoliberal technologies of the self into the two detective novels, the protagonists' brushes with ruin only transform them into more effective self-governing subjects who can lay greater claim to meritorious achievement. In the marketplace of competitive social relations, their newly acquired abilities to mobilize modes of disclosure make them all the fiercer opponents. If, however, *Finger of Suspicion* and *Red Ink* refuse to critique neoliberal reason outright, the novels nevertheless diagnose a critical problematic inherent to it. For as much as the novels normalize detective work as a foundational practice of vigilant self-governance, they illuminate the underlying tensions and contradictions of transparent self-disclosure as a neoliberal technology of the self. Thus, they make visible, even in their tacit consent to neoliberal reason, the ways that transparency is not all that it appears. In an era when sub-Saharan African nation-states including Nigeria and South Africa have witnessed popular mobilizations for specific policy measures associated with neoliberal rationalities, it is crucial then to acknowledge the central place of the detective genre, to repeat Sarah Nuttall's formulation, in the contested elevation of the individual 'within the work of liberation'. Questions about the extent to which detective novels stage the neoliberalized state, whether they implicitly or explicitly call for the naked power of the state, and how they figure normative citizenship are only just becoming decipherable and require careful consideration. But clearly these seemingly escapist entertainments are performing critical cultural work in the transformation of African communities. At the very least, as diagnostic texts that elucidate the tensions and contradictions inherent to neoliberalism, they make transparent in their own way not only the crises and conflicts confronting the readerships with the leisure time and resources, but also perhaps the pedagogical need to consume neoliberal noir.

Conclusion: The Future Imperfect

The locked-room mystery typically comes to its dramatic close with the detective gathering everyone together to reveal the identity of the culprit. To the captive audience the detective tells two stories. The first is that of the murderer's motivation and sequence of actions leading up to the seemingly perfect crime. The second is that of the detective's own investigation and reasoning through of the available evidence. This moment in the locked-room whodunit is, in Robert Champigny's (1977) formulation, the twinned story of 'what will have happened'. Champigny explains that it is the narrative equivalent of the grammatical future perfect in which the detective explains what will have happened in the lead up to the crime and what will have happened in the lead up to the detective's astonishing revelation. This narrative grammar puts the reader in the present tense of the moment of the crime's initial conception rather than that of the crime or the solution. From that temporal position, the detective, the gathered suspects, and the reader look forward in time to the execution of the murder and to the revelation of the murderer's identity, which is to say that it anticipates the moment of justice achieved. Few locked-room mysteries populate the history of Anglophone African detective fiction, and the few that do can hardly be argued to conform with the classic whodunits of Poe, Doyle, or Sayers. But it seems fitting to end this study of detective fiction by African writers with an analogous accounting of what will have happened to make the detective genre so productive for engaging with the problematics of the state, selfhood, and sovereignty, and for anticipating futures beyond them. What follows requires me to revisit and review a few key details that should be familiar by now but hopefully this denouement will fit the puzzle pieces into a clearer whole.

From the earliest experiments in the 1940s and 1950s, the story of Anglophone African detective fiction has been, at its most basic, a narrative of writers establishing and extending the boundaries of the detective story to make it serve African realities. As just a few examples indicate, African writers have been, and remain, endlessly innovative in domesticating the detective story for local, regional, and Africa-wide audiences. Writing during the era of 'boot-stamping' colonial constables, Cyprian Ekwensi's crime reporter is more likely to wield the discoveries of his investigations against the colonial state than he is to turn over to its judiciary hardworking African city-dwellers forced into criminal activity for reasons of pure survival. The fallibility of Nigerian and other African law courts of the 1970s leads Kole Omotoso and David G. Maillu to re-orient the detective story around supranational African defense forces untainted by the influence-peddling that characterized real-life institutions of law and order. When the police are complicit in acts of violence and dispossession, Unity Dow hands the work of criminal investigation over to a collective of feminist community activists. For Wahome Mutahi and Wahome Karengo, the postcolonial state is willing and eager to enforce its laws but lacks the capacity, resources, and at times the jurisdiction to rein in criminal syndicates that operate transnationally and whose economic activities blur distinctions between legal and illegal. Mukoma Wa Ngugi, Dan Fulani, Kalu Okpi, and Mwangi Ruheni tell similar stories. References and allusions to Sherlock Holmes abound, but Anglophone Africa's crime mysteries bear only superficial resemblance to Doyle's whodunits. In their reimagination of the detective story's building blocks, they represent something both familiar and distinct in the history of the genre and within African fiction.

As the above examples attest, the Africanization of the detective story has never been exclusively a matter of changed settings and character names. To preserve the locally contextual realism of any given crime mystery at any given time, the conditions under which criminality is defined, committed, and policed must be accounted for as well. Murder is murder, of course, but what constitutes justice or criminality is quite a different thing in the euphoric post-independence 1960s Ghanaian writing of Gilbert A. Sam, for instance, than it is for the African American Chester Himes writing about Harlem in the same period. Even within African detective fiction, Sam's police procedural surveys a radically distinct socio-structural milieu from that appearing in Black South African mystery writing only a few years earlier when the settler colony's white regime brutally enforced its apartheid laws. The differences are no less drastic when setting Sam's *Who Killed Inspector Kwasi Minta?* in comparison with Nigerian texts of two decades later, when Nigeria's government found itself hamstrung by IMF and World Bank loan conditionalities. Different state formations and different conceptualizations of the morality of the state demand, and produce, different kinds of detection narratives. For a realist genre such as the crime mystery, to Africanize plots, settings, conflicts, *and* the social-structural conditions against which those narrative elements are positioned have proved essential to providing suspenseful entertainment to the detective story's target readers. Supplying readers with recognizable conflicts in recognizable social milieux turns out to be just as important for producing compelling mysteries as setting the action in recognizable neighborhoods or filling them with local surnames.

I have endeavored to show throughout this study that, by taking account of the conditions under which laws are enacted and enforced, violence perpetrated, and privations experienced, African writers have, wittingly or not, turned the detective story into a highly productive mode of social and political critique. As the examples in previous paragraphs make evident, for many of the dozens of African detective fiction writers, individual abuses of power are less the central problem of African life than they are the primary symptom of the more substantial institutional and structural instabilities that characterize the African state. With the brief exception of the police procedurals produced in the euphoric 1960s, detective stories and novels written from the late 1940s to the present depict violation, dispossession, disorder, and insecurity as endemic to post-independence social life. To be clear, theirs is not the lawless phantasmagoria of the racist Western imaginary. These conditions are nevertheless suggested to be pervasive. The instabilities of private property rights, individual rights to possession-in-self, and the rule of law more broadly are understood to resist the easy rectification that follows the banishment of individual miscreants. The evolving crises of sovereign self-rule are depicted instead as structural. Some are rooted in the legacies of colonial authoritarianism or in the persistence of global economic inequalities long after independence. Others are rooted in the easy capture of the state by those with money or weapons, the unimpeded assertion of private power in the many spaces outside the state's reach, and/or the neoliberal dismantling of the centralized state. Consistently, they highlight the near impossibility of establishing robust governing institutions under any of these conditions. Because the self-ruled state is not, by any measure, sovereign as it was expected to be, governments in African detective fiction frequently lack the means to ensure rights and protections, to apply fair sanction, or to distribute resources in nominally equitable ways. As a 'biography of the state' (Olaniyan 2015), Anglophone Africa's detective fiction narrates political sovereignty as a moving target, more mythic than real, and never to be taken for granted.

In the crime mystery's most idealized form, the successful detective rescues and restores that which has been taken from the victim, be it private property, property in self, and when homicide has taken a life, the victim's right to legal recognition even in death. Writing about the golden age British whodunit, W.H. Auden explains that 'The job of the detective is to restore the state of grace in which the aesthetic and the ethical are as one' (1948: 409). G.K. Chesterton (1946) contends similarly that the ideal detective re-establishes society's fundamental equilibrium after its destabilization by the antisocial actions of a criminal. Because societal disequilibrium is instigated in the Golden Age whodunit of which these two speak by the isolated actions of an individual breaking the otherwise durable social contract, equilibrium is easily restored. All it requires is the expert ratiocination of the detective to identify said culprit.

Where social, economic, and political conditions are such that there is no state of grace to restore, no underlying social equilibrium to bring back into balance, let alone a fully self-sovereign state to authorize the detective's discovery, the detective's purpose becomes something different. As the novels and stories examined in the preceding chapters make evident, the simple work of investigative discovery is rarely sufficient to ensure any sort of social equilibrium or state of grace in Nigeria, Kenya, South Africa or anywhere else African writers have set their crime mysteries. To merely reveal the identities of individual criminals in these circumstances is to fail to deliver the justice that might be expected of a successful investigation. No matter how effective the detective is at uncovering the identities of villains in these contexts, the presumed mechanisms to punish them or to restore society to a state of grace are lacking, compromised, or hobbled. Even where the will to justice does persist, the presumed structural and institutional conditions for enforcing it remain significantly compromised. Disequilibrium is the norm rather than the exception.

In only rare examples, however, do Anglophone African writers abandon the ideal of the modernist nation-state as the best political formation for achieving security, social equilibrium, and above all freedom. Equally rare is their rejection of forms of political subjectivity predicated on Enlightenment conceptions of the rights-bearing liberal subject. Over and again, the stories and novels reaffirm the promise of the sovereign bodies of the state and citizen as articulated in the liberal democratic constitutions through which many of Africa's individual nation-states came into being. Despite all the structural impediments to the realization of sovereign self-rule catalogued in African detective fiction, sovereign statehood and its practices of citizenship hover as ideals against which lived reality is measured. In short, the sovereign modernist state remains the presumed ideal vehicle for collective decolonization, which is to say, for delivering the body politic to its anticipated decolonial future.

Anglophone Africa's writers repeatedly locate their detectives in the gap that separates the ideal from the reality. It is in the space between the expectation of legal justice as backed by the force of state and the lived experience of seemingly uncontainable violation, disorder, and dispossession where the detectives do their real work. By operating in that gap, the fictional detectives perform two critical functions. The first is to assess the reasons for the discrepancy between ideal and reality. Where decolonizing governing ideals persist but where there is no underlying stable social order to restore, African detective fiction writers put their protagonists to the work of social detection. In social detection, investigation and discovery serve not to reveal the identity of a single villain, but rather to make visible the conditions wherein violation in its multiple material manifestations and wherein legal exception and exclusion are the norm. Social detection assesses the social, political, and historical conditions that facilitate, and often normalize, violations against persons, property, and society. Much of what makes Anglophone African detective fiction so richly fertile is this diagnostic capability.

With the social-structural problems illuminated, Anglophone African detective fiction's second significant function is to re-animate the ideals of postcolonial sovereignty. The detective of Anglophone African fiction almost always stands in as a surrogate for the state, continually resurrecting its ideals in their absence. Individual criminals may occasionally slip the grasp of Anglophone Africa's many fictional detectives, but they never go unidentified. Like fictional detectives elsewhere, the detective thereby represents the Law as a moral authority. If the detective can contain the dispossession and disorder of the present for a more viable future, so too, the novels suggest, can the state. This dramatization of sovereign self-rule is what makes the African detective an African culture hero. In this role, the detective's work of social detection does not restore a prior state of grace or social equilibrium so much as rescue the promise of the sovereign, rights-guaranteeing state from the trash heap of history.

Anglophone African writers and readers of a more radical disposition might still cast a critical eye on African detective fiction for its persistent idealization of the modern nation-state as the pathway to decolonization. Apart from Lily Adaora Ulasi, who privileges the sovereign authority of Yoruba and Igbo deities, the novelists deflect questions about the nation-state's roots in European and American imperialist traditions. In this respect, there is some truth to Mukoma Wa Ngugi's assertion that Africa's detective fiction lacks the Fanonian impulses of some of the continent's more self-consciously political fiction (2018: 159). This reluctance serves as another reminder of the point I made at the beginning of this book that Anglophone African detective fiction's ideological articulations regularly blur the boundaries between conservative and radical. As a case in point, even as Anglophone African authors shy away from Fanonian critique, their resilient creativity in continually making use of the detective genre's historical elasticity and aesthetic liminality attests to their profound resistance to the colonial metropole's rigid classificatory taxonomies for both literary genres and political formations. The crime mystery has never been stable, monolithic, or ossified. Instead, and contrary to Aristotelian arguments to the contrary, the genre is both mutable and heterogeneous. It is simultaneously provisional and improvisatory. As with the detective genre, so too with the political genre of the nation-state. By rendering the mutability and heterogeneity of the former Anglophone African writers render the mutability and multiplicity of the latter.

Tsitsi Jaji and Lily Saint's contention, referenced at the beginning of this book, that 'genre, politics, and play in the postcolony not only coexist but are, in fact, co-constitutive' (2017: 152) underscores this point. Insofar as Anglophone African detective fiction has been shaped by the political conditions of the postcolony, the reverse relation is true as well. The playfulness at work in the writers' embrace of generic mutability suggests a radical openness to newness, to alternate configurations of familiar forms, in short, to local sovereignty over political self-definition. Only a few of the detective novels articulate what alternate formations of the sovereign postcolonial state might look like with any precision. Ulasi resuscitates Yoruba political cosmologies, and Diale Tlholwe explores governance models predicated on pan-African spiritual formations.

For Unity Dow and Tony Marinho, provisional democratic sodalities arising within the nation-state in response to specific needs offer the promise, although not always the actuality of widespread public justice. Kole Omotoso's and David G. Maillu's fantasies of African political unity do not rethink the contours of the state formation itself but do envision ways for those states to harness their collective power to achieve the dream of decolonization. But even in the absence of specific ideas about how to reformulate the postcolonial state for the needs of African polities, the texts remind their readers that if conditions demand inventiveness and improvisation, artistic and political genres alike can be reinvented and improvised. It is difficult to imagine a literary genre better suited to this articulation than the crime mystery. It is, after all, an ever-evolving and ever-fluid genre that takes as its raw material the fallibilities, contradictions, and excesses of the state and envisions a future free of them. It is a genre that continually shapes socio-political imaginaries.

As both an index of the crises of the state and a reminder of its capacity to underwrite liberty and security, Anglophone African detective fiction's hermeneutic value extends far beyond African borders. The crises of sovereignty and security illuminated by these novels take distinct local forms but are part of a larger global pattern in which the widespread retreat from the welfare state and Keynesian governance has entailed the privatization of risk and security. How humans narrate their anxieties about the resulting vulnerabilities, which is to say how they manage them by giving them cultural form, is thereby of global importance, as true for the United States, France, and Sweden as for Kenya, Nigeria, and South Africa. The crises prompted by the transformation of state sovereignty might be more acute in the African localities where African detective fiction is most robust, but understanding the resulting cultural forms can help us better analyze what, for example, the ubiquity of police procedurals on American television and the boom in Scandinavian crime fiction in the first decades of the twenty-first century might reveal about the reconceptualization of the state and democratic citizenship in those places. Additionally, one of the African detective story's most powerful aspects is its implicit futurity. The future perfect explains the genre's normative narrative grammar, but it also conjures a seemingly perfect future in which disruptions to a postcolonial social order have been contained, malefactors have been redeemed for the body politic, and everyday citizens secured in the promised state of decolonial grace. Here, too, African detective fiction offers rich possibilities for global comparison, especially across the Global South in places such as Central America and Southeast Asia where the crime mystery has blossomed under similar socio-political conditions.

The playfulness at work in Anglophone African detective fiction suggests another form of sovereignty as well. In the final analysis, all this serious critical engagement is packaged as entertainment written in no small part for readerly pleasure. Arthur Maimane's wily anti-hero O. Chester Morena, Hilary Ng'weno's dogged journalist Scoop Nelson, Victor Thorpe's 'Number One Kill-Master' Jack Ebony, Angela Makholwa's fearless Lucy Khambule, and Africa's many other detectives plunge their readers into head-spinning whorls of intrigue, mystery, and conflict. Their escapades inject suspense and adventure into everyday life. Above all, Anglophone Africa's detective fiction provides its readers the pleasures of familiarity. Whether it is the crime mystery's genre-specific satisfactions of culprits identified, of neat resolutions or cliff-hanger endings achieved, and justice promised, these detective stories fulfill recognizable desires. They do so moreover by giving their readers recognizably local settings, character types, villains, victims, conflicts, and thematic preoccupations. In short, Anglophone Africa's detective fiction has been produced and consumed far more often than not for local pleasure on local terms. This is not to suggest that these pleasures are absolute or unconditional or that they are not to varying degrees framed by the institutional imperatives of the various publishing and other cultural industries that produce detective novels as commodities. The histories and implications of Anglophone African detective fiction's status as a commodity, in fact, deserve a study of their own, one that future scholars might want to tease out. But, in the meantime, it is to suggest that, ultimately, Anglophone Africa's detective writers assert no small measure of self-determination over pleasure itself.

What does the future of African detective fiction hold in store? Some potential trajectories are becoming visible. Chris Abani's short story, 'Killer Ape' (2018b) points to a future in which detective stories unveil other kinds of hidden histories and unspeakable conflicts. Abani's constable, a closeted gay man, reads masked codes and telling silences to make visible traumas suffered by gay African men, traumas that he keeps hidden to protect the survivors from further violence. Liberian-South African H.J. Golakai's second Vee Johnson mystery, *The Score* (2015), concerns itself less with the crises of the state than with the violence lurking in gendered intimacies, suggesting a feminist take on old-fashioned stories of interpersonal conflict. In *A Spy in Time* (2018), South Africa's Imraan Coovadia makes the implicit futurity of the Anglophone detective novel explicit by melding mystery plotting with science fiction's speculative aesthetics. Africa's digital media entrepreneurs are also moving the crime mystery from the page to the screen in ways that suggest new aesthetic and thematic horizons. Nollywood movies such as *The Investigator* (Realnolly TV 2014), *Oga Detective* (Uwadi 2014), *The Detective* (2017), *Òlòtūré* (Gyang 2019), *Thirty Pieces of Silver* (Peters 2020), *Undercover* (Emelobe 2020), and *Grey Area* (Alexmoore 2020) bring fresh, uniquely West African perspectives to stories of neoliberal-era interpersonal conflict.[1] Ghanaian media impresario Shirley

---

1   See Moradewun Adejunmobi (2015).

Frimpong-Manso's investigative journalism webseries *Peep* narrates crises of neoliberal Africa that would be familiar to readers of Angela Makholwa, Diale Tlholwe, and Wahome Mutahi and Wahome Karengo, but does so in ways that expand the formal possibilities for interrogating what passes for truth in media-saturated twenty-first century life. Whether African writers and digital media creatives will continue to tease out any of these experiments is unknown of course. Only the African writers who embrace the genre in the coming decades will fully answer the question of what its future looks like, but no matter which directions African expressive artists take the crime mystery, it is a safe bet that they will continue to embrace its power to sustain anticipation for future justice.

An Anglophone African Detective Fiction Bibliography, 1940–2023

I compiled the following bibliography of Anglophone African detective fiction while writing this book. I offer it as a resource for scholars, genre aficionados, and lay readers alike. Please do not confuse it with a bibliography of African *crime* fiction, which is an impossibly broad category and which Christine Matzke (2012b) has already admirably charted. For reasons detailed in the early paragraphs of this book, my interest is in the narrower range of stories, novels, and films that make significant use of acts of mystery solving, crime investigation, detection in its various guises, and/or protagonists who bear resemblance to the global fictional and cinematic archetype of the private eye. The list includes puzzle-clue mysteries, whodunits, and hard-boiled investigations. It also includes thrillers that rely on investigation plotting – leaving out those thrillers that do not. As they are in all forms of expressive culture, African writers are endlessly innovative in their literary experimentation. Many works in this bibliography exemplify that creativity.

Interspersed throughout are children's books and secondary school readers as well as serial publications that feature mystery and detective stories. I have also included translated texts when they are available to African audiences. South African literature scholars will notice only a partial record of white South African-authored titles. Susan Friedland's (1972) and Elizabeth le Roux's (2013) excellent bibliographies of South African crime fiction make a fuller accounting unnecessary here. I make no claim to comprehensiveness. As is the nature of bibliographies, this one is partial and a work in progress. I see it as my individual contribution to the ongoing collective project of recording and preserving African literary culture.

Abani, Chris (2018). 'Killer Ape', in: C. Abani (ed.), *Lagos Noir* (Brooklyn: Akashic Books), 201–217.
—— (2014). *The Secret History of Las Vegas* (New York: Penguin).
Adenle, Leye (2022). *Unfinished Business* (Abuja: Cassava Republic).
—— (2018). *When Trouble Sleeps* (Abuja: Cassava Republic).
—— (2016). *Easy Motion Tourist* (Abuja: Cassava Republic).
Adeolu, Elizabeth Olushola (2018). *Chasing Facades* (Lagos: Farafina Breeze).
African Film [alt. title *Spear*] (1968-1972). [Serial photonovel]. (Johannesburg: Drum Publications).

Akwa, Kojo (1995). *Dela Boya African Detective* (London and Basingstoke: Macmillan Pacesetters).
Alily, Valentine (1980). *Mark of the Cobra* (Harare: The College Press/Macmillan Pacesetters).
Anuah, P.D. (1973). 'The Lost Corpse', *Sunday Spectator*, 11 August, 5.
Appiah, Kwame Anthony (1995). *Another Death in Venice* (London: Constable).
—— (1994). *Nobody Likes Letitia* (London: Constable).
—— (1991). *Avenging Angel* (New York: St. Martin's Press).
Ashun, Carlton (1967). 'Who Killed Rosi?', *Sunday Mirror*, 21 May, 11.
—— (1967). 'Who Killed Rosi?', *Sunday Mirror*, 14 May, 9.
Atalebe, Stephen (2014). *The Hour of Death in Harare* (CreateSpace Independent Publishing).
Awuah, A.K. (1968). 'Tobacco Trap', *Sunday Spectator*, 24 August, 4.
—— (1968). 'Tobacco Trap', *Sunday Spectator*, 17 August, 4.
—— (1968). 'Tobacco Trap', *Sunday Spectator*, 10 August, 4.
Badal, Sean (2010). *The Ice on Mars* (Alton: Wigan Pier Press).
Badoe, Yaba (2009). *True Murder* (London: Jonathan Cape).
Bah, Musa with Fatou Secka and Fatoumatta Drammeh (2013). *The Sledgehammer* (Banjul: Self-published).
Banda, Sekelani S. (2000). *Dead Ends (Crime, Cops, and a Renaissance)* (Lusaka: S & P).
Beukes, Lauren (2010). *Zoo City* (Auckland Park: Jacana Media).
Bilal, Parker (2017). *Dark Water* (New York: Bloomsbury).
—— (2016). *City of Jackals* (New York: Bloomsbury).
—— (2015). *The Burning Gates* (New York: Bloomsbury).
—— (2014). *The Ghost Runner* (New York: Bloomsbury).
—— (2013). *Dogstar Rising* (New York: Bloomsbury).
—— (2012). *The Golden Scales* (New York: Bloomsbury).
Bolaji, Omoseye (2018). *Tebogo and Uriah Heep* (Bloemfontein: Eselby Jnr Publications).
—— (2012). *Tebogo and the Bacchae* (Bloemfontein: Eselby Jnr Publications).
—— (2010). *Tebogo and the Pantophagist* (Bloemfontein: Eselby Jnr Publications).
—— (2009). *Tebogo and the Epithalamion* (Bloemfontein: Eselby Jnr Publications).
—— (2008). *Tebogo and the Haka* (Bloemfontein: Eselby Jnr Publications).
—— (2003). *Tebogo Fails* (Bloemfontein: Drufoma).
—— (2002). *Ask Tebogo* (Bloemfontein: Qoopane Literary Services).
—— (2001). *Tebogo's Spot of Bother* (Bloemfontein: Drufoma).
—— (2000). *Tebogo Investigates* (Bloemfontein: Drufoma).
Boom [alt. title *The Stranger*] (late 1960s – early 1970s). [Serial photonovel, no additional information]. (Johannesburg: Drum Publications).
Casley, D.J. (1995). *Death Undertow: A Chief Inspector Odhiambo Mystery* (New York: St. Martin's Press).
Chitambo, John (1984). *Secret Blood* (London and Basingstoke: Macmillan Pacesetters).
Coovadia, Imraan (2018). *A Spy in Time* (Los Angeles: Rare Bird Books).

Criminal. (1970s). [Serial publication]. (Kenya, no additional information).
David-West, T.M. (2018). *The Pearl Ring* (Nigeria: Self-published).
The Detective (2017). [Motion picture, no additional information]. Available at: https://watchnolly.com/the-detective, accessed 15 August 2021.
Dila, Dilman (2014). *A Killing in the Sun* (Johannesburg: Black Letter Media).
Dlovu, Nandi (1983). *Race Against Rats* (London and Basingstoke: Macmillan Pacesetters).
—— (1982). *Angel of Death* (London and Basingstoke: Macmillan Pacesetters).
Dow, Unity (2002). *The Screaming of the Innocent* (North Melbourne: Spinifex).
Dube, Hope (1981). *State Secret* (London and Basingstoke: Macmillan Pacesetters).
Duodu, S.O. (1968). 'Adventures of Annan-Clay', *Weekly Spectator*, 9 March, 4.
—— (1968). 'Adventures of Annan-Clay', *Weekly Spectator*, 2 March, 4–5.
—— (1968). 'Adventures of Annan-Clay', *Weekly Spectator*, 24 February, 4, 8.
—— (1967). 'Hot Money', *Weekly Spectator*, 12 August, 4.
—— (1967). 'Hot Money', *Weekly Spectator*, 5 August, 4.
—— (1967). 'Hot Money', *Weekly Spectator*, 29 July, 4.
—— (1967). 'Hot Money', *Weekly Spectator*, 22 July, 4.
—— (1967). 'Subversion at Poso', *Weekly Spectator*, 10 June, 5.
—— (1967). 'Subversion at Poso', *Weekly Spectator*, 3 June, 7.
Ebersohn, Wessel (1970). *A Lonely Place to Die* (London: Victor Gollancz).
—— (1980). *The Centurion* (Johannesburg: Ravan Press).
Ekwensi, Cyprian (1963). *People of the City* [Revised edition] (London: Heinemann African Writers Series).
—— (1962). *Yaba Round-about Murder* (Lagos: Tortoise Books).
—— (1954). *People of the City* (London: Andrew Dakers).
—— (1951). 'Death on the Bus', *West African Review*, March, 271–273.
—— (1948). 'The Case of the Howling Monkey', *West African Review*, December, 1452, 1455, 1457, 1459.
—— (1947). 'The Banana Peel', in: Cullen Young (ed.), *African New Writing* (London: Lutterworth), 11–20.
Emelobe, Timber (dir.) (2020). *Undercover* [Motion picture] (Lagos: ROK Studios).
Eni, Okey (2019). *DMI* (Self-published).
Eyo, Henri (2004). *The Dawn of Time* (Calabar: Wusen).
Fulani, Dan (2006). *The Power of Corruption* (London: Hodder Education).
—— (1983). *Flight 800* (Ibadan: Spectrum).
Garba, Mohmed Tukur (1983). *Stop Press: Murder* (London and Basingstoke: Macmillan Pacesetters).
—— (1981). *The Black Temple* (London and Basingstoke: Macmillan Pacesetters).
Genya, Monica (1996). *Links of a Chain* (Nairobi: East African Educational Publishers).
Gilpin, Tracy (2008). *Double Cross* (Richmond: Black Star Crime).
Golakai, H.J. (2015). *The Score* (Cape Town: Kwela).
—— (2011). *The Lazarus Effect* (Cape Town: Kwela).
Gyamfaa-Fofie, Akosua (1991). *Murder at Sunset* (Accra: Beginners Publishers).
Gyang, Kenneth (dir.) (2019). *Òlòtūré* [Motion picture] (Lagos: EbonyLife Films).

Henson, Pauline (2009). *Going Home* (Self-published: Lulu.com).
—— (2008). *Countdown* (Self-published).
—— (2004). *Case Closed* (Gweru: Mambo Press).
Ibe, Adimchinma (2012). *Cronies* (Self-published: CreateSpace Independent Publishing).
—— (2011). *Patron of Terror* (Self-published: Lulu.com).
—— (2010). *Treachery in the Yard* (New York: Minotaur).
Ifedigbo, Sylvia Nze (2022). *Believers and Hustlers* (Lehi, Utah: Iskanchi Press).
Ige, Muwiya (2010). *Dream Killers* (Ile-Ife: Serious Book Group Nigeria).
Ighavini, Dickson (1982). *Thief of State* (Zaria: Northern Nigeria Publishing Company).
Ike, Chukwuemeka (1980). *Expo '77* (London: Fontana-Collins).
Irungu, James (1987). *Circle of Betrayal* (London and Basingstoke: Macmillan Pacesetters).
Johnson, Louis Omotayo (1981). *Murder at Dawn* (Ibadan: Spectrum).
Kan, Toni (2018). *Carnivorous City* (Abuja: Cassava Republic).
Kangende, Kenneth (2002). *The Mistress* (Lusaka: Minta).
Kawegere, Fortunatus (1968). *Inspector Rajabu Investigates, and other stories* (Nairobi: East African Publishing House).
Kayode, Femi (2023). *Gaslight* (London: Raven Books).
—— (2021). *Lightseekers* (London: Raven Books).
Kibuuka, Ulysses Chuka (1991). *For the Fairest* (Kampala: Fountain Publishers).
Kimenye, Barbara (1978). *The Gemstone Affair* (Sunbury-on-Thames: Nelson).
Komey, Ellis Ayitey (1966). 'The Iron Box', *Sunday Mirror*, 19 June, 12.
Kubuitsile, Lauri (2012). *Claws of a Killer* (Self-published).
—— (2010). *Anything for Money* (Florida Hills: Vivlia).
—— (2008). *Murder for Profit* (Gaborone: Pentagon Publishers).
—— (2005). *The Fatal Payout* (Gaborone: Macmillan Botswana).
Kunzmann, Richard (2008). *Dead-end Road* (London: Macmillan).
—— (2007). *Salamander Cotton* (New York: St. Martin's Press).
—— (2004). *Bloody Harvests* (New York: St. Martin's Press).
Kwakye, Benjamin (2005). *The Sun by Night* (Trenton: Africa World Press).
Macgoye, Marjorie Oludhe (1972). *Murder in Majengo* (Nairobi: Oxford).
Machingauta, Rodwell Musekiwa (1994). *Detective Ridgemore Riva* (Harare: Zimbabwe Publishing House).
MacKenzie, Jassy (2018). *Bad Seeds* (New York: Soho Crime).
—— (2013). *Pale Horses* (New York: Soho Crime).
—— (2012). *The Fallen* (New York: Soho Crime).
—— (2011). *Stolen Lives* (New York: Soho Crime).
—— (2010). *Random Violence* (New York: Soho Crime).
Maillu, David G. (1986). *Benni Kamba 009 in Operation DXT* (Nairobi: Spear).
—— (1980). *Benni Kamba 009 in the Equatorial Assignment* (London and Basingstoke: Macmillan Pacesetters).
Maimane, Arthur [*published as* Arthur Mogale] (1953). 'You Can't Buy Me', *Drum*, December, 28–29.

—— (1953). 'You Can't Buy Me', *Drum*, October, 32–33.
—— (1953). 'You Can't Buy Me', *Drum*, September, 24–25.
—— (1953). 'You Can't Buy Me', *Drum*, August–September, Intl Edition, 30–31.
—— (1953). 'Hot Diamonds', *Drum*, July-August, Intl Edition, 29.
—— (1953). 'Hot Diamonds', *Drum*, June-July, Intl Edition, 31.
—— (1953). 'Hot Diamonds', *Drum*, May-June, Intl Edition, 30–31.
—— (1953). 'Hot Diamonds', *Drum*, April-May, Intl Edition, 30–31.
—— (2001). 'Crime for Sale [March 1953]', in: M. Chapman (ed.), *The Drum Decade: Stories from the 1950s* (Pietermaritzburg: University of Natal Press), 28–31.
—— (2001). 'Crime for Sale [January 1953]', in: M. Chapman (ed.), *The Drum Decade: Stories from the 1950s* (Pietermaritzburg: University of Natal Press), 24–27.
Makholwa, Angela (2007). *Red Ink* (Johannesburg: Pan Macmillan).
Manqupu, Mbokotwane (2001 [1955]). 'Love Comes Deadly', in: M. Chapman (ed.), *The Drum Decade: Stories from the 1950s* (Pietermaritzburg: University of Natal Press), 66–72.
Maredza, Claude (2002). *I Put it To You* (Harare: Norumedzo Enterprises).
Marinho, Tony (1992). *The Epidemic* (Ibadan: Heinemann).
—— (1987). *Deadly Cargo* (Ibadan: Spectrum Books).
Masemola, Thabo Nkosinathi (1993). *Mixed Signals* (Johannesburg: Skotaville).
Matjila, Andrew (2002). *Navachab Gold* (Windhoek: Gamsberg Macmillan).
McClure, James (1991). *The Song Dog* (New York: Mysterious Press).
—— (1984). *The Artful Egg* (New York: Pantheon).
—— (1980). *The Blood of an Englishman* (New York: Harper & Row).
—— (1977). *The Sunday Hangman* (New York: Harper & Row).
—— (1975). *Snake* (New York: Harper & Row).
—— (1974). *The Gooseberry Fool* (New York: Harper & Row).
—— (1972). *The Caterpiller Cop* (New York: Harper & Row).
—— (1971). *The Steam Pig* (New York: Harper & Row).
Mcimeli, Rayman (ed.) (1990). *UMakhwekhwetha! Xhosa Detective Stories* (Johannesburg: Educum Publishers).
Meyer, Deon (2021). *The Dark Flood*. K.L. Seegers (trans.) (New York: Atlantic Monthly Press).
—— (2016). *Icarus*. K.L. Seegers (trans.) (New York: Atlantic Monthly Press).
—— (2014). *Cobra*. K.L. Seegers (trans.) (New York: Atlantic Monthly Press).
—— (2012). *Seven Days*. K.L. Seegers (trans.) (New York: Atlantic Monthly Press).
—— (2011). *Trackers*. K.L. Seegers (trans.) (New York: Atlantic Monthly Press).
—— (2009). *Blood Safari*. K.L. Seegers (trans.) (New York: Grove Press).
—— (2007). *Devil's Peak*. K.L. Seegers (trans.) (New York: Little, Brown and Co.).
—— (2003). *Heart of the Hunter*. K.L. Seegers (trans.) (New York: Grove Press).
—— (2000). *Dead at Daybreak*. K.L. Seegers (trans.) (New York: Little, Brown and Co.).
—— (1999). *Dead before Dying*. K.L. Seegers (trans.) (New York: Little, Brown and Co.).
Mokae, Gomolemo (1995). *The Secret in My Bosom*. (Florida Hills: Vivlia).
Mtonga, Henry (1971). 'Hot Matter', *New Writing from Zambia*, vol. 7, 24–30.

—— (1970). 'Soft Things for Life', *New Writing from Zambia*, vol. 1, 21–31.
—— (1969). 'The Exact Man', *New Writing from Zambia*, vol. 1, 29–34.
Mukoma Wa Ngugi (2013). *Black Star Nairobi* (Brooklyn: Melville House).
—— (2010). *Nairobi Heat* (Brooklyn: Melville House).
Musodza, Masimba (2012). 'Lights, Camera, Murder', *Jungle Jim*, 14 & 15 (Afreak Publishing).
Mutahi, Wahome and Wahome Karengo (2003). *The Miracle Merchant* (Nairobi: Phoenix Publishers).
Mwangi, Meja (1979). *The Bushtrackers* (Nairobi: Longman Kenya).
Ndunguru, S. N. (1999). *Divine Providence* (Dar es Salam: Mkuki na Nyota Publishers).
Nfojoh, George Kofi (1972). 'Clue to the Unsolved Problem', *Sunday Spectator*, 4 March, 7.
Ng'weno, Hilary (1975). *The Men from Pretoria* (Nairobi: Longman Kenya).
Nicol, Mike (2021). *Rabbit Hole* (Johannesburg: Penguin South Africa).
—— (2013). *Of Cops and Robbers* (Exeter: Old Street Publishing).
—— (2010). *Payback* (Exeter: Old Street Publishing).
—— (1998). *The Ibis Tapestry* (New York: Knopf).
Nuhu, Abdul E. (1987). *The Lost Diamond: Ghanaian Detective* (Accra: Popular Publications).
—— (1987). *Crime Professionals: Ghanaian Detective* (Accra: Popular Publications).
Nunn, Malla (2014). *Present Darkness* (New York: Emily Bestler Books).
—— (2012). *Blessed Are the Dead* (New York: Emily Bestler Books).
—— (2010). *Let the Dead Lie* (New York: Washington Square Press).
—— (2009). *A Beautiful Place to Die* (Northlands: Picador Africa).
Nwokolo, Chuma (1988). *Dangerous Inheritance* (London and Basingstoke: Macmillan Pacesetters).
Nwokoma, Ibendiogwu (2012). *The Detective and the Ghostman* (Lagos: Moorhen Books).
Nzekwe, Amaechi (1985). *A Killer on the Loose* (Enugu: Fourth Dimension Press).
Obeng, Emmanuel (1942). *Issa Busanga*. (Ghana).
Odaga, Asenath Bole (1984). *The Shade Changes* (Kisumu: Lake Publishers).
Okoba, Matthew (2009). *Militants of the Niger Delta: A Detective Novel* (Lagos: Whiz-Kid Publishers).
Okpi, Kalu (1982). *The South African Affair* (London and Basingstoke: Macmillan Pacesetters).
—— (1977). *The Smugglers* (London and Basingstoke: Macmillan Pacesetters).
Oloyede, Sola (1981). *I Profess This Crime: The Brotherhood of the Silk Handcuffs* (Akure: Fagbamigbe).
Ominiabohs, Othuka (2016). *A Conspiracy of Ravens* (Lagos: Masobe).
Omotoso, Kole (1974). *Fella's Choice* (Benin City: Ethiope Publishing).
Opong, Peggy (2010). *The Red Heifer* (Accra: Peggy Opong Books).
Orford, Margie (2013). *Water Music* (Johannesburg: Jonathan Ball).
—— (2011). *Gallows Hill* (Johannesburg: Jonathan Ball).
—— (2009). *Daddy's Girl* (Johannesburg: Jonathan Ball).

—— (2009). *Blood Rose* (Johannesburg: Jonathan Ball).
—— (2008). *Like Clockwork* (Johannesburg: Jonathan Ball).
Orji, Gabriel (1994). *Baals of the Niger* (Enugu: Fourth Dimension Press).
Osofisan, Femi [*published as* Okinba Launko] (2009). *Pirates* (Lagos: Lantern Books).
Otter, Charlotte (2014). *Balthasar's Gift: A Maggie Cloete Mystery* (Cape Town: Modjaji Books).
—— (2016). *Karkloof Blue* (Cape Town: Modjaji Books).
Owusu-Ansah, F.A. (1971). 'The Tragedy of Essie', *The Mirror*, 28 August, 11.
—— (1971). 'The Tragedy of Essie', *The Mirror*, 21 August, 11.
Oyebanji, Adam (2022). *A Quiet Teacher* (London: Severn House).
Parkes, Nii Ayikwei (2010). *Tail of the Blue Bird* (New York: Flipped Eye).
Peters, Robert (dir.) (2020). *Thirty Pieces of Silver* [Motion picture] (Lagos: Charles Granville Productions, Genesis Pictures, and Whitestone Films).
Quartey, Kwei (2023). *Last Seen in Lapaz* (New York: Soho Crime).
—— (2021). *Sleep Well My Lady* (New York: Soho Crime).
—— (2020). *The Missing American* (New York: Soho Crime).
—— (2017). *Death by His Grace* (New York: Soho Crime).
—— (2016). *Gold of Our Fathers* (New York: Soho Crime).
—— (2014). *Murder at Cape Three Points* (New York: Soho Crime).
—— (2011). *Children of the Streets* (New York: Random House).
—— (2009). *Wife of the Gods* (New York: Random House).
Quaye, Cofie (1973). 'Copper Wire Conspiracy, pt. 2', *Pleasure: Ghana's Sunshine Magazine*, 5(5), November, 28–29.
—— (1970). *Murder in Kumasi* (Accra: Moxon).
—— (1970). *Sammy Slams his Gang* (Accra: Moxon).
Rabie, Sue (2011). *Fallout* (Cape Town: Human & Rousseau).
—— (2010). *Blood at Bay* (Cape Town: Human & Rousseau).
—— (2008). *Boston Snow Plough* (Cape Town: Human & Rousseau).
Rowe, Michéle (2015). *Hour of Darkness* (Cape Town: Penguin Random House).
—— (2013). *What Hidden Lies* (Johannesburg: Penguin).
Ruheni, Mwangi (1975). *The Mystery Smugglers* (Nairobi: Spear).
Ruzindana, Anaclet (2015). *Murder in the Toilet* (Kigali: Vision Publishers).
Sabelo, George (1983). *Scar of the Tiger: A Skip Dlamini Thriller* (Pietermaritzburg: Shuter & Shooter; Johannesburg: Collins).
—— (2015). *Target: The President* (Pietermartitzburg: Shuter & Shooter; Johannesburg: Collins).
Sam, Gilbert A. (1960). *Who Killed Inspector Kwasi Minta?* (Accra: Gilisam Publishing Syndicate).
Sibale, Grieve (1998). *Murder in the Forest* (Lusaka: Tupelo Honey Industries).
Singhateh, Sally (1998). *Christie's Crises* (Nairobi: East African Educational Publishers).
Slovo, Gillian (2000). *Red Dust* (London: Virago).
—— (1995). *Close Call* (London: Michael Joseph).
—— (1994). *Catnap* (New York: St. Martin's Press).
—— (1987). *Death Comes Staccato* (New York: Doubleday).

—— (1986). *Death by Analysis* (London: Women's Press).
—— (1984). *Morbid Symptoms: A Murder Mystery* (New York: Dembner).
Sparrow Productions (2011). *Peep* [Web video series].
Stanley, Michael (2020). *Facets of Death (Detective Kubu #7)* (Naperville: Poisoned Pen).
—— (2009). *A Carrion Death (Detective Kubu #1)* (New York: Harper Perennial).
Staunton, Irene (ed.) (2015). *Writing Mystery and Mayhem: Story Anthology* (Harare: Weaver Press).
Swingler, Shaun and Jenna Bass (eds) (2010s). *Jungle Jim* [Serial pulp fiction magazine]. (Afreak Publishing).
Tawfik. M.M. (2008). *Murder in the Tower of Happiness* (Cairo: American University in Cairo Press).
Thompson, Constable E.J. (1966). 'Point of No Return', *Sunday Mirror*, 27 February, 12, 14.
—— (1966). 'Point of No Return', *Sunday Mirror*, 20 February, 12.
—— (1966). 'Point of No Return', *Sunday Mirror*, 13 February, 10.
Thorpe, Victor (1979). *The Worshippers* (London and Basingstoke: Macmillan Pacesetters).
Tlholwe, Diale (2011). *Counting the Coffins* (Cape Town: Kwela Books).
—— (2008). *Ancient Rites* (Cape Town: Kwela Books).
True Crime Monthly (1992–). [Serial publication]. (Lagos: Media Agency International).
Turner, Jann (2002). *Southern Cross* (London: Orion).
Ukah, John (2016). *Murder at Midnight* (The Fearless Storyteller House).
Ulasi, Adaora Lily (1978). *The Man from Sagamu* (London: Fontana-Collins).
—— (1971). *Many Thing Begin For Change* (London: Fontana-Collins).
—— (1970). *Many Thing You No Understand* (London: Fontana-Collins).
Umbhali (1994). *Francie Molala and the Mercedes Affair* (London and Basingstoke: Macmillan Pacesetters).
Umelo, Rosina (1984). *Finger of Suspicion* (London and Basingstoke: Macmillan Pacesetters).
Uwadi, Francis (dir.) (2014). *Oga Detective* [Motion picture] (Basildon/Nigeria: Nolly Rocky TV).
Utley, David Jasper (1995). *Ngoma and Click: Namibian Detective Stories* (Windhoek: Gamsberg Macmillan).
Wanjikũ wa Ngũgĩ (2014). *The Fall of Saints* (New York: Atria Books).
Yemoh, Ali (1973). 'Oko & Ebo in "Slaves of the Lens"', *Pleasure: Ghana's Sunshine Magazine*, 5(1), July, 30–31.

Bibliography

Abani, Chris (2018a). 'Introduction', in: C. Abani (ed.), *Lagos Noir* (Brooklyn: Akashic Books), 14–22.
—— (2018b). 'Killer Ape', in: C. Abani (ed.), *Lagos Noir* (Brooklyn: Akashic Books), 201–217.
—— (2014). *The Secret History of Las Vegas* (New York: Penguin).
Achebe, Chinua (1989). 'Interviewed by Bill Moyers', in: B.S. Flowers (ed.), *Bill Moyers: A World of Ideas* (New York: Doubleday), 333–344.
—— (1987). *Anthills of the Savannah* (New York: Anchor).
Adejunmobi, Moradewun (2017). 'Afterword: Genre Queries, African Studies', *Cambridge Journal of Postcolonial Literary Inquiry*, 4(2), 258–264.
—— (2015). 'Neoliberal Rationalities in Old and New Nollywood', *African Studies Review*, 58(3), 31–53.
Adenle, Leye (2022). *Unfinished Business* (Abuja: Cassava Republic).
—— (2018). *When Trouble Sleeps* (Abuja: Cassava Republic).
—— (2016). *Easy Motion Tourist* (Abuja: Cassava Republic).
Aderinto, Saheed (2015). *When Sex Threatened the State: Illicit Sexuality, Nationalism, and Politics in Colonial Nigeria, 1900–1958* (Urbana: University of Illinois Press).
Adesokan, Akin (2009). 'Practicing "Democracy" in Nigerian Films', *African Affairs*, 108(433), 599–619.
Adomako, K. Bamfi (1988). *From Undergraduate to Prostitution* (Accra: Adwinsa).
Agamben, Giorgio (1998). *Homo Sacer: Sovereign Power and Bare Life* (Stanford: Stanford University Press).
Ahire, Philip T. (1990). 'Policing and the Construction of the Colonial State in Nigeria, 1860–1960', *Journal of Third World Studies*, 7(2), 151–172.
Akwa, Kojo (1995). *Dela Boya African Detective* (London and Basingstoke: Macmillan Pacesetters).
Alemika, Etannibi E.O. (1993). 'Colonialism, State, and Policing in Nigeria', *Crime, Law, and Social Change*, 20, 187–219.
Alexmoore, Uche (2020). *Grey Area*. [Motion picture] (Lagos: Rok Studios).
Alily, Valentine (2022). *The Supreme Undercover* (Self-published).
—— (1980). *Mark of the Cobra* (Harare: The College Press/Macmillan Pacesetters).
Amoke, Anene Kevin (2018). 'Cosmologies of the Sovereign in Chinua Achebe's *Anthills of the Savannah*', *Research in African Literatures*, 49(3), 35–57.
Amoko, Apollo (2010). *Postcolonialism in the Wake of the Nairobi Revolution: Ngugi wa Thiong'o and the Idea of African Literature* (New York: Palgrave).
Anderson, Benedict (1991). *Imagined Communities: Reflections on the Origin and Spread of Nationalism* (New York: Verso).
Anuah, P.D. (1973). 'The Lost Corpse', *Sunday Spectator*, 11 August, 5.

Appiah, Kwame Anthony (1995). *Another Death in Venice* (London: Constable).
—— (1994). *Nobody Likes Letitia* (London: Constable).
—— (1991). *Avenging Angel* (New York: St. Martin's Press).
Apter, Andrew (2005). *The Pan-African Nation: Oil and the Spectacle of Culture in Nigeria* (University of Chicago Press).
—— (2000). 'IBB=419: Nigerian Democracy and the Politics of Illusion', in: John L. and Jean Comaroff (eds), *Civil Society and the Political Imagination in Africa* (University of Chicago Press), 267–307.
Armillas-Tiseyra, Magalí (2022). 'Secret Histories: Detective Fiction, Hermeneutic Skepticism, and Bad Readers in the Contemporary African Novel', *Ariel: A Review of International English Literature*, 52(3), 49–79.
Arrighi, Giovanni (2002). 'The African Crisis: World Systemic and Regional Aspects', *New Left Review*, 15, 5–36.
Asante, Samuel K.B. (1965). 'Interests in Land in the Customary Law of Ghana – A New Appraisal', *Yale Law Journal*, 74(4), 848–885.
Asare, Abena Ampofoa (2018). *Truth Without Reconciliation: A Human Rights History of Ghana* (Philadelphia: University of Pennsylvania Press).
Ashforth, Adam (2005). *Witchcraft, Violence, and Democracy in South Africa* (University of Chicago Press).
Ashun, Carlton (1967). 'Who Killed Rosi?', *Sunday Mirror*, 21 May, 11.
—— (1967). 'Who Killed Rosi?', *Sunday Mirror*, 14 May, 9.
Asong, Linus (2012). *Detective Fiction and the African Scene: From Whodunit to Whydunit* (Bamenda: Langaa).
Assefa, Taye (1989). 'Detective Fiction in Amharic', *Northeast African Studies*, 1(3), 13–33.
Atalebe, Stephen (2014). *The Hour of Death in Harare* (CreateSpace Independent Publishing).
Auden, W.H. (1948). 'The Guilty Vicarage: Notes on the Detective Story', *Harper's Magazine*, May, 406–412.
Augart, Julia (2018). 'Kenya Noir: Crime Fiction's Critique', *Journal of African Cultural Studies*, 30(1), 81–92.
Awoonor, Kofi and Geormbeeyi Adale-Mortty (eds) (1971). *Messages: Poems from Ghana* (London: Heinemann African Writers Series).
Awuah, A.K. (1968). 'Tobacco Trap', *Sunday Spectator*, 24 August, 4.
—— (1968). 'Tobacco Trap', *Sunday Spectator*, 17 August, 4.
—— (1968). 'Tobacco Trap', *Sunday Spectator*, 10 August, 4.
Ball, Tyler Scott (2018). 'Sof-town Sleuths: The Hard-Boiled Genre Goes to Jo'burg', *The Cambridge Journal of Postcolonial Literary Inquiry*, 5(1), 20–35.
Banda, Sekelani S. (2000). *Dead Ends (Crime, Cops, and a Renaissance)* (Lusaka: S & P).
Barber, Karin (1987). 'Popular Arts in Africa', *African Studies Review*, 30(3), 1–78.
Barnard, Rita (2008). 'Tsotsis: On Law, the Outlaw, and the Postcolonial State', *Contemporary Literature*, 49(4), 541–572.
Baxter, Elizabeth Isobel (2019). *Imagined States: Law and Literature in Nigeria* (Edinburgh University Press).

Bayart, Jean-Francois (1993). *The State in Africa: The Politics of the Belly* (New York: Longman).
Bayart, Jean-Francois, Stephen Ellis, and Beatrice Hibou (eds) (1999). *Criminalization of the State in Africa* (Oxford: James Currey; Bloomington: Indiana University Press).
Benjamin, Walter (2006). *Selected Writings*, vol. 4. Howard Eiland and Michael W. Jennings (eds). (Cambridge: Belknap Press).
—— (1999). *The Arcades Project*. Howard Eiland and Kevin McLaughlin (trans.) (Cambridge: Belknap Press).
Bennett, Tony and Janet Woollacott (1987). *Bond and Beyond: The Political Career of a Popular Hero* (Basingstoke: Macmillan).
Berglund, Karl (2017). 'With a Global Market in Mind: Agents, Authors, and the Dissemination of Contemporary Swedish Crime Fiction', in: L. Nilsson, D. Damrosch, and T. D'Haen (eds), *Crime Fiction as World Literature* (New York: Bloomsbury), 77–90.
Beukes, Lauren (2010). *Zoo City* (Auckland Park: Jacana Media).
Bevan, Elizabeth (1958). 'Review of *People of the City*', *Black Orpheus*, October, 53–55.
Bgoya, Walter and Mary Jay (2013). 'Publishing in Africa from Independence to the Present Day', *Research in African Literatures*, 44(2), 17–34.
Bilal, Parker (2017). *Dark Water* (New York: Bloomsbury).
—— (2016). *City of Jackals* (New York: Bloomsbury).
—— (2015). *The Burning Gates* (New York: Bloomsbury).
—— (2014). *The Ghost Runner* (New York: Bloomsbury).
—— (2013). *Dogstar Rising* (New York: Bloomsbury).
—— (2012). *The Golden Scales* (New York: Bloomsbury).
Binder, Sabine (2021). *Women and Crime in Post-transitional South African Crime Fiction* (Leiden: Brill).
Bird, S. Elizabeth and Rosina Umelo (2018). *Surviving Biafra: A Nigerwife's Story* (London: Hurst & Company).
Black, Shameem (2011). 'Truth Commission Thrillers', *Social Text*, 29(2) (107), 47–66.
Blacklaws, Troy (2014). 'John Wayne in Sophiatown: The Wild West Motif in Apartheid Prose', *English in Africa*, 41(1), 127–142.
Bolaji, Omoseye (2000). *Tebogo Investigates* (Bloemfontein: Drufoma).
Bolaño, Roberto (2009). *2066*, Natasha Wimmer (trans.) (New York: Picador).
Bosch Santana, Stephanie (2014). 'Migrant Forms: *African Parade*'s New Literary Geographies', *Research in African Literatures*, 45(3), 167–187.
Braham, Persephone (2004). *Crimes Against the State, Crimes Against Persons: Detective Fiction in Cuba and Mexico* (Minneapolis: University of Minnesota Press).
Brown, Matthew H. (2021). *Indirect Subjects: Nollywood's Local Address* (Durham: Duke University Press).
Bruce, John Edward (2002 [1907]). *The Black Sleuth*. John Cullen Gruesser (ed.) (Boston: Northeastern University Press).
de Bruijn, Esther (2017). 'Sensationally Reading Ghana's *Joy-Ride* Magazine', *Cambridge Journal of Postcolonial Literary Inquiry*, 4(1), 27–48.

Bryce, Jane (1988). *A Feminist Study of Fiction by Nigerian Women Writers*. PhD Dissertation (Ile-Ife: Obafemi Awolowo University).
Burns, James (2002). 'John Wayne on the Zambezi: Cinema, Empire, and the American Western in British Central Africa', *The International Journal of African Historical Studies*, 35(1), 103–117.
Callaci, Emily (2017). *Street Archives and City Life: Popular Intellectuals in Postcolonial Tanzania* (Durham: Duke University Press).
Cawelti, John G. and Bruce A. Rosenberg (1987). *The Spy Story* (University of Chicago Press).
Chakava, Henry (1997). 'Selling Books in Africa: A Publisher's Reflections', *Logos*, 3, 159–164.
—— (1977). 'Publishing in a Multilingual Situation: the Kenya Case', *The African Book Publishing Record*, 3(2), 83–90.
Chalfin, Brenda (2010). *Neoliberal Frontiers: An Ethnography of Sovereignty in West Africa* (University of Chicago Press).
Champigny, Robert (1977). *What Will Have Happened: A Philosophical and Technical Essay on Mystery Stories* (Bloomington: Indiana University Press).
Chapman, Michael (2001). 'More than Telling a Story: *Drum* and its Significance in Black South African Writing', in: M. Chapman (ed.), *The Drum Decade: Stories from the 1950s* (Pietermaritzburg: Natal University Press), 181–232.
Chesterton, G.K. (1946). 'A Defence of Detective Stories', in: H. Haycraft (ed.), *The Art of the Mystery Story: A Collection of Critical Essays* (New York: Grosset and Dunlap), 3–6.
Chigidi, William Lugisani (1997). The Emergence and Development of the Shona Detective Story as a Fictional Genre in Zimbabwean Literature [MA Thesis] (Pretoria: University of South Africa).
Christensen, Matthew J. (2013). 'African Popular Crime Genres and the Genres of Neoliberalism', *Social Text*, 31(2) (115), 103–121.
—— (2012). 'Violable States: Sovereignty, Neoliberalism, and Generic Failure in Tony Marinho's Nigerian Biothriller *The Epidemic*', in: A. Oed and C. Matzke (eds), *Life is a Thriller: Investigating African Crime Fiction* (Köln: Rüdiger Köppe Verlag), 77–88.
Christian, Ed (ed.) (2001). *The Postcolonial Detective* (New York: St. Martin's Press).
Christie, Agatha (1934, 2011). *Murder on the Orient Express* (New York: Harpers).
Clapham, Christopher (1996). *Africa and the International System: The Politics of State Survival* (Cambridge University Press).
Close, Glen (2018). *The Female Corpse: A Transatlantic Perspective* (New York: Palgrave Macmillan).
—— (2008). *Contemporary Hispanic Crime Fiction: A Trans-Atlantic Discourse on Urban Violence* (New York: Palgrave).
Coleman, Nancy (2020). 'Why We Are Capitalizing Black', *New York Times*, 5 July. Available at: https://www.nytimes.com/2020/07/05/insider/capitalized-black.html, accessed 23 April 2023.
Comaroff, Jean (2007). 'Beyond Bare Life: AIDS, (Bio)Politics, and the Neoliberal Order', *Public Culture*, 19(1), 197–219.
Comaroff, Jean and John L. (2016). *The Truth about Crime: Sovereignty, Knowledge, Social Order* (University of Chicago Press).

—— (2006). 'Criminal Obsessions, after Foucault: Postcoloniality, Policing, and the Metaphysics of Disorder', in: J. Comaroff and J.L. Comaroff (eds), *Law and Disorder in the Postcolony* (University of Chicago Press), 273–298.
—— (2000). 'Millennial Capitalism: First Thoughts on a Second Coming', *Public Culture*, 12(2) 291–343.
—— (1999). 'Occult Economies and the Violence of Abstraction: Notes from the South African Postcolony', *American Ethnologist*, 26(2), 279–303.
Condouriotis, Eleni (2017). 'Memory and the Popular: Rwanda in Mukoma Wa Ngugi's Fiction', *Cambridge Journal of Postcolonial Literary Inquiry*, 4(3), 382–397.
Cooper, Frederick (1996). *Decolonization and African Society: The Labor Question in French and British Africa* (Cambridge: Cambridge University Press).
Coovadia, Imraan (2018). *A Spy in Time* (Los Angeles: Rare Bird Books).
Copjec, Joan (ed.) (1993). *Shades of Noir: A Reader* (New York: Verso).
Crace, John (2013). 'Jamal Mahjoub: "My Wife Says Parker Bilal Is Much Nicer Than You"', *The Guardian*, 17 March. Available at: www.theguardian.com/books/2013/mar/17, accessed 18 April 2023.
Darko, Kari (2001). 'Introduction', in: R.E. Obeng, *Eighteenpence* (Accra: Sub-Saharan Publishers).
Darlington, Sonja (2013). '"Fiat Justitia, Ruat Caelum": Justice Juxtaposed to Questions of Maturity, Community, Gender, and Moral Action in the Novels by Unity Dow', *Journal of the African Literature Association*, 8(1), 74–86.
Dash, Leon (1983). 'Mysterious Fires Plague Nigerian Investigation', *Wall Street Journal*, 27 February.
Daymond, M.J. and Margaret Lenta (2004). '"It Was like Singing in the Wilderness": An Interview with Unity Dow', *Kunapipi*, 26(2), 47–60.
Denning, Michael (1987). *Cover Stories: Narrative and Ideology in the British Spy Thriller* (London and New York: Routledge; Kegan Paul, 1987).
Derrida, Jacques (2009). *The Beast and the Sovereign*, vol. 1, Geoffrey Bennington (trans.), Michel Lisse, Marie-Louise Mallet, and Ginette Michaud (eds). (University of Chicago Press).
Diabate, Naminata (2020). *Naked Agency: Genital Cursing and Biopolitics in Africa* (Durham: Duke University Press).
Diawara, Manthia (1993). 'Noir by Noirs: Towards a New Realism in Black Cinema', *African American Review*, 27(4), 525–537.
Dimock, Wai Chee (2006). 'Genre as World System: Epic and Novel on Four Continents', *Narrative*, 14(1), 85–101.
Dodson, Don (1974). 'The Four Modes of *Drum*: Popular Fiction and Social Control in South Africa', *African Studies Review*, 17(2), 317–343.
Dow, Unity (2002). *The Screaming of the Innocent* (North Melbourne: Spinifex).
Driver, Dorothy (2002). '*Drum* Magazine (1951–9) and the Spatial Configurations of Gender', in: S. Newell (ed.), *Readings in African Popular Fiction* (Oxford: James Currey; Bloomington: Indiana University Press), 156–159.
Dube, Hope (1981). *State Secret* (London and Basingstoke: Macmillan Pacesetters).
Duodu, S.O. (1968). 'Adventures of Annan-Clay', *Weekly Spectator*, 9 March, 4.
—— (1968). 'Adventures of Annan-Clay', *Weekly Spectator*, 2 March, 4–5.
—— (1968). 'Adventures of Annan-Clay', *Weekly Spectator*, 24 February, 4, 8.
—— (1967). 'Hot Money', *Weekly Spectator*, 12 August 4.

—— (1967). 'Hot Money', *Weekly Spectator*, 5 August, 4.
—— (1967). 'Hot Money', *Weekly Spectator*, 29 July, 4.
—— (1967). 'Hot Money', *Weekly Spectator*, 22 July, 4.
—— (1967). 'Subversion at Poso', *Weekly Spectator*, 10 June, 5.
—— (1967). 'Subversion at Poso', *Weekly Spectator*, 3 June, 7.
Eco, Umberto (1985). 'Innovation and Repetition: Between Modern and Post-Modern Aesthetics', *Daedalus*, 114(4), 161–184.
Ekwensi, Cyprian (1986). 'Why Hadley Chase? An Examination of Compulsive Versus Compulsory Reading', in: E. Emenyonu (ed.), *Literature and Society: Selected Essays on African Literature* (Oguta: Zim Pan African Publishers), 104–111.
—— (1962). *Yaba Round-about Murder* (Lagos: Tortoise Books).
—— (1954). *People of the City* (London: Andrew Dakers).
—— (1951). 'Death on the Bus', *West African Review*, March, 271–273.
—— (1948). 'The Case of the Howling Monkey', *West African Review*, December, 1452, 1455, 1457, 1459.
—— (1947). 'The Banana Peel', in: C. Young (ed.), *African New Writing* (London: Lutterworth), 11–20.
Elliott, Jane (2018). *The Microeconomic Mode: Political Subjectivity in Contemporary Popular Aesthetics* (New York: Columbia University Press).
Emelobe, Timber (dir.) (2020). *Undercover* [Motion picture] (Lagos: ROK Studios).
Emenyonu, Ernest (2006). 'Lagos (*People of the City*, Cyprian Ekwensi, 1954)', in: F. Moretti (ed.), *The Novel*, vol. 2. (Princeton University Press), 700–705.
—— (1974). *Cyprian Ekwensi* (London: Evans Brothers).
English, Daylanne K. (2009). 'Being Black There: Racial Subjectivity and Temporality in Walter Mosley's Detective Novels', *Novel*, 42(3), 361–365.
Eyo, Henri (2004). *The Dawn of Time* (Calabar: Wusen).
Fair, Laura (2018). *Reel Pleasures: Cinema Audiences and Entrepreneurs in Twentieth-Century Urban Tanzania* (Athens: Ohio University Press).
Fanon, Frantz (2014). *The Wretched of the Earth*, Richard Wilcox (trans.) (New York: Grove).
Fay, Jennifer and Justus Nieland (2009). *Film Noir: Hard-boiled Modernity and the Cultures of Globalization* (London: Routledge).
Fenwick, Mac (1996). '"Tough Guy, eh?" The Gangster-figure in *Drum*', *Journal of Southern African Studies*, 22(4), 617–632.
Ferguson, James (2006). *Global Shadows: Africa in the Neoliberal World Order* (Durham: Duke University Press).
—— (1999). *Expectations of Modernity: Myths and Meanings of Urban Life on the Zambian Copperbelt* (Berkeley and Los Angeles: University of California Press).
Fleming, Tyler and Toyin Falola (2005). 'Africa's Media Empire: *Drum*'s Expansion to Nigeria', *History in Africa*, 32, 133–164.
Foucault, Michel (1977). *Discipline and Punish: The Birth of the Prison*. Alan Sheridan (trans.). (New York: Vintage).
Fox, Patricia (2019). 'Not Your Grandparents' Flaneur: The Afropolitan Detective in the Urban Crime Novels of Quartey and Crompton', *Africa Today*, 65(4), 61–82.
Friedland. Susan (1972). 'South African Detective Stories in English and Afrikaans from 1951–1971', University of Witwatersrand Department of Bibliography and

Typography.
Fukuyama, Francis (1992). *The End of History and the Last Man* (New York: Free Press).
Fulani, Dan (2006). *The Power of Corruption* (London: Hodder Education).
—— (1983). *Flight 800* (Ibadan: Spectrum).
Gagiano, Annie (2004). 'Getting Under the Skin of Power: The Novels of Unity Dow', *English Academy Review*, 21(1), 36–50.
Ganiyu, Muftau (1974). 'Children Picking Up Bad Practice "Karate" Films Blamed', *Weekly Spectator*, 23 November, 1.
Garba, Mohmed Tukur (1983). *Stop Press: Murder* (London and Basingstoke: Macmillan Pacesetters).
Garritano, Carmela (2020). 'The Entrepreneurial Feminist Subject of New Screen Media from Ghana: Labor, Pleasure, and Power', *South Central Review*, 37(2), 4–15.
—— (2013). *African Video Movies and Global Desires: A Ghanaian History* (Athens: Ohio University Press).
Genya, Monica (1996). *Links of a Chain* (Nairobi: East African Educational Publishers).
Geshiere, Peter (1997). *The Modernity of Witchcraft* (Charlottesville: University of Virginia Press).
Getachew, Adom (2019). *Worldmaking after Empire: The Rise and Fall of Self-Determination* (Princeton University Press).
Gikandi, Simon (2001). 'Globalization and the Claims of Postcoloniality', *South Atlantic Quarterly*, 100(3), 627–658.
—— (1991). *Reading Chinua Achebe: Language and Ideology in Fiction* (Oxford: James Currey).
Golakai, H.J. (2015). *The Score* (Cape Town: Kwela).
—— (2011). *The Lazarus Effect* (Cape Town: Kwela).
Gondola, Didier (2016). *Tropical Cowboys: Westerns, Violence, and Masculinity in Kinshasa* (Bloomington: Indiana University Press).
Goodlad, Lauren (2021). 'The Ontological Work of Genre and Place: Wuthering Heights and the Case of the Occulted Landscape', *Victorian Literature and Culture*, 49(1), 107–138.
Gramsci, Antonio (1985). *Selections from Cultural Writings*, William Boelhower (trans.), David Forgacs and Geoffrey Nowell-Smith (eds.) (Cambridge University Press).
Gready, Paul (1990). 'The Sophiatown Writers of the Fifties: The Unreality of Their World', *Journal of South African Studies*, 1, 139–164.
Guldimann, Colette (2019). 'Against the Law: Arthur Maimane's Pioneering Hard-boiled Black Detective Fiction in *Drum* Magazine', *Safundi: The Journal of South African and American Studies*, 20(3), 259–276.
—— (2009). '"Imported from America" or Fugitive Forgeries? *Drum* Magazine and Black Popular Culture in 1950s South Africa', in: T. Falola and F. Ngom (eds), *Oral and Written Expressions of African Cultures* (Durham: Carolina Academic Press), 47–67.
van Gulik, Robert (1976). 'Preface', in: R. van Gulik (ed.), *Celebrated Cases of Judge Dee (Dee Goong An)* (New York: Dover), i-xxiii.
Gyamfaa-Fofie, Akosua (1991). *Murder at Sunset* (Accra: Beginners Publishers).
Gyang, Kenneth (dir.) (2019). *Òlòtūré* [Motion picture] (Lagos: EbonyLife Films).

Habila, Helon (2013). 'Crime Fiction and the African Zeitgeist: Interview with Ainehi Edoro', *Brittle Paper*, 26 August. Available at: www.brittlepaper.com/2013/08/crime-fiction-african-zeitgeista-brittle-paper-interview-helon-habila-crime-writing-project, accessed 18 April 2023.

Harvey, David (1991). *The Condition of Postmodernity: An Enquiry into the Origins of Cultural Change* (Cambridge: Wiley-Blackwell).

Hassan, Robert (2017). 'Time and Sovereignty in the Neoliberal Hegemony', in: P. Heubner, S. O'Brien, T. Porter, L. Stockdale, and Y.R. Zhou (eds), *Time, Globalization, and Human Experience* (New York: Routledge), 26–46.

Haycraft, Howard (ed.) (1946). *The Art of the Mystery Story: A Collection of Critical Essays* (New York: Grosset and Dunlap).

—— (1941). *Murder for Pleasure: The Life and Times of the Detective Story* (New York: D. Appleton-Century Company).

Haynes, Jonathan (2016). *Nollywood: The Creation of Nigerian Film Genres* (University of Chicago Press).

Hefner, Robert W. (2010). 'Religious Resurgence in Contemporary Asia: Southeast Asian Perspectives on Capitalism, the State, and the New Piety', *The Journal of Asian Studies*, 69(4), 1031–1047.

Hepburn, Allan (2020). 'World Citizens: Espionage Literature in the Cold War', in: A. Hammond (ed.), *The Palgrave Handbook of Cold War Literature* (Cham: Palgrave Macmillan), 303–322.

Higginson, Pim (2017). 'What and Where is Francophone African Popular Fiction?', *Cambridge Journal of Postcolonial Literary Inquiry*, 4(2), 207–221.

—— (2011). *The Noir Atlantic: Chester Himes and the Birth of the Francophone African Crime Novel* (Liverpool University Press).

Hirst, Terry (1979). 'Interview', *African Book Publishing Record*, 5(2), 88–91.

Holquist, Michael (1971). 'Whodunit and Other Questions: Meta-physical Detective Stories in Postwar Fiction', *New Literary History*, 3(1), 135–156.

Horsley, Kate (2013). 'Interrogations of Society in Contemporary African Crime Writing', *Moving Worlds: A Journal of Transcultural Writings*, 13(1), 62–76.

Ibe, Adimchinma (2010). *Treachery in the Yard* (New York: Minotaur).

Ighavini, Dickson (1982). *Thief of State* (Zaria: Northern Nigeria Publishing Company).

Ike, Chukwuemeka (1980). *Expo '77* (London: Fontana-Collins).

Ince, Onur (2020). *Colonial Capitalism and the Dilemmas of Liberalism* (Oxford: Oxford University Press).

Irele, Abiola (1975). 'The Ethiope Experience', in: E. Oluwasanmi, E. McLean, and H. Zell (eds), *Publishing in Africa in the Seventies* (Ile-Ife: Ife University Press), 143–165.

Irungu, James (1987). *Circle of Betrayal* (London and Basingstoke: Macmillan Pacesetters).

Jaji, Tsitsi Ella (2014a). 'Cassava Westerns: Ways of Watching Abderrahmane Sissako', *Black Camera*, 6(1), 154–177.

—— (2014b). *Africa in Stereo: Modernism, Music, and Pan-African Solidarity* (Oxford: Oxford University Press).

Jaji, Tsitsi and Lily Saint (2017). 'Introduction: Genre in Africa', *Cambridge Journal of Postcolonial Inquiry*, 4(2), 2017, 151–158.
James, C.L.R. (1993). *American Civilization* (Cambridge: Blackwell).
James, Deborah (2012). 'Money-Go-Round: Personal Economies of Wealth, Aspiration, and Indebtedness', *Africa: Journal of the International Africa Institute*, 82(1), 20–40.
Jameson, Fredric (1993). 'The Synoptic Chandler', in: J. Copjec (ed.), *Shades of Noir: A Reader* (New York: Verso), 33–56.
—— (1979). 'Reification and Utopia in Mass Culture', *Social Text*, 1, 130–148.
Jefferson, Roland S. (1984). 'Review [*The Bushtrackers*]', *The Black Scholar*, 15(6), 61–63.
Johnson, Louis Omotayo (1981). *Murder at Dawn* (Ibadan: Spectrum).
Jondot, Jacqueline (2015). 'Displacement, Authority and Identity in Jamal Mahjoub's *In the Hour of Signs* and *Nubian Indigo*', in: F. Labaune-Demeule (ed.), *Authority and Displacement in the English-Speaking World* (Newcastle-upon-Tyne: Cambridge Scholars), 117–125.
Joseph, May (1999). *Nomadic Identities: The Performance of Citizenship* (Minneapolis: University of Minnesota Press).
Kalua, Fetson (2009). 'Identities in Transition Unity Dow's *Far and Beyon*' and *The Screaming of the Innocent*', *Scrutiny2*, 14(2), 48–58.
Katz, Cynthia (2005). 'Partners in Crime? Neoliberalism and the Production of New Political Subjectivities', *Antipode*, 37(3), 623–631.
Kawegere, Fortunatus (1968). *Inspector Rajabu Investigates, and other stories* (Nairobi: East African Publishing House).
Khamis, Said (2012). 'Is Abdulla's Bwana Msa in *Mzimu wa Watu wa Kale* Conan Doyle's Sherlock Holmes in Disguise?' in: A. Oed and C. Matzke (eds), *Life is a Thriller: Investigating African Crime Fiction* (Rüdiger Köppe Verlag), 161–172.
Khumalo, Fred (2018). 'Books and Belonging – Fred Khumalo Reflects on How James Hadley Chase and Alan Patton Changed His Life', *Johannesburg Review of Books*. Available at: https://johannesburgreviewofbooks.com/2018/10/01, accessed 18 April 2023.
Kibuuka, Ulysses Chuka (2009). 'Interview with Ambrose Musiyiwa', *Conversations with Writers*, October. Available at: www.conversationswithwriters.blogspot.com/2009/10, accessed 18 April 2023.
—— (1991). *For the Fairest* (Kampala: Fountain Publishers).
Kimenye, Barbara (1978). *The Gemstone Affair* (Sunbury-on-Thames: Nelson).
King, Stewart (2014). 'Crime Fiction as World Literature', *Clues: A Journal of Detection*, 32(2), 8–19.
de Kock, Leon (2016). *Losing the Plot: Crime, Reality, and Fiction in Postapartheid Writing*. (Johannesburg: Wits University Press).
Kokotovic, Misha (2006). 'Neoliberal Noir: Contemporary Central American Crime Fiction as Social Criticism', *Clues: A Journal of Detection*, 24(3), 15–29.
Komey, Ellis Ayitey (1966). 'The Iron Box', *Sunday Mirror*, 19 June, 12.
Komey, Ellis Ayitey and Ezekiel Mphalele (eds) (1964). *Modern African Stories* (London: Faber and Faber).

ten Kortenaar, Neil (1993). '"Only Connect": *Anthills of the Savannah* and Achebe's *Trouble with Nigeria*', *Research in African Literatures*, 24(3), 59-72.
Krige, Detlev (2012). 'Fields of Dreams, Fields of Schemes: Ponzi Finance and Multi-level Marketing in South Africa', *Africa: Journal of the International Africa Institute*, 82(1), 69-92.
Krings, Matthias (2015). *African Appropriations: Cultural Difference, Mimesis, and Media* (Bloomington: Indiana University Press).
Krishnan, Madhu (2018). *Writing Spatiality in West Africa: Colonial Legacies in the Anglophone/Francophone Novel* (Woodbridge: James Currey).
Kubuitsile, Lauri (2018). *Murder for Profit* (Gaborone: Pentagon Publishers).
Lindfors, Bernth (2002). *Africa Talks Back: Interviews with Anglophone African Writers* (Trenton: Africa World Press).
—— (1994). *Comparative Approaches to African Literatures* (Amsterdam: Rodopi).
—— (1991). *Popular Literatures in Africa* (Trenton: Africa World Press).
—— (1982). *Early Nigerian Literature* (New York: Holmes and Meier Publishers).
—— (1980). *Mazungumzo: Interviews with East African Writers, Publishers, Editors, and Scholars* (Athens: Ohio University Center for International Studies, Africa Program).
Loimeier, Manfred (2012). 'Life is a Thriller: Crime Fiction in West Africa', in: A. Oed and C. Matzke (eds), *Life is a Thriller: Investigating African Crime Fiction* (Köln: Rüdiger Köppe Verlag), 139-147.
Lynn, Martin (2006). 'The Nigerian Self-Government Crisis of 1953 and the Colonial Office', *The Journal of Imperial and Commonwealth History*, 34(2), 245-261.
MacDonald, Michael (2004). 'The Political Economy of Identity Politics', *South Atlantic Quarterly*, 103(4), 629-656.
Macgoye, Marjorie Oludhe (1972). *Murder in Majengo* (Nairobi: Oxford).
Machingauta, Rodwell Musekiwa (1994). *Detective Ridgemore Riva* (Harare: Zimbabwe Publishing House).
Maillu, David G. (1986). *Benni Kamba 009 in Operation DXT* (Nairobi: Spear).
—— (1980). *Benni Kamba 009 in the Equatorial Assignment*. (London and Basingstoke: Macmillan Pacesetters).
Maimane, Arthur [*published as* Arthur Mogale] (2001a). 'Crime for Sale (January 1953)', in: M. Chapman (ed.), *The Drum Decade: Stories from the 1950s* (Pietermaritzburg: University of Natal Press), 24-27.
—— (2001b). 'Crime for Sale (March 1953)', in: M. Chapman (ed.), *The Drum Decade: Stories from the 1950s* (Pietermaritzburg: University of Natal Press), 28-31.
—— (1953a). 'Hot Diamonds', *Drum*, April-May, Intl Edition, 30-31.
—— (1953b). 'Hot Diamonds', *Drum*, May-June, Intl Edition, 30-31.
—— (1953c). 'Hot Diamonds', *Drum*, July-August, Intl Edition, 29.
Mains, Daniel (2007). 'Neoliberal Times: Progress, Boredom, and Shame among Young Men in Urban Ethiopia', *American Ethnologist*, 34(4), 659-673.
Makholwa, Angela (2014). *Black Widow Society* (Johannesburg: Pan Macmillan).
—— (2012). 'Interview with Manfred Loimeier', in: A. Oed and C. Matzke (eds), *Life is a Thriller: Investigating African Crime Fiction* (Köln: Rüdiger Köppe Verlag), 233-234.

—— (2007). *Red Ink* (Johannesburg: Pan Macmillan).
Mamdani, Mahmood (1996). *Citizen and Subject: Contemporary Africa and the Legacy of Late Colonialism* (Princeton University Press).
Mandel, Ernest (1985). *Delightful Murder: A Social History of the Crime Story* (Minneapolis: University of Minnesota Press).
Manqupu, Mbokotwane (2001 [1955]). 'Love Comes Deadly', in: M. Chapman (ed.), *The Drum Decade: Stories from the 1950s* (Pietermaritzburg: University of Natal Press), 66–72.
Marenin, Otwin (1985). 'Policing Nigeria: Control and Autonomy in the Exercise of Coercion', *African Studies Review*, 28(1), 73–93.
—— (1982). 'Policing African States: Toward a Critique', *Comparative Politics*, 14(4), 379–396.
Marinho, Tony (1992). *The Epidemic* (Ibadan: Heinemann).
—— (1987). *Deadly Cargo* (Ibadan: Spectrum Books).
Marshall, Ruth (2009). *Political Spiritualities: The Pentecostal Revolution in Nigeria* (University of Chicago Press).
Martin, Theodore (2012). 'The Long Wait: Timely Secrets of the Contemporary Detective Novel', *Novel*, 45(2), 165–183.
Masemola, Thabo Nkosinathi (1993). *Mixed Signals* (Johannesburg: Skotaville).
Matolino, Bernard and Wenceslaus Kwindingwi (2013). 'The End of Ubuntu', *South African Journal of Philosophy*, 32(2), 197–205.
Matzke, Christine (2012a). 'Girls with Guts: Writing a South African Thriller – Angela Makholwa in Conversation', in: A. Oed and C. Matzke (eds), *Life is a Thriller: Investigating African Crime Fiction* (Köln: Rüdiger Köppe Verlag), 227–232.
—— (2012b). 'A Preliminary Checklist', in: A. Oed and C. Matzke (eds), *Life is a Thriller: Investigating African Crime Fiction* (Köln: Rüdiger Köppe Verlag), 205–212.
—— (2006). '"A Good Woman in a Good Country" or The Essence Is in the Pumpkin: Alexander McCall Smith's Mma Ramotswe Novels as a Case of Postcolonial Nostalgia', *Wasafiri*, 21(1), 64–71.
Matzke, Christine and Susanne Mühleisen (eds) (2006). *Postcolonial Postmortems: Crime Fiction from a Transcultural Perspective* (Amsterdam: Rodopi).
Maupeu, Hervé and Patrick Mutahi (eds) (2005). *Wahome Mutahi's World* (Nairobi: Transafrica Press).
Mayer, Ruth (2017). 'In the Nick of Time? Detective Film Serials, Temporality, and Contingency Management, 1919-1926', *The Velvet Light Trap*, 79, 21–35.
—— (2007). 'Virus Discourse: The Rhetoric of Threat and Terrorism in the Biothriller', *Cultural Critique*, 66, 1–20.
Mbembe, Achille (2019). *Necropolitics*. Steven Corcoran (trans.) (Durham: Duke University Press).
—— (2003). 'Necropolitics', Libby Meintjes (trans.), *Public Culture*, 15(1), 11–40.
—— (2001). *On the Postcolony* (Berkeley and Los Angeles: University of California Press).
McCann, Sean (2000). *Gumshoe America: Hard-Boiled Crime Fiction and the Rise and Fall of New Deal Liberalism* (Durham: Duke University Press).

Merivale, Patricia and Susan Elizabeth Sweeney (eds) (1998). *Detective Texts: The Metaphysical Detective Story from Poe to Postmodernism* (Philadelphia: University of Pennsylvania Press).

Meyer, Birgit (2007). 'Pentecostalism and Neo-Liberal Capitalism: Faith, Prosperity and Vision in African Pentecostal-Charismatic Churches', *Journal for the Study of Religion*, 20(2), 5–28.

—— (1998). '"Make a Complete Break with the Past": Memory and Post-colonial Modernity in Ghanaian Pentecostalist Discourse', *Journal of Religion in Africa*, 28(3), 316–349.

Meyer, Deon (2000). *Dead at Daybreak*. K.L. Seegers (trans.) (New York: Little, Brown and Co.).

Modisane, William 'Bloke' (1963). *Blame Me on History* (New York: Dutton & Co.).

Mohammad, Yasemin (2017). 'Reconfiguring European History and Cultural Memory in Jamal Mahjoub's *Travelling with Djinns*', *Journal of Commonwealth Literature*, 52(2), 316–330.

Mohsen, Caroline A. (2000). 'Narrating Identity & Conflict: History, Geography, and the Nation in Jamal Mahjoub's Portrayal of Modern-Day Sudan', *World Literature Today*, 74(3), 541–554.

Mokae, Gomolemo (1995). *The Secret in My Bosom* (Florida Hills: Vivlia).

Moretti, Franco (ed.) (2006), *The Novel*, vol. 2 (Princeton University Press),

—— (1983). *Signs Taken for Wonders: Essays in the Sociology of Literary Forms*, Susan Fischer, David Forgacs, and David Miller (trans.) (New York: Verso).

Moreton, Bethany E. (2007). 'The Soul of Neoliberalism', *Social Text*, 25(3) (92), 103–123.

Moyola, Yemi (1989). 'The Novels of Adaora Lily Ulasi', in: H.C. Otokunefor (ed.), *Nigerian Female Writers: A Critical Perspective* (Lagos: Malthouse Press), 37–46.

Msiska, Mpalive-Hangson (2009). 'Detecting Globalisation, Modernity, and Gender Subjectivity in David Maillu's *Benni Kamba 009 in Operation DXT*', *Journal of Eastern African Studies*, 3(1), 132–152.

Mtobwa, Ben R. (1985). *Najisikia Kuua Tena* (Nairobi: East African Educational Publishers).

Mukoma Wa Ngugi (2018). *The Rise of the African Novel: Politics of Language, Identity, and Ownership* (Ann Arbor: University of Michigan Press).

—— (2013). *Black Star Nairobi* (Brooklyn: Melville House).

—— (2010). *Nairobi Heat* (Brooklyn: Melville House).

Mutahi, Wahome and Wahome Karengo (2003). *The Miracle Merchant* (Nairobi: Phoenix Publishers).

Mwangi, Meja (1979). *The Bushtrackers* (Nairobi: Longman Kenya).

Naidu, Sam (2022). 'How Black is African Noir? Defining Blackness through Crime Fiction', *Cultural Studies*, 37(2), 263–279.

Naidu, Sam and Elizabeth le Roux (2017). *A Survey of South African Crime Fiction* (Pietermaritzburg: University of KwaZulu Natal Press).

National Reconciliation Commission (2005). *Final Report of the National Reconciliation Commission*, vol. 1 (Government of Ghana).

Ndebele, Njabulo (2002 [1991]). 'Rediscovery of the Ordinary', in S. Newell (ed.), *Readings in African Popular Fiction* (Oxford: James Currey; Bloomington: Indiana University Press), 134–140.

Newell, Sasha (2012). *The Modernity Bluff: Crime, Consumption, and Citizenship in Côte d'Ivoire* (University of Chicago Press).

—— (2007). 'Pentecostal Witchcraft: Neoliberal Possession and Demonic Discourse in Ivorian Pentecostal Churches', *Journal of Religion in Africa*, 37, 461–490.

Newell, Stephanie (2002a). "Introduction" in: S. Newell (ed.), *Readings in African Popular Fiction* (Oxford: James Currey; Bloomington: Indiana University Press), 1–10.

—— (2002b). *Literary Culture in Colonial Ghana: 'How to Play the Game of Life'* (Indiana University Press).

—— (2000). *Ghanaian Popular Fiction: 'Thrilling Discoveries in Conjugal Life'* (Oxford: James Currey; Athens: Ohio University Press).

Nfojoh, George Kofi (1972). 'Clue to the Unsolved Problem', *Sunday Spectator*, 4 March, 7.

Ng'weno, Hilary (1979). 'Interview with Bernth Lindfors', *The African Book Publishing Record*, 5(3), 157–161.

—— (1975). *The Men from Pretoria* (Nairobi: Longman Kenya).

Nichols, Robert (2020). *Theft is Property: Dispossession and Critical Theory* (Durham: Duke University Press).

Nilsson, Louise, David Damrosch, and Theo D'Haen (2017). 'Introduction: Crime Fiction as World Literature', in L. Nilsson, D. Damrosch, and T. D'Haen (eds), *Crime Fiction as World Literature* (New York: Bloomsbury), 1–9.

Nixon, Rob (1994). *Homelands, Harlem, and Hollywood: South African Culture and the World Beyond* (New York: Routledge).

Nunn, Malla (2014). *Present Darkness* (New York: Emily Bestler Books).

—— (2012). *Blessed Are the Dead* (New York: Emily Bestler Books).

—— (2010). *Let the Dead Lie* (New York: Washington Square Press).

—— (2009). *A Beautiful Place to Die* (Northlands: Picador Africa).

Nuttall, Sarah (2004). 'Stylizing the Self: The Y Generation in Rosebank, Johannesburg', *Public Culture*, 16(3), 430–452.

Nwankwo, Nkem (1975). *My Mercedes is Bigger than Yours* (New York: Harper & Row).

Nwokolo, Chuma (2015). 'Interview with Adaobi Nkeokelonye', *Fiction & Development*. Available at: https://fictioningdevelopment.org/fictions-in-diaspora/on-bribecode-an-interview-with-chuma-nwokolo, accessed 19 April 2023.

—— (1988). *Dangerous Inheritance* (London and Basingstoke: Macmillan Pacesetters).

Nyman, Jopi (2011). 'Beyond Liverpool, 1957: Travel, Diaspora, and Migration in Jamal Mahjoub's *The Drift Latitudes*', *Journal of Commonwealth Literature*, 46(3), 493–511.

Nzekwe, Amaechi (1985). *A Killer on the Loose* (Enugu: Fourth Dimension Press).

Obeng, Emmanuel (1942). *Issa Busanga* (Ghana: Publisher n.k.).

Obiechina, Emmanuel (1973). 'Ekwensi as Novelist', *Présence Africaine*, 83(2e Trimestre), 152–164.

Ochiagha, Terry (2015). *Achebe and Friends at Umuahia: The Making of a Literary Elite* (Woodbridge: James Currey).

Odhiambo, Tom (2011). 'Inventing Africa in the Twentieth Century: Cultural Imagination, Politics, and Transnationalism in *Drum* Magazine', *African Studies*, 5(2), 157–174.

—— (2008). 'The Romantic Detective in Two Kenyan Popular Novels', *Social Dynamics*, 30(2), 190–206.

Oed, Anja (2012). '"The World Has Changed": Modernity in Kolá Akínlàdé's Detective Novel *Owó ẹje*', in: A. Oed and C. Matzke (eds), *Life is a Thriller: Investigating African Crime Fiction* (Rüdiger Köppe Verlag), 113–128.

Oed, Anja and Christine Matzke (2012). 'Introduction', in: A. Oed and C. Matzke (eds), *Life is a Thriller: Investigating African Crime Fiction* (Köln: Rüdiger Köppe Verlag), 9–15.

Ogola, George (2005). 'Wahome Mutahi: (Hi)story and Popular Literature in Kenya', in: H. Maupeu and P. Mutahi (eds), *Wahome Mutahi's World* (Nairobi: Transafrica Press), 49–72.

Ogunyemi, Chikwenye Okonjo (1996). *African Wo/man Palava: The Nigerian Novel by Women* (University of Chicago Press).

Okpi, Kalu (1982). *Biafra Testament* (London: Macmillan).

—— (1982). *The South African Affair* (London and Basingstoke: Macmillan Pacesetters).

—— (1977). *The Smugglers* (London and Basingstoke: Macmillan Pacesetters).

Olaniyan, Tejumola (2017). 'Introduction: State and Culture in Africa – The Possibilities of Strangeness', in: T. Olaniyan (ed.), *State and Culture in Postcolonial Africa: Enchantings* (Bloomington: Indiana University Press), 1–24.

—— (2015). 'A Biography of the State in Africa: Some Literary Notes on a Method' [Conference presentation]. African Studies Association Annual Meeting, 20 November.

—— (2004). *Arrest the Music! Fela and his Rebel Art and Politics* (Bloomington: Indiana University Press).

Olaniyan, Tejumola and Peter Limb (eds) (2018). *Taking African Cartoons Seriously: Politics, Satire, and Culture* (Michigan State University Press).

Oloyede, Sola (1981). *I Profess This Crime: The Brotherhood of the Silk Handcuffs* (Akure: Fagbamigbe).

Omanga, Duncan (2016). '"Akokhan Returns": Kenyan Newspaper Comics and the Making of an "African" Superhero', *Journal of African Cultural Studies*, 28(3), 262–274.

Ominiabohs, Othuka (2016). *A Conspiracy of Ravens* (Lagos: Masobe).

Omotoso, Kole (1979). 'Interview with Bernth Lindfors', *The African Book Publishing Record*, 5(3), 157–161.

—— (1974). 'Publishing in Africa', *Afriscope*, February, 6–10.

—— (1974). *Fella's Choice* (Benin City: Ethiope Publishing).

—— (1973). 'The Missing Apex: A Search for the Audience', in: E. Oluwasanmi, E. McLean, and H. Zell (eds), *Publishing in Africa in the Seventies* (Ile-Ife: Ife University Press), 251–261.

Onoja, Adoyi (2013). 'A Reappraisal of the Historiography of the Police in Nigeria during the Colonial Period', *Journal of the Historical Society of Nigeria*, 22, 1–32.

Orford, Margie (2013). *Water Music* (Johannesburg: Jonathan Ball).

—— (2011). *Gallows Hill* (Johannesburg: Jonathan Ball).

—— (2009). *Daddy's Girl* (Johannesburg: Jonathan Ball).

—— (2009). *Blood Rose* (Johannesburg: Jonathan Ball).

—— (2008). *Like Clockwork* (Johannesburg: Jonathan Ball).

Orwell, George (1944). 'Raffles and Miss Blandish' (Orwell Foundation). Available at: www.orwellfoundation.com/the-orwell-foundation/orwell/essays-and-other-works/raffles-and-miss-blandish, accessed 21 June 2020.

Osofisan, Femi (2008). 'Domestication of an Opiate: Western Paraesthetics and the Growth of the Ekwensi Tradition', in: G.G. Darah (ed.), *Radical Essays on Nigerian Literature* (Lagos, Malthouse), 309–325.

—— [*published as* Okinba Launko] (2009). *Pirates* (Lagos: Lantern Books).

Otiso, Wycliffe Nyachoti and Ruth Joyce Kaguta (2016). 'Kenya at Fifty: State Policing Reforms, Politics, and Law, 1963–2013', in: Michael Mwenda Kithinji, Mickie Mwanzia Koster, and Jerono P. Rotich (eds), *Kenya After Fifty: Reconfiguring Historical, Political, and Policy Milestones* (New York: Palgrave Macmillan), 221–244.

Owusu-Ansah, F.A. (1971). 'The Tragedy of Essie', *The Mirror*, 28 August, 11.

—— (1971). 'The Tragedy of Essie', *The Mirror*, 21 August, 11.

Pahl, Miriam (2018). 'Reframing the Nation-State: The Transgression and Redrawing of Borders in African Crime Fiction', *Research in African Literatures*, 49(1), 84–102.

Paleker, Gairoonisa (2010). 'The B-Scheme Subsidy and the "Black Film Industry" in Apartheid South Africa, 1972–1990', *Journal of African Cultural Studies*, 22(1), 91–104.

Paren, Elizabeth (1978). 'The Multinational Publishing Firm in Africa: The Macmillan Perspective', *The African Book Publishing Record*, 4(1), 15–17.

Pearson, Nels and Marc Singer (2009). 'Open Cases: Detection, (Post)Modernity, and the State', in: N. Pearson and M. Singer (eds), *Detective Fiction in Postcolonial and Transnational World* (Burlington: Ashgate), 1–14.

Pepper, Andrew (2016). *Unwilling Executioner: Crime Fiction and the State* (Oxford: Oxford University Press).

Peters, Robert (dir.) (2020). *Thirty Pieces of Silver* [Motion picture] (Lagos: Charles Granville Productions, Genesis Pictures, and Whitestone Films).

Piccato, Pablo (2017). *A History of Infamy: Crime, Truth, and Justice in Mexico* (Berkeley and Los Angeles: University of California Press).

Poe, Edgar Allan (1845). 'The Purloined Letter', *The Gift* (Philadelphia).

—— (1841). 'Murders in the rue Morgue', *Graham's Magazine*, April (Philadelphia).

Porter, Dennis (1981). *The Pursuit of Crime: Art and Ideology in the Detective Novel* (New Haven: Yale University Press).

Prashad, Vijay (2002). *Everybody Was Kung Fu Fighting: Afro-Asian Connections and the Myth of Cultural Purity* (Boston: Beacon).

Primorac, Ranka (2012). 'Nation, Detection, and Time in Contemporary Southern African Fiction' in: A. Oed and C. Matzke (eds), *Life is a Thriller: Investigating African Crime Fiction* (Köln: Rüdiger Köppe Verlag), 21–34.

—— (2011). 'The Modern City and Citizen Efficacy in a Zambian Novel', *Journal of Postcolonial Writing*, 44(1), 49–59.

—— (2010). 'Cosmopolitanism and Social Change in a Zambian Thriller', *Research in African Literatures*, 41(3), 49–61.

—— (2005). 'The Eye of the Nation: Reading Ideology and Genre in a Zimbabwean Thriller', in: R. Mupande and R. Primorac (eds), *Versions of Zimbabwe: New Approaches to Literature and Culture* (Harare, Weaver Press), 161–176.

Quartey, Kwei (2019). 'Magic and Murder in African Crime Fiction', *Kwei Jones Quartey Blog*, 19 November. Available at: www.kweiquartey.com/post/african-crime-fiction, accessed 5 June 2021.
—— (2017). *Death by His Grace* (New York: Soho Crime).
—— (2016). *Gold of Our Fathers* (New York: Soho Crime).
—— (2014). *Murder at Cape Three Points* (New York: Soho Crime).
—— (2011). *Children of the Streets* (New York: Random House).
—— (2009). *Wife of the Gods* (New York: Random House).
Quaye, Cofie (1973). 'Copper Wire Conspiracy, pt. 2', *Pleasure: Ghana's Sunshine Magazine*, 5(5), November, 28–29.
—— (1970). *Murder in Kumasi* (Accra: Moxon).
—— (1970). *Sammy Slams his Gang* (Accra: Moxon).
Quinn, Mary Lou and Eugene Schleh (1989). 'Popular Crime in Africa: The Macmillan Education Program', *Clues: A Journal of Detection*, 10(2), 37–48.
Realnolly TV (2015). *The Investigator* [Motion picture]. Available at: https://www.youtube.com/watch?v=zpuHH8_YKAQ, accessed 9 September 2023.
Ribic, Peter (2021). '"When It Comes to Crime, I'm a Nationalist": National Integrity, Neocolonialism, and the Kenyan Thriller', *The Journal of Popular Culture*, 54(6), 1271–1290.
Robbins, Bruce (2015). 'The Detective is Suspended: Nordic Noir and the Welfare State', *Post45*. Available at: http://post45.research.yale.edu/2015/05, accessed August 2015.
Rodriguez, Ralph E. (2005). *Brown Gumshoes: Detective Fiction and the Search for Chicana/o Identity* (Austin: University of Texas Press).
le Roux, Elizabeth (2013). 'South African Crime and Detective Fiction in English: A Bibliography and Publishing History', *Current Writing: Text and Reception in Southern Africa* [Special issue: Crime Fiction, South Africa], 25(2), 136–152.
Ruheni, Mwangi (1975). *The Mystery Smugglers* (Nairobi: Spear).
Rushing, Robert A. (2007). *Resisting Arrest: Detective Fiction and Popular Culture* (New York: Other Press).
Saint, Lily (2013). '"You Kiss in Westerns": Cultural Translation in Moustapha Alassane's *Le retour d'un aventurier*', *Journal of African Cinemas*, 5(2), 203–217.
Salzani, Carlo (2007). 'The City as Crime Scene: Walter Benjamin and the Traces of the Detective', *New German Critique*, 34(1) (100), 165–187.
Sam, Gilbert A. (1960). *Who Killed Inspector Kwasi Minta?* (Accra: Gilisam Publishing Syndicate).
Sampson, Anthony (1957). *DRUM: The Newspaper that Won Africa* (Boston: Houghton Mifflin).
Sandwith, Corinne (2018). 'The Appearance of the Book: Towards a History of the Reading Lives and Worlds of Black South African Readers', *English in Africa*, 45(1), 11–38.
Sayers, Dorothy (1947 [1929]). 'The Omnibus of Crime', in: H. Haycraft (ed.), *The Art of the Mystery Story: A Collection of Critical Essays* (New York: Grosset and Dunlap), 71–109.
Shapiro, Matan (2019). 'Brajisalem: Biblical Cosmology, Power Dynamics and the Brazilian Political Imagination', *Ethnos*, 86(5), 832–852.

Sharma, Sarah (2014). *In the Meantime: Temporality and Cultural Politics* (Durham: Duke University Press).
—— (2011). 'The Biopolitical Economy of Time', *Journal of Communication Inquiry*, 35(4), 439–444.
Shaw, Rosalind (2002). *Memories of the Slave Trade: Ritual and the Historical Imagination in Sierra Leone* (University of Chicago Press).
Shih, Shu-mei (2004). 'Global Literature and the Technologies of Recognition', *PMLA*, 119(1), 16–30.
Siddiqi, Yumna (2008). *Anxieties of Empire and the Fiction of Intrigue* (New York: Columbia University Press).
Slaughter, Joseph (2007). *Human Rights, Inc.: The World Novel, Narrative Form, and International Law* (New York: Fordham University Press).
Slovo, Gillian (2000). *Red Dust* (London: Virago).
Smith, James Howard (2008). *Bewitching Development: Witchcraft and the Reinvention of Development in Neoliberal Kenya* (University of Chicago Press).
Soederberg, Susan (2001). 'Grafting Stability onto Globalisation: Deconstructing the IMF's Recent Bid for Transparency', *Third World Quarterly*, 22(5), 849–864.
Soitos, Stephen (1996). *The Blues Detective: A Study of African American Detective Fiction* (Amherst: University of Massachusetts Press).
Sorkin, Andrew Ross (2013). 'How Mandela Shifted Views on Freedom of Markets', *New York Times*, 9 December.
Soyinka, Wole (2003). *Death and the King's Horseman*, Simon Gikandi (ed.) (New York: Norton)
Sparrow Productions (2011). *Peep* [Web video series].
Steiner, Tina (2018). 'Temporal Aftermaths and Ruined Spaces in the African Metropolis: Cairo in the Crime Fiction of Parker Bilal', *English in Africa*, 45(3), 99–117.
Sternberg, Meir (1978). *Expositional Modes and Temporal Ordering in Fiction* (Baltimore: Johns Hopkins University Press).
Stiebel, Lindy (2002). 'Black "Tecs": Popular Thrillers by South African Black Writers in the Nineties', in: S. Newell (ed.), *Readings in African Popular Fiction* (Oxford: James Currey; Bloomington: Indiana University Press), 187–192.
Taiwo, Oladele (1984). *Female Novelists of Modern Africa* (New York: St. Martin's Press).
Tamuno, Tekena N. (1970). *The Police in Modern Nigeria 1861-1965: Origins, Development, and Role* (Ibadan University Press).
Tankebe, Justice (2013). 'In Search of Moral Recognition? Policing and Eudaemonic Legitimacy in Ghana', *Law & Social Inquiry*, 38(3), 576–597.
Tchumkam, Hervé (2012). 'Of Murder and Love: Peregrinations of the African Detective Writer', *Research in African Literatures*, 43(4), 38–49.
Thompson, Constable E.J. (1966). 'Point of No Return', *Sunday Mirror*, 27 February, 12, 14.
—— (1966). 'Point of No Return', *Sunday Mirror*, 20 February, 12.
—— (1966). 'Point of No Return', *Sunday Mirror*, 13 February, 10.
Thorpe, Victor (1979). *The Worshippers* (London and Basingstoke: Macmillan Pacesetters).

Tlholwe, Diale (2011). *Counting the Coffins* (Cape Town: Kwela Books).
—— (2008). *Ancient Rites* (Cape Town: Kwela Books).
Todorov, Tzvetan (1977). *The Poetics of Prose*. Richard Howard (trans.) (Ithaca: Cornell University Press).
Tomaselli, Keyan (1988). *The Cinema of Apartheid: Race and Class in South African Film* (London: Routledge).
Turner, Jann (2002). *Southern Cross* (London: Orion).
Tutu, Desmond Mpilo (1999). *No Future Without Forgiveness* (New York: Doubleday).
Ulasi, Adaora Lily (1978). *The Man from Sagamu* (London: Fontana-Collins).
—— (1971). *Many Thing Begin For Change* (London: Fontana-Collins).
—— (1970). *Many Thing You No Understand* (London: Fontana-Collins).
Umeh, Marie (2001). 'Ulasi, Adaora Lily', in: J.E. Miller (ed.), *Who's Who in Contemporary Women's Writing* (New York: Routledge), 328.
Umelo, Rosina (1984). *Finger of Suspicion* (London and Basingstoke: Macmillan Pacesetters).
Uwadi, Francis (dir.) (2014). *Oga Detective* [Motion picture] (Basildon/Nigeria: Nolly Rocky TV).
Visser, N.W. (1976). 'The Renaissance that Failed', *Journal of Commonwealth Literature*, 11(1), 42–57.
Walton, Patricia and Manina Jones (1999). *Detective Agency: Women Rewrite the Hard-boiled Tradition* (Berkeley and Los Angeles: University of California Press).
Wanjohi, Samuel Wambugu (2015). 'Narrating Transnational Violence and Crime in Mukoma Wa Ngugi's Novels' [MA Thesis] (Department of Literature, University of Nairobi).
Wenzel, Jennifer (2009). *Bulletproof: Afterlives of Anticolonial Prophesy in South Africa and Beyond* (University of Chicago Press).
Williams, John A. and Lori Williams (eds) (2008). *Dear Chester, Dear John: Letters between Chester Himes and John A. Williams* (Detroit: Wayne State University Press).
Williams, Raymond (1977). *Marxism and Literature* (Oxford: Oxford University Press).
Willis, Justin (2015). '"Peace and Order are in the Interest of Every Citizen": Elections, Violence and State Legitimacy in Kenya, 1957–1974', *International Journal of African Historical Studies*, 48(1), 99–116.
Wilson, Edmund (1944). 'Why Do People Read Detective Stories', *New Yorker*, 14 October, 78–84.
Winston, Robert P. and Nancy C. Mellerski (1992). *The Public Eye: Ideology and the Police Procedural* (New York: St. Martin's Press).
Woods, Paula (ed.) (1995). *Spooks, Spies, and Private Eyes: Black Mystery, Crime and Suspense Fiction of the Twentieth Century* (New York: Doubleday).
Yemoh, Ali (1973). 'Oko & Ebo in Slaves of the Lens', *Pleasure: Ghana's Sunshine Magazine*, 5(1), 30–31.
Žižek, Slavoj (1991). *Looking Awry: An Introduction to Jacques Lacan through Popular Culture* (Cambridge: MIT University Press).

Index

Abani, Chris 77, 78 n.17, 191
Achebe, Chinua 5, 31, 99, 120
   Arrow of God 107
   Things Fall Apart 10, 104
Adenle, Leye 118 n.4, 153
Adomako, K. Bamfi 5
'Adventures of Annan-Clay'
   (Duodu) 65
African detective fiction
   archive of 24–6
   capitalism and 21, 117
   citizenship and 188
   as conservative 10–13, 15–16
   criminality in 1
   decolonization and 2, 26
   development of 23
   dispossession in 32, 43, 187, 188–9
   future of 191–2
   futurity of 190
   historical context of 185–7
   influence of Doyle on 31, 186
   justice in 1, 139, 187–8, 192
   law and courts in 1, 15, 87–92, 187, 189
   liberalism and 21, 117
   misogyny in 21
   modernity and 56
   neoliberalism and 117, 120–6, 130, 134–5
   playfulness of 14, 190–1
   political efficacy of 9
   postcoloniality and 189–90
   power and 1
   as progressive 14–15
   social detection in 9, 9 n.7, 188–9
   sovereign authority in 13, 22–3, 26, 87 n.30, 187–9
   the state, critique of 5–9, 13, 15, 21–2, 87
   transnational influences on 18–22
   urban life in 39–42
   See also detective fiction
African Film (photonovel)
   Lance Spearman stories 19, 77–8, 152
African National Congress
   (ANC) 62–3
Africanness 25
Afrikaner Nationalist Party 23
Agamben, Giorgio 131
Alily, Valentine 77, 78
Althusser, Louis 11
Ancient Rites (Tlholwe) 118, 123, 132–4
   class in 124–5, 132–3
   economic subjectivity in 131
   gender in 132–3
   justice in 140–1
   occult economics in 128, 137–8, 189
   Pentecostalism in 138
   role of detective in 135, 137–9
Anderson, Benedict 156
Anuah, P.D. 65, 66 n.6
apartheid 74
   Black South African writing and 14
   in *Chief* series 44–5
   dispossession and 36, 45
   escalation of 23
   policing under 62–3
   property and 52
   resettlement 58
   violence and 36, 178
Appiah, Kwame Anthony 119
Apter, Andrew 71, 99–100, 120, 175–6
Armillas-Tiseyra, Magalí 7–8

Ashun, Carlton   65
Auden, W.H.   187
Augart, Julia   7
Awuah, A.K.   65

Babangida, Ibrahim Badamosi   121, 172
Banda, Sekelani S.   19
Bayart, Jean-Francois   15 n.16
Beautiful Place to Die, A (Nunn)   178, 179
Benjamin, Walter   40, 47, 47 n.20, 53, 170, 175
Bennett, Tony   81
Benni Kamba 009 novels (Maillu)   74, 76, 78–9, 82, 153
   state institutions in   85, 87
Berglund, Karl   154
Beukes, Lauren   119
Bilal, Parker (Jamal Mahjoub)   24, 149, 149 n.3, 154 n.7
   See also Makana mysteries (Bilal)
bildung   156–7, 162, 165
bildungsroman   21–2, 38
Binder, Sabine   7, 11 n.11
Black, Shameem   178–9
Blacklaws, Troy   31 n.5
Blaxploitation   76–7, 77 n.16
Bolaji, Omoseye   119, 153
Bolaño, Roberto   131
Borges, Jorge Luis   15 n.15
Braddon, Mary Elizabeth   6
Brown, Matthew H.   33
Bryce, Jane   103–4
Bushtrackers, The (Mwangi)   19, 74, 77

Cain, James M.   17
capitalism
   African detective fiction and   21, 117
   colonial   22, 32, 143–5, 153–4
   detective fiction and   39–40, 102
   Doyle and   43
   Ghana and   146
   global   18
   neoliberal   147, 169
   police procedurals and   22
   Protestantism and   126 n.12
   seriality and   155
   temporality of   143–5
Casanova, Pascale   20
Chakava, Henry   10, 10 n.9
Chalfin, Brenda   116, 147
Champigny, Robert   94, 159, 185
Chandler, Raymond   6, 17, 18, 48 n.21
Charteris, Leslie   18, 35
Chase, James Hadley   12, 153
   fascist aesthetics of   22
   influence on African writers   18–19, 19 n.20, 36
   misogyny in   22
Chesterton, G.K.   187
Cheyney, Peter   18
Chief series (Maimane as Arthur Mogale)   22, 29, 33, 37–8, 50–2, 152, 191
   apartheid in   44–5
   colonial dispossession in   49–50, 56–7
   entrepreneurialism in   41
   independence in   51
   liberal selfhood in   41
   scientific rationalism in   43–4, 50
   self-possession in   56–7
   surveillance in   44
   See also Maimane, Arthur
Christie, Agatha   6, 16
   African readership of   18, 152
   repetition in   165
citizenship   2, 59
   African detective fiction and   188
   neoliberal   117, 134, 184
   the state and   5
class   132–5
   in *Ancient Rites*   124–5, 132–3
Close, Glen   130–1
'Clue to the Unsolved Problem' (Nfojoh)   65
colonialism
   authoritarianism and   18
   capitalism and   32
   criminality and   29

dispossession and   23, 29, 32, 39, 43, 46 n.18, 46–50, 56–7, 62
  labor and   48–54
  modernity and   112
  neocolonialism   7
  policing   60–1, 84–5
  property, protection of   48
  state sovereignty and   2
  subjecthood and   32
  temporality of   102, 107–11
  violence of   47
  See also decolonization, postcoloniality
Comaroff, Jean   48, 49, 92, 132
  on pharmaceutical industrial complex   132
Comaroff, John   48, 49, 92, 132
Condouriotis, Eleni   10 n.10
Coovadia, Imraan   191
courtroom drama   2, 88, 91–2
crime fiction
  v. detective fiction   3
  development of   6
  implicit futurity of   23
  Scandinavian   153, 154–5, 166 n.16, 190
  seriality in   151–2
  See also detective fiction
criminalization
  false accusations   170
  of state institutions   1, 15, 95–7, 112

Damrosch, David   20
Dangerous Inheritance (Nwokolo)   94–5, 101–2, 112, 118 n.4, 166
Darko Dawson procedurals (Quartey)   17, 119, 146–9, 153, 155 n.11
  efficiency in   157–8, 159–60
  labor in   148
  meritocracy in   158–9, 160
  neoliberal temporality in   146–7, 159–60
  Pentecostal Christianity in   147–8
  policing in   148
  seriality and   156–7
  victims in   147

Darlington, Sonja   7
Deadly Cargo (Marinho)   74, 120 n.6
decolonization
  African detective fiction and   2, 26
  kleptocracy and   93–4, 120
  modernity and   93
  nationalism and   127
  nation-building   80, 98, 120
  of Nigeria   98, 99, 101, 106–7
  police procedurals and   22
  of policing   62, 71
  state power and   71–2, 91–2, 118
  state role in   62–3, 93–5, 141, 145, 148, 166–7, 189–90
  teleology of   143–4
  temporality of   24, 105
  tradition and   111
  See also colonialism, postcoloniality
Denning, Michael   80
Derrida, Jacques   67
detective fiction
  Africanization of   1–2
  Benjamin on   40, 47, 47 n.20, 53, 170, 175
  capitalism and   39–40, 102
  characters in   30, 162–3
  colonial dispossession in   39, 43, 102
  delayed exposition in   95, 143
  future perfect narration of   94, 95, 100–1, 112, 143, 185, 190
  futurity of   185, 190
  generic attributes of   3–4
  as ideologically conservative   10–13, 15–16
  individual rights in   39
  justice and   4
  liberalism and   102
  liberal society, restoration of   42–3, 187
  modernity and   42
  narratology of   94–5, 185
  neoliberalism and   184
  realism of   103, 186
  repetitive looping in   162–3
  sovereign power in   39, 96

the state and 5–6
surveillance and 109
temporality of 95, 165
urban life in 39–40, 42
violence and 10
See also African detective fiction
Detective Ridgemore Riva
  (Machingauta) 17, 77
developmentalism 115–16, 143–4
  de-developmentalism 145–6, 156–7
  modernization and 93, 95
  in police procedurals 83–4, 91
D'Haen, Theo 20
Dhlakama, Afonso Marceta
  Macacho 135
Dimock, Wai Chee 20–1
dispossession
  in African detective fiction 32, 43, 187, 188–9
  apartheid and 36, 45
  of Black selfhood 16, 22, 45
  colonial 23, 29, 32, 39, 43, 46–50, 46 n.18, 56–7, 62
  in *People of the City* 45–6, 52–5
  settler colonial 52
Dow, Unity 19, 121–2, 122 n.9, 186, 190
  feminist critique of 7, 16–17
  graphic violence in 129–30
  neoliberal governance, critique of 24
  political subjectivity in 140
  See also Screaming of the Innocent,
    The (Dow)
Doyle, Arthur Conan 6, 16, 20, 152, 185
  African readership of 18
  bourgeois liberal selfhood in 45
  capitalism and 43
  The Hound of the Baskervilles 175
  influence of 31, 186
  repetition in 165
Driver, Dorothy 50 n.23
Drum (magazine) 9, 19, 29, 60
  criticism of 30
  futurity of 34–5
  gender roles in 50 n.23

influences on 35–6
modernity and 33–4
outlawing of 58
political writing 30
Dube, Hope 81, 153
Duodu, S.O. 65, 67 n.7, 69

Ebersohn, Wessel 58 n.25
Eco, Umberto 15 n.15, 162–3, 165
Ekwensi, Cyprian 1, 19, 185
  on Chase's influence 19 n.20
  colonial dispossession in 43
  critiques of 30–1
  Drum stories 29, 60
  gender in 50 n.23
  influences on 31 n.7, 153
  justice in 30
  liberal individualism and 31
  limits of detection 32
  possession in 32
  resistance in 23
  reviews of 33 n.8
  See also People of the City (Ekwensi),
    Yaba Round-about Murder
    (Ekwensi)
Elliot, C.M. 65 n.5
Ellis, Stephen 15 n.16
Emenyonu, Ernest 68
entrepreneurialism
  in *Chief* series 40–1
  in *Finger of Suspicion* 172, 180, 182–3
  in *People of the City* 40–1
  in *Red Ink* 182–3
  subjectivity and 169–70
Epidemic, The (Marinho) 118, 120–1, 122
  class in 132
  collective detection in 139
  economic subjectivity in 131
  justice in 140–1
  neoliberal governance in 132, 134–5
Erdmann, Eva 154
escapism 9–10
espionage thrillers
  See spy thrillers

Expo '77 (Ike)   99–101, 102, 112, 176
  future perfect narration of   94, 95, 100
  static temporality of   100–1
Eyo, Henri   119

Fanon, Frantz   12, 111–12, 189
Fay, Jennifer   17
Fella's Choice (Omotoso)   19, 72–4, 75 n.12, 76, 77, 80
  influence of James Bond novels   18
  state institutions in   85, 185–6
femmes fatales   35
  in Maimane   50 n.23
Ferguson, James   93, 116 n.1, 143–4
Finger of Suspicion (Umelo)
  entrepreneurialism in   172, 180, 182–3
  meritocracy in   172, 173, 174–5
  mystification in   170, 174–7
  neoliberal ethos of   170, 172–4, 180
  occult violence, accusations of   174
  personal transparency in   169–70, 174–7, 182–4
Fleming, Ian   81, 82, 152
Flight 800 (Fulani)   77, 85–6, 87
Forsyth, Frederick   12
For the Fairest (Kibuuka)   17
Foucault, Michel   67, 68, 91
Friedman, Milton   150
Frimprong-Manso, Shirley   153, 155 n.11, 191–2
Fukuyama, Francis   165
Fulani, Dan   76, 186
  Flight 800   77, 85–6, 87
futurity
  of African detective fiction   190
  of crime fiction   23
  of detective fiction   185, 190
  in *Drum*   34–5

Gaboriau, Émile   6, 20
Gagiano, Annie   122 n.10
Ganiyu, Muftau   77 n.16

gender
  in *Ancient Rites*   132–3
  in *Drum* stories   50 n.23
  labor and   116
  masculinity, African   11 n.11
  in police procedurals   84 n.24
  in *Screaming of the Innocent*   132, 133–5
  in Ulasi   104
genre
  global   20–2
  of *People of the City*   38–9
  postcoloniality and   14
  Ulasi and   105
Genya, Monica   74, 76
Getachew, Adom   80
Ghana
  capitalism and   146
  customary law in   89–90
  independence of   23, 59, 118
  neoliberalization of   147, 157
  newspaper fiction in   66, 66 n.7
  policing in   62
Gide, André   20
Gikandi, Simon   98, 102
globalization   7, 127
Golakai, H.J.   119, 153
  The Lazarus Effect   178
  The Score   191
Goodlad, Lauren   154 n.7
governance   2
  neoliberal   24, 132, 134–5, 137, 141, 177, 183–4
  state sovereignty and   59
  transparency   177, 183–4
Gramsci, Antonio   47, 47 n.20, 53, 136
Guldimann, Colette   44–5, 45 n.17

Habila, Helon   19, 153–4
Hammett, Dashiell   6, 17, 18, 48 n.21, 134, 152, 154 n.7
hard-boiled fiction   17–18, 82 n.21, 136
  influence on African detective fiction   35, 46
  skepticism of liberalism   46

Harvey, David 143
Hassan, Robert 144, 161 n.14
Hayek, Friedrich von 150
Henson, Pauline 65 n.5
Hibou, Beatrice 15 n.16
Higginson, Pim 13–14, 20
Himes, Chester 20, 155, 186
Hirst, Terry 76 n.13
'Hot Money' (Duodu) 65
Hour of Death in Harare, The
  (Atalebe) 86

Ibe, Adimchinma 65, 118 n.4, 153
Ike, Chukwuemeka 99
  Expo '77 94, 95, 99–101
independence, African 2
  in *Chief* series 51
  Ghanaian 23, 59, 118
  Nigerian 37, 37 n.13, 106
  police procedurals and 68
International Monetary Fund
  (IMF) 115, 121
  impact on publishing 153–4
  reform mandates 117, 169, 186
I Profess This Crime (Oloyede) 94
Irele, Abiola 75 n.12
'Iron Box, The' (Komey) 65, 87–91
Irungu, James 119

Jaji, Tsitsi 14, 189
Jameson, Frederic 83, 136–7
Joe (magazine) 76 n.13
juju fiction 104
justice
  in African detective fiction 1, 30,
    139–41, 186–8, 192
  detective fiction and 4
  neoliberal 135
  restorative justice 7, 187
  the state and 4

Kalua, Festus 7 n.5
Karengo, Wahome 24
Kariamiti, John 12
Katalambulla, F. 78 n.17

Katz, Cynthia 169
Khumalo, Fred 36
Kibuuka, Ulysses Chuka 18–19, 11
  For the Fairest 17
'Killer Ape' (Abani) 191
Killer on the Loose, A (Nzekwe) 25,
  93–4, 95, 98, 118 n.4
  as necropornographic 130
Kipling, Rudyard 103, 103 n.4
de Kock, Leon 8, 182 n.9
Kokotovic, Misha 23
Komey, Ellis Ayitey 65
  poems 88 n.31
Krings, Matthias 152
Krishnan, Madhu 37
Kubuitsile, Lauri 119, 153
kung fu films 77 n.16

labor
  colonialism and 48–54
  in Darko Dawson procedurals 148
  feminization of 116
  gender and 116
La Guma, Alex 5
Lance Spearman stories 19, 77–8, 152
law
  in African detective fiction 1, 15,
    87–92, 187, 189
  customary v. common 89–90
  postcoloniality and 89–91
  in spy thrillers 87
Leavis, F.R. 9
le Carré, John 82
liberalism 16–18
  African detective fiction and 21,
    117
  of detective fiction 42–3, 187
  See also neoliberalism
liberalization
  of Nigeria 121, 169, 172, 175–6, 186
  Pentecostal Christianity and 125–9
Lindfors, Bernth 30, 79
Links of a Chain (Genya) 74, 76
Locke, John 32
Loimeier, Mannfred 103

'Lost Corpse, The' (Anuah)   65
'Love Comes Deadly' (Manqupu)   29,
    33, 36, 38
  the city in   42
  as necropornographic   130
Ludlum, Robert   12, 153
Lynn, Martin   37 n.13

Machingauta, Rodwell Musekiwa   65,
    67 n.7, 77
  Detective Ridgemore Riva   17
MacKenzie, Jassy   153
Mahjoub, Jamal (pseud. Parker
    Bilal)   24, 149, 149 n.3, 154 n.7
  See also Makana mysteries (Bilal)
Maillu, David G.   12, 18, 185–6, 190
  Benni Kamba 009 novels   74, 76,
    78–9, 82, 131, 153
Maimane, Arthur
  colonial dispossession in   43, 49–50
  critiques of   30–1
  femmes fatales in   50 n.23
  influence of Doyle on   31
  influence of hard-boiled fiction
    on   35, 46
  justice in   30
  liberal selfhood in   31, 44–5
  limits of detection in   32
  possession in   32
  resistance in   23
  See also Chief series (Maimane as
    Arthur Mogale)
Mains, Daniel   161 n.14
Makana mysteries (Bilal)   146, 149–51, 153
  Islamist militancy in   161–2
  neoliberal capitalism and   147
  neoliberal social relations in   165–7
  neoliberal time in   160–1, 161 n.14
  recurring characters   151
  seriality and   156–7
  stasis in   160–5, 161 n.14
Makholwa, Angela   24, 119, 172–3, 192
  Black Widow Society   181–2, 182 n.9
  See also Red Ink (Makholwa)
Mamdani, Mahmood   90

Mandel, Ernest   47 n.20
Man from Sagamu, The (Ulasi)   95, 102,
    104, 105–12
  delayed exposition in   108
  generic codes of   105, 109
  sovereign authority in   109
  state power in   106
  Yoruba cosmology in   95, 107–8,
    110–11, 189
  See also Ulasi, Adaora Lily
Manqupu, Mbokotwane
  critiques of   30–1
  influence of hard-boiled fiction
    on   35
  justice in   30
  'Love Comes Deadly'   29, 33, 36, 38
  possession in   32
Marinho, Tony   23–4, 81, 190
  neoliberal governance, critique
    of   24
  See also Epidemic, The (Marinho)
Mark of the Cobra (Alily)   77, 78
Masemola, Thabo Nkosinathi
  Mixed Signals   64, 69, 70, 83, 181
    n.8
Matzke, Christine   7, 9, 25 n.25
Mayer, Ruth   121, 155
Mbembe, Achille   131
McCall Smith, Alexander   153, 155 n.11
McCann, Sean   16, 17, 130–1
McClure, James   58 n.25, 65 n.5, 85 n.27,
    153
Mellerski, Nancy C.   67, 68
Men from Pretoria, The (Ng'weno)   19,
    74–6, 76 n.14, 79, 79 n.18, 166, 191
Meyer, Birgit   116 n.1, 126–7, 126 n.12
Meyer, Deon   153, 155 n.11
  Dead at Daybreak   178
Miracle Merchant, The (Mutahi and
    Karengo)   118, 119–20, 134, 186, 192
  class in   132
  critique of neoliberal
    governance   137
  economic subjectivity in   131
  justice in   140–1

neoliberalism in   126
Pentecostalism in   125–8
role of detective in   135–7, 138–9
sovereign power, expropriation of   131–2
zombies in   127–8
misogyny
in African detective fiction   21, 130
in Chase   22
Mixed Signals (Masemola)   64, 69, 70, 84 n.26, 91, 181 n.8
economic development in   83
modernity
African   33
African detective fiction and   56
colonialism and   112
decolonial   93
detective fiction and   42
Drum magazine and   33–4
Nigeria and   95
noir and   17–18
police procedurals and   70
seriality and   155
temporality and   102, 111, 143–4, 155, 165–6
modernization
development telos of   93, 95
retreat from   116
Modisane, Bloke   9–10, 12, 51
influences on   35, 153
on Sophiatown   34
Mohsen, Caroline A.   149
Moi, Daniel arap   115
Mokae, Gomolemo   64–5, 119
Secret in my Bosom, The   64–5, 83, 84–5, 181 n.8
Monsiváis, Carlos   11
Moretti, Franco   20
on detective fiction   30, 162–3, 165
Mosely, Walter   19
Mphalele, Ezekiel   88 n.31
Msiska, Mpalive-Hangson   11
Mtobwa, Ben R.   5
Mudavadi, Musalia   115
Mühleisen, Susanne   9

Mukoma Wa Ngugi   10–11, 19, 26, 153–5, 186, 189
Murder at Dawn (Johnson)   94
Murder at Sunset (Gyamfaa-Fofie)   94, 118 n.4
Murder in Majengo (Macgoye), 76 n.14, 94
Mutahi, Wahome   135, 135 n.22
neoliberal governance, critique of   24
See also *Miracle Merchant, The* (Mutahi and Karengo)
Mwangi, Meja   12, 74
The Bushtrackers   19, 74, 77
Mystery Smugglers, The (Ruheni)   74, 79 n.18
mystery stories   15
See also African detective fiction, detective fiction

nationalism
decolonization and   127
liberation rhetoric   101
Nasserist   146, 151, 160, 165
neoliberalism and   120
Nigerian   101
postcolonial   96–7, 138
teleology of   146
Ndebele, Njabulo   30–1, 33, 51
necropornography   129–31
neocolonialism   7
neoliberalism
African detective fiction and   117, 120–6, 130, 134–5, 170, 172–4, 180
capitalism and   147, 169
citizenship and   117, 134, 184
detective fiction and   184
evangelical Christianity and   126
governance and   24, 132, 134–5, 137, 141, 177, 183–4
justice and   135
nationalism and   120
Nigerian cheating scandal   100, 176
postcolonial African state and   2
publishing and   117, 143, 167

privatization of risk   112
sovereign selfhood and   170, 177
state sovereignty and   8–9, 115–17, 131, 135, 138, 140, 160, 164–5, 187
subjectivity and   173–4, 177
temporality of   24, 145–7, 155–6, 158–61, 161 n.14
violence of   120, 131
neoliberalization   123
  of African state   143
  of Egypt   150–1
  of Ghana   147, 157
  of Nigeria   175–6
neoliberal noir   23–4, 118, 119–20, 184
neopoliciaco   12 n.13
Newell, Stephanie   20–1, 84 n.24
Nfojoh, George Kofi   65
Ngũgĩ wa Thiong'o   5, 12
Ng'weno, Hilary   10, 74–5, 75 n.12
  The Men from Pretoria   19
Nicol, Mike   26, 155 n.11
Nieland, Justus   17
Nigeria
  arson wave in   95–6, 96 n.1
  cheating scandal   100, 176
  decolonization of   98, 99, 101, 106–7
  independence   37, 37 n.13, 106
  liberalization of   121, 169, 172, 175–6, 186
  modernity and   95
  nationalism   101
  oil boom   71, 72, 95, 104, 120, 171, 172, 176
  post-independence writing in   59
Nilsson, Louise   20
Nkrumah, Kwame   146
  address to police graduates   61–2, 63, 66, 71
noir
  modernity and   17–18
  neoliberal   23–4, 118, 119–20, 184
Nollywood films   141, 191
Nunn, Malla   119 n.5, 153, 154 n.9, 156
  A Beautiful Place to Die   178

Nuttall, Sarah   173, 184
Nwankwo, Nkem   5
Nwapa, Flora   152
Nxumalo, Henry   51

Obeng, R.E.   1
  Issa Busanga   29
Obiechina, Emmanuel   30, 37, 39
Odhiambo, Tom   34 n.10
Odoi, Frank   76 n.13
Oed, Anja   7
Ogunyemi, Chikwenye Okonjo   104–5
Okara, Gabriel   120
Okigbo, Christopher   99
Okpi, Kalu   186
  The Smugglers   74
  The South African Affair   74, 79 n.18, 86 n.28
Olaniyan, Tejumola   4–5, 15
Oloyede, Sola   94, 153
Omotoso, Kole   1, 18, 75 n.12, 190
  See also *Fella's Choice* (Omotoso)
Onwueme, Tess Akaeke   119
Orford, Margie   153, 178
Orwell, George   22
Osofisan, Femi   10, 31
  Pirates (as Okinba Launko)   12, 118 n.4
Osundare, Niyi   120
Owusu-Ansah, F.A.   65, 66 n.6

Pacesetters novels   19, 75, 96, 152 n.5, 171–2
Pahl, Miriam   8
Parks, Gordon, Jr.   19, 77
pass laws   48
Peep (webseries)   153, 192
Pentecostalism   125–9, 138, 147–8, 161
People of the City (Ekwensi)   25, 29–30, 37–9, 166
  AWS edition   38, 46 n.18, 68 n.10
  critiques of   30
  dispossession of self in   45–6, 52–5
  entrepreneurialism in   40–1
  genre of   38–9

labor in   52–4
liberal selfhood in   40–1, 44–6
police officers in   69, 70
residential labor controls in   48 n.21
self-possession in   54–6, 57
urban life in   40–2
violence in   44
See also Ekwensi, Cyprian
Pepper, Andrew   5–6, 13, 15, 19–20
photonovels   77–8, 152
Pirates (Osofisan as Okinba Launko)   12, 118 n.4
Pleasure: Ghana's Sunshine Magazine   152
Poe, Edgar Allen   6, 20, 185
  Dupin stories   15 n.15, 16, 152
  'The Purloined Letter'   87 n.30
'Point of No Return, The' (Thompson)   65
police procedurals   59–60, 118
  beneficent state in   64–71, 72–3, 83
  capitalism, affirmation of   22
  conservatism of   22
  decolonization and   22
  economic development in   83–4, 91
  gender in   84 n.24
  independence and   68
  law enforcement in   63
  modernity and   70
  policing in   69, 84–5
  popularity, decline of   92
  post-independence   64
  state sovereignty in   63–4, 67, 80
  state violence in   63
  surveillance in   68–70
  violence in   70
policing
  under apartheid   60–1
  colonial   60–1, 84–5
  decolonization of   62, 71
  in Darko Dawson procedurals   148
  in Ghana   62
  in police procedurals   69, 84–5
  post-apartheid   62–3

post-independence   61–2
in *Yaba Round-about Murder*   69–70, 84–5
Porter, Dennis   11, 22, 106
postcoloniality
  in African detective fiction   189–90
  genre and   14
  the law and   89–91
  nationalism   96–7, 138
  neoliberalism and   2
  sovereignty and   2, 102, 117
  temporality and   102, 111, 143–4
Primorac, Ranka   9, 26
publishing
  asymmetric economic conditions of   75 n.12
  global capitalism and   153–4
  neoliberalism and   117, 143, 167
  popular genre series   75, 120, 143, 152 n.5

Quartey, Kwei   19, 24, 65
  critique of Dow   129–30
  Wife of the Gods   10
  See also Darko Dawson procedurals (Quartey)
Quaye, Cofi   152

racism, colonial   18
Red Dust (Slovo)   178
Red Ink (Makholwa)   191
  entrepreneurialism in   182–3
  mystification in   170, 177, 180
  neoliberal ethos of   170, 172–4, 180–1
  neoliberal selfhood in   180
  personal transparency in   169–70, 174, 177, 181, 182–4
  See also Makholwa, Angela
resistance
  in Africa   23
  genre fiction and   13
  seriality and   24
resistant reading   35–6
restorative justice   7, 187

Revenge (film)   19
Robbins, Bruce   166 n.16
Ruheni, Mwangi   12, 81, 186
   The Mystery Smugglers   74, 79 n.18

Sabelo, George   58 n.25
Saint, Lily   14, 189
Sam, Gilbert A.   59, 60
   See also *Who Killed Inspector Kwasi Minta?* (Sam)
Sayers, Dorothy   11, 11 n.12, 154 n.8, 185
Scandinavian crime fiction   153, 154–5, 166 n.16, 190
Screaming of the Innocent, The (Dow)   7 n.5, 118, 121–3, 134
   class in   132, 133–5
   collective detection in   139–40
   economic subjectivity in   131
   gender in   132, 133–5
   justice in   140–1
   occult economics in   128–30, 129 n.17
Secret History of Las Vegas, The (Abani)   7
Secret in my Bosom, The (Mokae)   64–5, 83–5, 84 n.26, 181 n.8
   economic development in   83
selfhood
   liberal   31, 40–1, 44–5
   neoliberal   170, 177
   as property   49
self-possession
   anticolonialism and   57
   in *Chief* series   56–7
seriality
   capitalism and   155
   in crime stories   151–2
   in Darko Dawson procedurals   156–7
   economics of   153–5
   imagined communities and   156
   in Makana mysteries   156–7
   modernity and   155
   novel series   151–3
   resistance and   24

   stasis and   156, 160–5
   temporality of   143–7
serialization
   neoliberal time and   146–7
Sharma, Sarah   144–5, 161 n.14
Shih, Shu-mei   24
Slovo, Gillian   58 n.25
Smugglers, The (Okpi)   74
Sophiatown   33, 34–5, 58
South Africa
   crime in   181
   economic liberalization of   174, 178
   pass laws in   48, 51
   popularity of Westerns in   31 n.5
   post-apartheid   173, 178, 181–2
   resistant reading in   35–6
   Sophiatown   33, 34–5, 58
   transparency in   179
   Truth and Reconciliation Commission (TRC)   178–9
South African Affair, The (Okpi)   74, 79 n.18, 82
   state institutions in   86 n.28
Southern Cross (Turner)   178
sovereignty, personal   2
   sovereign selfhood   16, 170, 177
sovereignty, state   2, 190
   in African detective fiction   2–3, 13, 22–3, 26, 87 n.30, 187–9
   the African state and   4
   coloniality and   2
   in detective fiction   39, 96
   expropriation of   131–2
   governance and   59
   in *Man from Sagamu*   109
   neoliberalism and   8–9, 115–17, 131, 135, 138, 140, 160, 164–5, 187
   in police procedurals   63–4, 67, 80
   postcoloniality and   2, 102, 117
   in spy thrillers   63–4, 72, 82
   state power and   63–4, 109
   See also state, the
Soyinka, Wole   5, 31
   Death and the King's Horseman   61
Spy in Time, A (Coovadia)   191

spy thrillers   60, 118
    apartheid government in   74
    beneficent state in   83
    Blaxploitation, influence of   76–7
    Bond thrillers, influence of   18, 76, 76 n.14, 81
    British   82 n.21
    Empire and   80–2
    as fantasy   78–80
    humor and spectacle in   79 n.18
    the law in   87
    law enforcement in   63
    neocolonial threat in   80
    popularity, decline of   92
    post-independence   64
    sovereignty and   72, 80, 82
    state institutions in   85–7
    state sovereignty in   63–4, 72, 82
    state violence in   63
    surveillance in   86
Stanley, Michael   153
state, the
    in African detective fiction   5–9, 13, 15, 21–2, 85–7, 86 n.28, 185–6
    in classic whodunits   67
    in detective fiction   5–6
    as guarantor of rights   59
    citizenship and   5
    criminalization of institutions   1, 15, 95–7, 112
    decolonization, role in   62–3, 93–5, 141, 145, 148, 166–7, 189–90
    decolonization, state power and   71–2, 91–2, 118
    detective fiction and   5–6
    justice and   4
    liberation projects   60, 67, 86, 91, 95, 98, 101
    in *Man from Sagamu*   106
    neoliberalism and   115–17
    sovereignty and   4, 102
    surveillance and   109
    See also sovereignty, state
State Secret (Dube)   74
Steiner, Tina   160
Sternberg, Meir   108

Stop Press: Murder (Garba)   79, 94, 166
subjecthood
    colonialism and   32
    victims' loss of   130–1
subjectivity
    economic   131
    entrepreneurialism and   169–70
    neoliberalism and   173–4, 177
    political   140
'Subversion at Poso' (Duodu)   65
Sue, Eugène   38
surveillance
    in *Chief* series   44
    in detective fiction   109
    in Maimane   44
    in police procedurals   68–70
    in spy thrillers   86
    the state and   109

temporality
    of capitalism   143–5
    colonial   102, 107–12
    decolonial   24, 105
    of detective fiction   95, 165
    Enlightenment   95, 105, 110
    of *Expo '77*   100–1
    of global capitalism   143–5
    modernity and   102, 111, 143–4, 155, 165–6
    neoliberal   24, 145–7, 155–6, 158–61, 161 n.14
    network time   144, 155, 158
    postcolonial   102, 111, 143–4
    of seriality   143–7
    sovereignty and   105
    Yoruba   95, 107–8, 110–12
ten Kortenaar, Neil   98
Thief of the State (Ighavini)   94
Things Fall Apart (Achebe)   10, 104
Thompson, Constable E.J.   65, 66 n.6, 69–70
Thorpe, Victor   153, 191
Tlholwe, Diale   121–2, 153, 192
    Counting the Coffins   119, 123, 178, 181 n.8
    neoliberal governance, critique of   24

neoliberalization in   123
See also Ancient Rites (Tlholwe)
'Tragedy of Essie, The' (Owusu-Ansah)   65
transparency
  in *Finger of Suspicion*   169–70, 174, 175, 176–7, 182–4
  meritocracy in   173
  neoliberal self-governance and   177, 183–4
  in *Red Ink*   169–70, 174, 177, 181, 182–4
  in South Africa   179
truth commission thrillers   178–9
Tutu, Desmond   178

Ulasi, Adaora Lily   22, 102–3
  colonial past in   103
  critical responses to   103–5
  gender in   104
  genre and   105
  Many Thing Begin for Change   108
  politics of   103–4, 111
  supernatural forces in   103, 189
  See also Man from Sagamu, The (Ulasi)
Umelo, Rosina   19, 24, 171–2
  See also Finger of Suspicion (Umelo)

Vidocq, Eugène-François   6, 20, 38
violence
  apartheid and   36, 178
  colonial   47
  in detective fiction   10
  in Dow   129–30
  neoliberal   120, 131
  in neoliberal noir   118, 130–2
  occult   174
  in *People of the City*   44
  in police procedurals   63, 70
  state   52–3, 63, 178

Weber, Max   126 n.12
Wenzel, Jennifer   101
Westerns   31 n.5
whiteness   179
whodunits   1
  bourgeois values of   16
  liberal capitalist values of   44
  locked-room mysteries   185
  self-sovereignty in   32
  the state in   67
  See also African detective fiction, detective fiction
Who Killed Inspector Kwasi Minta? (Sam)   59, 64–5, 66 n.6, 79, 82, 91
  economic development in   83
  justice in   186
  police-public encounters in   66, 70
  the state in   67–8
  subjectivity in   131
'Who Killed Rosi?' (Ashun)   65
Wife of the Gods (Quartey)   10
Williams, Raymond   21
Winston, Robert P.   67, 68
witchcraft, accusations of   125, 127–8, 127 n.14
Woollacott, Janet   81
World Bank   115, 121, 153–4, 186

Yaba Round-about Murder (Ekwensi)   59, 64, 65, 66 n.6, 67, 91
  critical reception   68 n.9
  economic development in   83
  policing in   69–70, 84–5
  realism of   79
  the state in   68, 90
  subjectivity in   131
Yemoh, Ali   152

Žižek, Slavoj   136
zombies   127–8

AFRICAN ARTICULATIONS

ISSN 2054-5673

Previously published

Achebe & Friends at Umuahia: The Making of a Literary Elite
Terri Ochiagha, 2015. Winner of the ASAUK Fage & Oliver Prize 2016

A Death Retold in Truth and Rumour: Kenya, Britain and the Julie Ward Murder   Grace A. Musila, 2015

Scoring Race: Jazz, Fiction, and Francophone Africa   Pim Higginson, 2017

Writing Spatiality in West Africa: Colonial Legacies in the Anglophone/Francophone Novel   Madhu Krishnan, 2018. Winner of the ALA Book of the Year Award – Scholarship 2020

Written under the Skin: Blood and Intergenerational Memory in South Africa   Carli Coetzee, 2019. Winner of the ALA Book of the Year Award – Scholarship 2021

Experiments with Truth: Narrative Non-fiction and the Coming of Democracy in South Africa   Hedley Twidle, 2019

At the Crossroads: Nigerian Travel Writing and Literary Culture in Yoruba and English   Rebecca Jones, 2019. Shortlisted for the ASAUK Fage & Oliver Prize 2020, 'Honorable Mention' for the ALA First Book Award – Scholarship 2021

Cinemas of the Mozambican Revolution: Anti-Colonialism, Independence and Internationalism in Filmmaking, 1968-1991   Ros Gray, 2020

African Literature in the Digital Age: Class and Sexual Politics in New Writing from Nigeria and Kenya   Shola Adenekan, 2021

Newsprint Literature and Local Literary Creativity in West Africa, 1900s–1960s   Stephanie Newell, 2023

Keorapetse Kgositsile & the Black Arts Movement: Poetics of Possibility
Uhuru Portia Phalafala, 2024

www.ingramcontent.com/pod-product-compliance
Lightning Source LLC
Chambersburg PA
CBHW070800230426
43665CB00017B/2438